Marketing Fundamentals
2002–2003

Marketing Fundamentals 2002–2003

Geoff Lancaster
Frank Withey
Ruth Ashford

OXFORD AMSTERDAM BOSTON LONDON NEW YORK PARIS
SAN DIEGO SAN FRANCISCO SINGAPORE SYDNEY TOKYO

Butterworth-Heinemann
An imprint of Elsevier Science
Linacre House, Jordan Hill, Oxford OX2 8DP
225 Wildwood Avenue, Woburn MA 01801-2041

First published 2002

British Library Cataloguing in Publication Data
A catalogue record for this book is available from the British Library

ISBN 0 7506 5702 2

For information on all Butterworth-Heinemann publications
visit our website at www.bh.com

Typeset by Integra Software Services Pvt. Ltd, Pondicherry, India
www.integra-india.com
Printed and bound in Italy

Contents

Preface

The Chartered Institute of Marketing has recently introduced updated syllabuses for all its professional examinations, together with changes to how some of these examinations are structured. This coursebook has been designed to cover the new Marketing Fundamentals Syllabus at the Certificate level of the CIM examinations and is one of a series of such coursebooks that have been specially commissioned. It is important to stress at the outset that this is not a textbook but rather is designed to complement the recommended reading for this subject suggested by The Chartered Institute of Marketing.

As in many areas of study, and certainly one such as marketing where there is much to learn and often different perspectives, as much reading around the subject as possible is to be recommended. Again, we would stress therefore, that this coursebook should be used in conjunction with the other recommended reading for this subject, as in The Chartered Institute of Marketing syllabus for this subject. The full reading list for this subject is contained in Appendix 3.

Essentially the coursebook, like the others in the series, presents an overview of the main concepts and techniques encompassed by the Marketing Fundamentals syllabus. These are presented in Units 'The development of marketing and marketing orientation' to 'Marketing in context' of the coursebook. In addition to reviewing these main concepts and techniques, through a series of questions, activities, and exam hints, you will be encouraged to apply the concepts and techniques to the 'real world' of marketing. These activities, etc., are the driving force of the coursebook and you should make every effort to complete them. As you would expect from the professional body for marketing, candidates for any of the CIM's examinations are expected to be able to 'apply' the tools and techniques of marketing. The coursebook is designed to help you in these application skills and hence better prepare you for the examination.

We wish you every success in your studies and careers in marketing.

Geoff Lancaster

Frank Withey

Ruth Ashford

An introduction from the academic development advisor

Over the past few years there have been a series of syllabus changes initiated by the Chartered Institute of Marketing to ensure that their qualifications continue to be relevant and of significant consequence in the world of marketing, both within industry and academia. As a result Butterworth-Heinemann and I have rigorously revised and updated the Coursebook series to make sure that every title is the best possible study aid and accurately reflects the latest CIM syllabus.

The revisions to the series this year include both restructuring and the inclusion of many new mini cases and examples. There are a number of new and accomplished authors in the series commissioned both for their CIM course teaching and examining experience, and their wide general knowledge of the latest marketing thinking.

We are certain that you will find the new-look books a highly beneficial study tool as you prepare for the CIM examinations. They will guide you in a structured and logical way through the detail of the syllabus, providing you with the required underpinning knowledge, understanding and application of theory.

The editorial team and authors wish you every success as you embark upon your studies.

Karen Beamish

Academic Development Advisor

How to use these coursebooks

Everyone who has contributed to this series has been careful to structure the books with the exams in mind. Each unit, therefore, covers an essential part of the syllabus. You need to work through the complete coursebook systematically to ensure that you have covered everything you need to know.

This coursebook is divided into units each containing a selection of the following standard elements:

- **Objectives** tell you what part of the syllabus you will be covering and what you will be expected to know, having read the unit. These objectives relate to the key areas of the syllabus which are identified in the objectives element. The objectives also encompass the key learning outcomes and associated key skills specified in the syllabus for this subject.
- **Study guides** include a brief introduction to the areas covered in the chapter, tell you how long the unit is and how long its activities take to do.
- **Questions** are designed to give you practice; all the questions are similar to those you get in the exam. Because of this, they are included in the Further Study section of the units. In this section of each unit we have also taken the opportunity to include an actual exam question from a previous examination paper. As with all the questions in the units, these 'real life' exam questions are accompanied by an answer debrief in the answers and debriefings appendix. You should note, however, that for these actual exam questions you may also access a full specimen answer from the relevant paper in the www.bh.com website. The full website address is www.bh.com/marketing or www.marketingonline.co.uk. Details of which exam paper these questions are taken from are therefore provided in full with each actual exam question in each of the units.
- **Answers** (at the end of the book) give you a suggested approach for answering questions. *Remember* there is no such thing as a model answer — you should use these examples only as guidelines.
- **Activities** give you a chance to put what you have learned into practice.
- **Debriefings** (at the end of the activities and questions) shed light on the methodologies involved in the activities.
- **Exam hints** are tips from the senior examiner or examiner which are designed to help you avoid common mistakes made by previous candidates.
- **Study tips** give you guidance on improving your knowledge base.
- **Insights** encourage you to contextualize your academic knowledge by reference to real-life experience.
- **Definitions** may be used for words you must know to pass the exam.
- **Summaries** cover what you should have picked up from reading the unit.
- **Bibliography and references** contains a list of all sources used in the chapter and encompasses, as appropriate, not only books but journal and newspaper/magazine articles as well as website addresses.
- **Further study** is intended to help you consolidate your knowledge. It includes suggestions for further reading and you are strongly recommended to read as widely as possible using this guide. While you will find that each section of the syllabus has been covered within this text, you might find that the order of some of the topics has been changed.

This is because it sometimes makes more sense to put certain topics together when you are studying, even though they might appear in different sections of the syllabus itself. If you work through each of the units in order, completing all the activities and following up with additional reading and study, together with examination preparation based around the end of unit questions, your coverage of the syllabus will be just fine.

About MarketingOnline

With this year's coursebooks Butterworth-Heinemann is offering readers free access to MarketingOnline (www.marketingonline.co.uk), our premier online support engine for the CIM marketing courses. On this site you can benefit from:

- Tutorials on key topics every two weeks during the term, comprehensive revision support material and access to revision days from Tactics – the highly acclaimed independent trainer for CIM courses.
- Fully customizable electronic versions of the coursebooks – annotate, cut and paste sections of text to create your own tailored learning notes.
- Access to the e-Library – electronic versions of eight classic BH marketing texts to enrich and extend your knowledge.
- Instant access to specimen papers and answers, as well as other extra material and weblinks related to the coursebooks.
- Capacity to search the coursebook online for instant access to definitions and key concepts.

Logging on

Before you can access MarketingOnline you will first need to get a password. Please go to www.marketingonline.co.uk where you will find registration instructions for coursebook purchasers. Once you have got your password, you will need to log on using the onscreen instructions. This will give you access to the various functions outlined below.

Using MarketingOnline

MarketingOnline is broadly divided into six sections which can each be accessed from the front page after you have logged on to the system:

1. **The coursebooks**: buttons corresponding to the three levels of CIM marketing qualification are situated on the home page. Select your level and you will be presented with the four coursebook titles for each module of that level. Click on the desired coursebook to access the full online text (divided up by chapter). On each page of text you have the option to add an electronic bookmark or annotation by following the onscreen instructions. You can also freely cut and paste text into a blank word document to create your own learning notes.

2. **The e-Library**: click on the 'BH Library' button on the front page to access the eight titles in the e-Library. Again you can annotate, bookmark and copy text as you see fit.

3. **Revision material**: click on the 'Revision material' link and select the appropriate CIM level and coursebook to access revision material.

4. **Useful links**: click on 'Useful links' to access a list of links to other sites of interest for further reading and research.

5 **Glossary**: click on the 'Glossary' button to access our online dictionary of marketing terms.

6 **Discussion**: click on the 'Discussion' button to access our various online noticeboards. All users can access and put up entries on our public noticeboard using onscreen instructions. If your college has registered as a MarketingOnline user you may also have access to your own 'Tutor Group Discussion' where you can interact with your fellow students and tutors.

If you have specific queries about using MarketingOnline then you should consult our fully searchable FAQ section – again, this is accessible through the appropriate link on the front page of the site. Please also note that a **full user guide** can be downloaded by clicking on the link on the opening page of the website.

Unit 1
The development of marketing and marketing orientation

Objectives

By the end of this unit you will:

- Understand the development of marketing as an exchange process, a philosophy of business and a managerial function (1.1).
- Recognize the contribution of marketing as a means of creating customer value and as a form of competition (1.2).
- Appreciate the importance of a market orientation to organizational performance and identify the factors that promote and impede the adoption of a market orientation (1.3).
- Understand the role of marketing in co-ordinating organizational resources both within and outside the marketing function (1.4).
- Understand the impacts of marketing actions on society and the need for marketers to act in an ethical and socially responsible manner (1.5).
- Appreciate the significance of buyer–seller relationships in marketing and the role of relationship marketing in facilitating the retention of customers (1.6).

Study guide

Clearly this first unit is an introduction to the development, meaning, and role of marketing in the contemporary organization. In short, this unit sets the scene for the remaining units in the guide. In a way the unit reflects the process that must occur in an organization if it is to improve its performance in marketing, in as much as the first step in this improvement is an understanding of what marketing means and how it can be implemented. We shall start by looking at definitions of marketing, moving on to consider the so-called 'marketing concept' and 'marketing orientation'. We shall look at marketing's development and the notion of marketing as an exchange process, a philosophy of business, and a managerial function. We shall look at the importance of a marketing orientation to organizational performance and the issues and problems in implementing a marketing orientation through building and enhancing a marketing culture. The important contribution of marketing as a means of creating customer value and as a form of competition is considered, together with the role of marketing in coordinating organizational resources both within and outside the marketing function. We shall consider the changing role of marketing, and in particular the wider range of applications for marketing these days; the importance of environmental, ethical and social issues in marketing; and the growth of so-called 'relationship marketing'. Finally, we shall introduce you to the increasing importance of new technology in marketing these days, a theme that will be explored in each of the units in the coursebook.

We would expect it to take you about 3 hours to work through this first unit, and suggest you allow a further 3–4 hours to undertake the various activities suggested. Other than your notebook and writing equipment you will not need anything further to complete this unit.

This first unit will also help familiarize you with the approach and style of our coursebooks. Of course if you are studying other subjects using the Butterworth-Heinemann coursebooks you will be used to the approach. However, in case you are new to the coursebook series, you will find that the coursebooks have been developed to ensure that you acquire not only the knowledge necessary for examination success but also the skills to apply that knowledge, both in the examination and in your work as a practising marketer. Some of the elements, outlined at the start of the coursebook and especially the activities and questions etc. are designed of course to help you develop these application skills. Remember then, these activities etc. are central to the design of the coursebooks and you are therefore advised to avoid the temptation to leave them out.

What is marketing?

We don't expect a formal definition at this stage but do you really know what marketing is?

Study tip

Organize your study materials from the beginning of your course:

- Use file dividers to keep broad topic areas indexed and relevant materials and articles with the relevant notes.
- Look out for relevant articles, newspaper reports, etc. that you feel provide good examples of the key concepts and techniques covered in the coursebook. You will find these useful to illustrate examination answers.

Activity 1.1

In your own words describe what you think marketing is all about.

Different people will have different views of what marketing is but it would be surprising if many did not have one or more of the following in their description.

Marketing is about:

- Selling.
- Market research.
- Advertising.

Or perhaps for those of you who work in marketing it is about 'Selling products that don't come back to customers who do'.

For those of you who prefer a more formal approach marketing may be about 'Analysis, Planning, Implementation and Control in order to develop a competitive advantage'.

The common theme that runs through this variety of viewpoints about what marketing entails is that marketing is a set of activities or, more specifically, a set of managerial activities or functions required to be performed in an organization. Certainly marketing does encompass activities such as selling, researching markets, attracting and keeping customers, and developing and implementing plans. In short, it is true that it is a managerial function. In fact, this managerial function of marketing is enshrined in the CIM's own definition of marketing as follows:

> **Definition**
>
> **Marketing**
>
> Marketing is 'The management process which identifies, anticipates and satisfies customer requirements efficiently and profitably'.

We can see, though, that the CIM definition, in addition to confirming marketing as a management process, also highlights the fact that the central focus of this process is the 'customer' and the aim is 'satisfying' his/her requirements or 'needs'. Finally, all this must be done in the most efficient way possible with a view to achieving maximum profitability.

In fact, as you would expect, most of the formal definitions of marketing are very similar. Here, for example, are two more for you to consider.

> **Definition**
>
> **Marketing**
>
> 'Marketing consists of individual and organizational activities that facilitate and expedite satisfying exchange relationships in a dynamic environment through the creation, distribution, promotion and pricing of goods, services and ideas.' *Dibb, Simkin, Pride and Ferrell, 1997*

> **Definition**
>
> **Marketing**
>
> 'Marketing means working with markets to bring about exchanges for the purpose of satisfying human needs and wants. It is a process by which individuals and groups obtain what they need and want creating and exchanging products and value with others.' *Kotler, Armstrong, Saunders and Wong, 2000*

So, then, if we are to understand the fundamentals of marketing, we must learn about what this management process consists of. We need to know the key tasks of marketing management and the marketing tools that are used in these tasks. Indeed in the following units we shall be exploring both tasks and tools more closely. However, marketing is not only or even primarily a management function or set of activities. First and foremost marketing is a way of thinking, or, as it is often called, a 'concept' for running a business. Some have even argued that marketing is essentially a 'philosophy'. The point is that only by first understanding and accepting this way of thinking (concept, or philosophy) can a company begin to develop a marketing culture or orientation and, hence, ultimately become effective at marketing.

So what is this so-called marketing concept and how does it relate to the development of a marketing culture?

The marketing concept: marketing orientation

Put simply, the marketing concept focuses on customers. A company that adopts the marketing concept puts the customer at the centre of all business decision-making and planning, and not just marketing department decision-making and planning. A company with this approach is said to be marketing-oriented. In order to understand the meaning and implications of being marketing-oriented we need to examine briefly the background to the development of the marketing concept and the distinction between a marketing versus a production-, product-, or sales-oriented company. We shall start by highlighting the distinctions between these orientations in a company.

Activity 1.2

Marketing-oriented vs other possible orientations of an organization

A company can be:

- Production-oriented.
- Product-oriented.
- Sales-oriented.
- Marketing-oriented.

Using the following statements from the management of our hypothetical organizations, can you assess which of these four possible orientations for a company best fits the organization described by each statement. Read each of the descriptions and then place a number in the circles to indicate the following:

1. This company is marketing-oriented.
2. This company is sales-oriented.
3. This company is production-oriented.
4. This company is product-oriented.

Company A

'We believe that our products are the most innovative on the market. Our quality is second to none and we've gone all out to develop the best design team in the business.'

No. ◯

Company B

'Our salespeople understand how to get the customer to sign on the dotted line. Most customers really want to purchase our product when they see it; they just need a little push to make up their mind.'

No. ◯

Company C

'Customers can be very fickle sometimes. We've just had to change a specification because the customer wanted something else at the last minute. This also affected our production schedules and our delivery department, and everything had to be recosted. Still at least everyone pulled together on this one.'

No. ◯

Company D

'The customer can have any colour so long as its black.'

No. ◯

Of course some of you will have recognized in Company D our old friend Henry Ford, the founder of the Ford Motor Company. Allegedly Henry Ford was said to have uttered this much quoted phrase about the world's first mass-produced motor car.

At the time, the 1920s, Ford's major concern was with the problems of producing cars in sufficient volume and at a price the huge latent mass market, which he rightly perceived to exist, could afford. The colour of his cars therefore mattered little to Henry Ford other than the fact that only producing one colour enabled both output to be greater and prices lower.

Interestingly, at the time, Ford's focus on production rather than the colour preferences of his customers was right. Customers at the time were less interested in colour than in availability and affordability. Henry Ford's approach was right for the time.

This is an important lesson to learn. The need to be marketing-oriented (Company C in our example) is a function of the market and competitive conditions now faced by companies. Put another way, marketing orientation is the result of a gradual process of evolution that many, if not all, companies have passed through as societies, manufacturing economies, and customers themselves have evolved.

The stages of evolution are shown in simple form below.

Era (Approx)	Orientation/Emphasis
1900–1930s	Production orientation
1930s–1960s	Selling orientation
1960s–today	Marketing orientation

A good summary of the differences between the production, selling and marketing concepts is provided (by Kotler) as follows:

The production concept concentrates on production and distribution economies. This in turn is based on the notion that consumers will choose lower priced products that are readily available.

The selling concept is of course based on the notion that customers need to be persuaded to buy through aggressive selling and promotion.

The marketing concept is based on the notion that organizations can best meet their objectives by concentrating on customer needs and satisfying these needs better than competitors.

NB Perhaps there have always been, and always will be, those inventors/companies who dangerously believe that product orientation is the secret of commercial success.

In fact, as we shall see later, societies and therefore markets are still evolving and so too is marketing thought and practice. For example, many developed economies have now become service economies, giving rise to additional considerations in 'services marketing'. Similarly, many consumers are much more concerned about the environment and the possible effects of marketing activities, giving rise to 'social marketing'. Finally, organizations other than 'for-profit' ones are embracing the marketing concept and marketing practices. Charities, churches, political parties and personalities are only some of these wider applications of what is sometimes termed 'meta marketing'.

We shall therefore be considering some of the implications of this evolving nature of the marketing culture later in this, and subsequent, units. In addition to these wider applications of marketing, however, marketing practices too are evolving and changing. In this respect, several recent developments in marketing are particularly worthy of note, namely: the growth of so-called 'relationship marketing'; and the development of 'network marketing'. Perhaps one of the most significant developments affecting all marketing managers in recent years, however, is the changing nature of marketing due to an increased use, and application, of information technology. As in many areas of business, IT, in all its forms, is having a significant impact on management practice. In the area of marketing, examples of this impact would include: the growth of the Internet with its implications for areas such as home shopping, marketing communications, and so on; increasing sophistication in the use of databases for marketing purposes with its implications for areas such as direct mail; increasingly powerful computer-based techniques for analysing customers and markets with its implications for areas such as market segmentation and targeting, and brand positioning. Again, we shall look at the evolving and changing nature of marketing practices in more detail in this and the units which follow as appropriate.

Exam hint

As this is the Marketing Fundamentals paper, the examiners are unlikely to expect you to be an expert in the more specialized applications of marketing. However, the examiners will expect you to have a good basic grasp of how marketing and its applications are widening and changing in the modern world. It is vital, therefore, that you try to keep as up to date as possible with what is going on in the world of marketing. The examiners will expect you to be familiar with current thinking and practices in marketing. This coursebook, of course, is designed, as far as possible, to encompass and reflect this thinking and practices but the marketing world is very dynamic and you should try to keep up to date with current industry practices. A good general purpose magazine on marketing designed for the marketing practitioner, such as *Marketing Today*, or even the financial pages of a good quality newspaper will help you in keeping up to date and in providing you with lots of examples that will potentially earn you higher marks in the examination.

Factors contributing to the need to be marketing-oriented

Many factors have contributed to the requirement to be marketing-oriented in today's business environment, but to appreciate some of the more important of these you should complete the activity below before proceeding.

Activity 1.3

Factors underpinning the need to be market-oriented

Below are listed some of the key factors that have contributed to the need to be marketing-oriented. In order to help you in this activity we have described the 'state' of each factor when, as it was in the days of Henry Ford, production orientation was appropriate for organizations.

What you should do is to assess the 'state' of these factors today, which in turn underpin the need to be marketing-oriented.

Look carefully at each factor as it related to the production-oriented era and then decide how you feel each factor is likely to have changed in the era of marketing orientation.

Factor	Production-oriented era	Marketing-oriented era
Demand	Latent – demand high	
Average disposable income	Low	
General level of education	Low	
Mass media/access to information	Underdeveloped/low	
Supply/industry capacity	Insufficient	
Competition	Negligible/local	

You should now compare your descriptions for each of the factors, with those shown in the Activity debriefing.

Broad economic, political, social and technological factors have all contributed to the development of marketing orientation; however, you will not be surprised if we say that, in summarizing these factors, the overriding reason underpinning the need to be marketing-oriented is customer choice. Quite simply, the organization most effectively identifying and supplying customer needs will get the business.

Again it is important to stress that both production and sales orientation were probably the right approaches to markets for their times. However, not only does it now make more sense to focus the whole of the business and hence product design, pricing policies, distribution and everything else, on a careful analysis of customer needs, i.e. to start the planning process around those needs, but the fact is that in today's environment being market-oriented is an essential – perhaps the essential – ingredient in organizational survival and success. Business planning must now start and end with the customer.

We shall be looking at marketing planning shortly, but it is important to recognize that marketing plans and business plans are different albeit totally interrelated.

The business plan, perhaps as you would expect, relates to the organization as a whole and therefore encompasses objectives and strategies for the whole company embracing all functions and activities. Marketing plans however, again as one would expect, relate to marketing objectives and strategies and primarily involve the functions and activities of the marketing department. One could perhaps readily understand that marketing plans must start and end with customers, but under the marketing concept, and where a marketing culture exists in an organization, then business plans too, despite their wider remit, must also start and end with customers. The simple reason for this is that in the final analysis it is the customer's needs, and the importance of identifying and satisfying these which lie at the heart of the success or failure of business plans.

Again, it is acknowledged that business plans necessarily have a broader remit than just the marketing part of the business and must seek to co-ordinate every key function in the organization. However, the primary input into and focus for all the elements of the business plan in the company which has a true marketing culture must centre on the needs of the customer.

The truly marketing-oriented organization then is one that places the customer and his or her needs at the centre of everything the company does. Not only marketers and the marketing function must accept this central importance of customers and hence the need to develop plans and activities to satisfy them, but every department, even every individual, in the marketing-oriented organization must be attuned to the importance of satisfying customer needs. We shall return to this aspect later.

This then is what is meant by being marketing-oriented.

Definition

Marketing orientation

Marketing orientation is a philosophy that places customer satisfaction at the centre of all organizational planning and procedures. (Withey, 2001)

Marketing as a form of competition: creating customer value

Although marketing and being marketing oriented is essentially, as we have seen, about thinking customers and focusing all the company's efforts and resources on customer needs and their satisfaction, increasingly marketers are recognizing that it is as important to be competitor as customer oriented. This does not detract from the importance of customer orientation but is simply a recognition that with so much competition about these days, and with so many of those competitors themselves being very customer and marketing oriented, very often the achievement of organizational and marketing objectives rests on whether or not a company can beat the competition. Beating the competition of course, should still be viewed from a customer perspective, competitors are beaten where customers perceive a company's offerings or more specifically the value of those offerings to be superior to competitor offerings. In this sense then, although still oriented around customers, marketing can be thought of as a form of competition. The marketer's task is to out-compete other potential suppliers by creating and maintaining superior customer value through the effective application and co-ordination of the marketing mix. Obviously there are numerous ways in which a company can attempt to create superior customer value including, for example, low prices, better service, higher quality, speedier delivery, etc. The ways in which a company creates superior value should reflect customer needs but also needs to be based on marketing assets and strengths which are superior to competitors and which can be defended and sustained in the market place. Marketers often refer to this process, then, as creating a sustainable competitive advantage (an SCA). The sustainable competitive advantage, then, represents the objective and the output of successful marketing activities in the contemporary organization.

Building a marketing culture

We have seen that in today's environment it is vital to become marketing-oriented. But we have also seen that, although perhaps the identification of customer needs and the development of plans and programmes to meet these needs is the responsibility of the marketing function, all functions and individuals in organizations need to accept the central importance of the customer. In other words, we need to establish and encourage the right (marketing-oriented) attitudes and practices throughout the company. What is required therefore is a marketing culture. Needless to say, this is easier said than done. While most managers, even non-marketing ones, would accept the importance of the customer/client to their organizations, in practice many do not 'think customers' in their day-to-day activities or even longer-term planning. So the questions are:

- How can we establish the extent to which an organization has the basics for building a marketing culture?
- How can we assess the extent to which this culture has permeated organizational thinking and planning?
- How, if necessary, can we instil and enhance a marketing culture in an organization?

These are not simple questions, and the last one, in particular, has no easy solution. Let us examine each question in turn.

Business definition and a marketing culture

The starting point for building a marketing culture in an organization is quite simply to 'think customers'. Perhaps one of the most fundamental ways in which the extent to which the management of an organization is 'thinking customers' can be assessed is in how it defines what business the organization is in.

Activity 1.4

In your own words, and as briefly as you can, summarize what business the following organizations are in:

- The Ford Motor Company.
- IBM.
- Max Factor.
- The Catholic Church.
- Your own company (or an organization you are familiar with).

Again we each might have different ideas about what business the organizations listed in the activity are in, but what really matters is our perspective or basis for defining each business. The non-marketing-oriented manager will base the definition of each of these organizations essentially on the products or services they produce. So, for example, Ford = cars and trucks; Max Factor = cosmetics/perfume; IBM = computers; the Catholic Church = religion, and so on. In the marketing-oriented company, however, business definitions will be based on a customer perspective, i.e. the definition will stem from the benefits that the customer is seeking. So now, Ford = Transport (or perhaps for some products, status); Max Factor = beauty; IBM = solutions to business problems; and the Catholic Church = hope or salvation.

Any organization that sees and hence defines its business in anything other than customer benefit terms has simply not reached first base in developing a marketing culture. An organization that defines its business in terms of what it produces is said to be suffering from what a famous marketing pundit and writer, Theodore Levitt, called 'marketing myopia'.

Definition

Marketing myopia

Marketing myopia results from a company having a short-sighted and narrow view of the business it is in as a result of product or service based business definitions rather than customer need based ones.

Assessing the extent of the marketing culture

Thinking customers, then, through how we view and define the business is the first step in developing a marketing culture. But, as we have seen, 'thinking customers', must permeate all functions and levels of the organization and not just the marketing function or even senior management. Certainly talking to managers from different functions to assess how they define the business (as you have done in the previous activity in this unit) will give us the first indication of how widespread or otherwise is the marketing culture. However, given the importance of developing this culture company-wide, not surprisingly, more formal methods of assessing the extent to which a marketing culture has permeated organizational thinking and planning are available. Many organizations now enshrine this assessment in annual marketing audits, parts of which are often the measurement of the extent to which there is a marketing or customer culture. Such measurement may entail the use of formal questionnaires in a marketing effectiveness rating review. Areas/aspects covered by such reviews include, for example:

- Evidence of market and customer research.
- Co-ordination between functions based on customer needs.
- Evidence of long- versus short-term planning and plans.
- Company-wide communication on customer needs.

Extending knowledge

Although space does not permit the inclusion of a full marketing effectiveness questionnaire, exposure to (and even completion of) an example of such a comprehensive and widely applied questionnaire would be very useful to understanding and knowledge in this area.

An excellent example of a questionnaire-based marketing effectiveness instrument is contained in P. Kotler: *Marketing Management*, 8th edition, pp. 756–7. If you possibly can, you should read through this, and, better still, complete the questionnaire for an organization of your choice.

Instilling and enhancing a marketing culture: factors that promote and impede the adoption of a market orientation

We have seen that a marketing culture essentially means putting the customer first and 'thinking customers'. We have also seen that this must permeate the organization at all levels and all functions. Finally, we have seen that it is possible to assess the extent of such a marketing culture in an organization. But what if we find that no such culture exists and we wish therefore to instil a marketing culture? Or, as is more usual, what if we wish to enhance and extend a marketing culture throughout an organization? As mentioned earlier, this is probably the most difficult step for the majority of companies, especially when it comes to instilling such a culture into non-marketing staff. But a number of steps can be taken to grow a marketing culture.

Activity 1.6

Think about an organization you know – any organization will do. Use these questions to prompt your thoughts about the key steps in growing a marketing culture:

- Is senior management in the organization totally committed to customers and improved marketing?
- Has anyone the specific responsibility and authority for enhancing a marketing culture in the organization?

- Do job descriptions in functions other than marketing include reference to customer satisfaction?
- Are marketing staff regularly trained in developments in contemporary marketing concepts and techniques?
- Are non-marketing staff trained in customer appreciation and care?
- Are non-marketing and sales staff ever given a chance to meet customers/clients?
- Do reward and motivation systems in all jobs encourage employees to serve customers better?

If the answer to any of the questions in the activity is no, then there are opportunities to enhance the marketing culture in the organization.

It is important to recognize that this sort of culture cannot be achieved overnight. Indeed there is often antagonism and resistance on the part of individuals outside the marketing or sales departments. Such resistance should be anticipated and planned for. Often the persuasive (rather than authoritative) powers of a respected senior executive committed to building a marketing culture are essential here.

The development of a marketing culture and, in particular, the training and motivation of all the individuals in an organization to achieve this is now often referred to as internal marketing.

Definition

Internal marketing

'Internal marketing is the creation of an Internal Environment which supports customer-consciousness and sales-mindedness amongst all personnel within an organization.' *Christian Gröonroos*

Some authors now suggest that plans should include activities for marketing internally as well as externally. In other words, the marketing skills and techniques of the marketing manager should be used to market plans for customer satisfaction to target 'customers' within the organization.

Although internal marketing is important for all organizations it has proved particularly popular in service organizations, e.g. banks, hotels and so on, where a wide range of staff are often in contact with customers.

Difficulties in managing the introduction of a customer oriented culture

Needless to say, achieving a customer oriented culture is not always easy. Some of the major difficulties and barriers in the introduction of such a culture are as follows:

- Managers fail to realize or understand the true concept.
- The structure of the organization may require changing and this can lead to other managers' resistance and costs.
- People are frightened and reluctant to change.

- The power struggle between the different departments within an organization can hinder the process, e.g. the production department.
- In some organizations the responsibility for marketing strategy and implementation are separated, and this may offer many problems.

Marketing's co-ordinating role

Effective marketing, as we shall see when we consider marketing planning and the management of the marketing mix, requires that all marketing and sales activities within the marketing function be co-ordinated. Unfortunately the degree of co-ordination required in some organizations, particularly between sales and marketing, is not all that it should be. So, for example, in some organizations the sales department often functions almost independently of the marketing department. In part this is because of the traditional structure and position of the sales function in many organizations and also because some organizations even now are not truly marketing oriented. Sales and selling activities should be part of an overall co-ordinated marketing effort. As with achieving a marketing culture, this can and does give rise to problems of conflict and antagonism between sales and marketing. The senior management of a company need to ensure that the sales personnel understand their relationship to marketing and the fact that all marketing activities including selling need to be marketing department led and in the process, customer driven. This is not to suggest that selling is in any way inferior or should be subservient to marketing, but rather stresses the co-ordinating role of marketing. Other marketing activities, too, need to be co-ordinated including activities encompassing marketing research, promotion and advertising, customer service and of course the marketing mix.

In addition, and often even more problematical, marketing also has a role and responsibility in co-ordinating organizational efforts and resources outside of the marketing function – hence the need for a company-wide marketing culture. In particular, marketing should help co-ordinate the efforts and activities of the other key functional areas of the business that impinge on and affect customers. This includes, then, for example the production and quality control functions, accountancy and finance, research and development, and even personnel. Again, this is not to suggest that these other functions should be subservient to marketing, rather only that marketing should play the co-ordinating role in the efforts of these other functions, again centred on achieving customer satisfaction.

Finally, marketing also has a role to play in co-ordinating resources and activities not only outside of the marketing function in the organization but also outside of the organization itself. Often marketing strategies and plans encompass and involve other individuals and organizations external to an organization. A simple example would include the need to co-ordinate the activities and resources of, say, distributors. After all, distributors play a key part in achieving marketing objectives and in the levels of customer satisfaction achieved. In many ways in fact, effective marketing requires the efforts of very many parties both internal and external to the organization to be co-ordinated. Sometimes the external parties are external marketing agencies such as, for example, market research companies, advertising agencies, or the distributors and middle persons already mentioned. But also marketers must often play a co-ordinating role with other parties in the overall value chain including, for example, suppliers. In fact, increasingly, marketers build their marketing strategies and plans taking into account and having to co-ordinate the full set of activities in the value chain.

Achieving co-ordination, both inside and outside of the marketing function and including outside agencies and organizations, requires the marketer to have clear objectives and planning processes. The marketer must ensure that all parties concerned with customer satisfaction are aware of customer needs and the company's objectives and plans with respect to meeting these. Other parties must also be aware of their contribution and role in fulfilling these plans and the activities that will need to be performed. The marketer increasingly needs analysis and planning skills so as to be able to steer other parties in the right direction with regard to the use of resources to achieve customer satisfaction. In addition, the contemporary marketer must have good communication and inter-personal skills so as to be able to motivate these other parties.

Technology and the marketing culture

Developments in technology are affecting every facet of marketing. Indeed, these developments are amongst the most pervasive of factors influencing the practice of marketing. Because of this, remember, we shall be looking at some of the more important of these developments throughout the units of the course. At this point then it would be perhaps useful to point to some of the ways in which technology and particularly information technology is helping companies in their management of a customer oriented culture.

Some of the ways in which technology is helping in the management of a customer oriented culture are as follows:

- More effective and efficient internal communication via ICT.

- Speedier responses to customer needs and market changes.

- Better prepared analysis of data and statistics for market and customer intelligence.

- More powerful databases which helps customer profiling and therefore tailoring of products to customer needs.

- The use of intranets and extranets to keep staff and suppliers informed and to manage the value chain.

- Related to the above, the use of electronic data interchange (EDI) systems to facilitate communication through the value chain.

- Improved systems of stock control and management through use of computer applications enabling more effective customer service delivery etc.

- Automated telephone and call-centre systems potentially improving customer response.

- Increases in the number of channels through which customers and other stakeholders can communicate with an organization.

- The Internet and website developments which enable customers, for example, to shop in alternative ways, facilitates customer choice, and allows easier trading around the world.

- The use of database systems to facilitate more effective customer relationship management (CRM) through developments such as, for example, loyalty card systems etc.

Marketing as a management function

Early in this unit we looked at definitions of marketing, including the one proposed by the Chartered Institute of Marketing. We suggested that a common theme to all definitions of marketing is that it is a management function, which indeed it is. However, we also suggested that before we looked at the tasks of marketing management, we needed to explore marketing as a way of thinking or philosophy, the so-called marketing concept, and the importance of building a marketing culture in an organization. Having done this, we can now turn our attention to the tasks and tools of marketing management.

Activity 1.7

Look at the advertisement below for a marketing post. Study it carefully and then write down a list of what you see as the key activities in this post.

MARKETING MANAGER

South West circa £-

- Challenge of this new role is to develop creative approaches and long-range marketing plans while also adding immediate commercial value to the activities

---

of operations colleagues with strong bottom-line orientation and limited application of professional marketing.

- Major retail service group which leads their market with over 100 outlets nationwide and turnover of £1bn.

- Key accountabilities in the creation of an influential marketing function will include market analysis, building of customer database, new product/service development, corporate identity, business planning and developing co-operative relationships with suppliers.

- Operating company board member with additional line responsibility for two development businesses.

- Probably 35–45, graduate calibre and possibly MBA. Successful record in senior brand marketing role in blue-chip retailing, multi-site service or FMCG company. Any general management experience would be an advantage.

- Strategic visioning and business planning skills combined with ability to win credibility and make things happen with powerful line directors. Management skills to handle hybrid staff/line role and to lead change processes.

- Strong but subtle influencing style. Creative but pragmatic. Common touch as well as ability to develop senior relationships. General management potential.

Clearly the specific tasks of an individual marketing manager will vary from one organization to another but you will find that most of your list of key activities from this recruitment advertisement can be categorized under one of the following headings.

- Analysis.
- Planning.
- Implementation.
- Control.

Turn to activity 1.7 of this unit to find out what each of these tasks entails and examples of how the various activities referred to in the job description relate to the tasks.

Now you have considered Activity Debrief 1.7 we can now turn our attention to each of the key activities in our list.

Analysis

Analysis includes the assessment of both internal and external factors that affect and help shape, therefore, marketing plans. Analysis encompasses the analysis of the wider marketing environment including, for example, economic, political, social/cultural and technological factors and the nearer task environment factors such as competitors, and of course customers. Effective marketing ultimately stems from effective analysis. The marketer must understand how markets operate and the trends affecting them. The analysis tasks of marketing managers require them to make use of the tools and techniques of marketing research leading increasingly to the development of marketing information systems.

Planning

Based on careful analysis, the marketing manager is responsible for developing marketing plans.

Although the marketing manager will be required to perform all four of the key activities listed above, the planning element is in some ways the central activity. It is important therefore, that you understand the key steps in the planning process and how these fit together into a systematic framework.

A basic overview of the marketing planning steps is shown in Figure 1.1.

Figure 1.1 *Key steps in marketing planning*

Implementation

As we can see from our Figure 1.1, implementation represents the penultimate stage of the marketing planning process, though we have of course listed it separately. Implementation in fact is important enough in its own right to be considered one of the four key activities and responsibilities of the marketing manager. Implementation essentially involves getting things done. This in turn entails the marketing manager ensuring, for example, that resources and budgets are in place to implement marketing plans, plans are communicated and accepted, and that staff both within the marketing function and in other functional areas both inside and outside of the business are motivated.

Control

Again, part of our marketing planning framework in Figure 1.1, but again important enough to be considered in its own right. In fact monitoring and control of marketing activities is often a neglected area, both in the literature surrounding marketing activities but also, unfortunately, in many organizations. It is the marketer's responsibility to assess the extent to which marketing strategies and plans are working, achieving the objectives set and doing this in a cost-effective manner. In addition, the control process involves making any necessary changes to marketing activities and plans to take account of, say, any changed circumstances.

These, then, are the basic activities and responsibilities of the marketing manager. Within these broad areas of activity the marketing manager has several specific marketing activities and responsibilities to perform in the organization. Amongst some of the most important of these activities are those of market segmentation and the development and application of the so-called marketing mix. We shall now consider these two extremely important aspects of the marketing manager's job.

Market segmentation

Many feel that market segmentation lies at the heart of the contemporary marketing manager's task and it certainly represents a key facet of a marketing-oriented organization and hence a marketing culture. As with the marketing planning process, market segmentation including the related aspects of targeting and positioning are discussed in detail in Unit 2 'Marketing Planning and Budgeting'. Again, however, we feel it is useful to introduce you to the notion of market segmentation at this point as it is so central as a concept and technique to the marketing culture.

Essentially, market segmentation recognizes the fact that in most, if not all markets, all customers are not the same with respect to their needs and wants. Market segmentation is the process of identifying and classifying customers according to these different needs and wants. By doing so, the marketer is better able to decide which groups of customers or segments to serve, and on what basis. In particular, effective market segmentation enables the marketer to develop marketing mix programmes which are much more closely tailored to the needs of different customers. As such, then, we can see how market segmentation enables the marketer to translate the marketing concept into practical marketing programmes and because of this, market segmentation represents one of those powerful tools of the modern marketer.

The tools of marketing management: the marketing mix

In performing their key tasks marketing managers have at their disposal a number of tools or ingredients they can use to develop marketing plans, and to create customer satisfaction and, ultimately, profits for the organization. These tools or ingredients are often referred to as the 'marketing mix'.

Definition

The marketing mix: *the 4Ps*

The marketing mix is the set of controllable variables the marketer uses to develop marketing plans and programmes.
First proposed by Neil Borden, the original and still basic elements of the marketing mix are the 4Ps:

- Product,
- Price,
- Place,
- Promotion.

In the units that follow we shall be looking at each of these in detail.

Definition

A further 3Ps

More recently, however, largely because of the growth of services marketing, the original mix has been extended to include three further Ps, namely:

- People,
- Process,
- Physical evidence.

Again we shall also be looking at these further elements of the mix in later units. So at this stage you simply need to know what they are.

Overviewing the marketing process: marketing as an exchange process

So far in this unit we have looked at the evolution and meaning of the marketing concept, and the development of a marketing orientation or culture in an organization. We have also looked at the tasks of the marketing manager and the basic tools or ingredients with which to perform these tasks. It would be helpful at this stage, however, to outline briefly how all of this translates into the marketing process.

This can perhaps most easily be done by the use of a simple diagram (Figure 1.2).

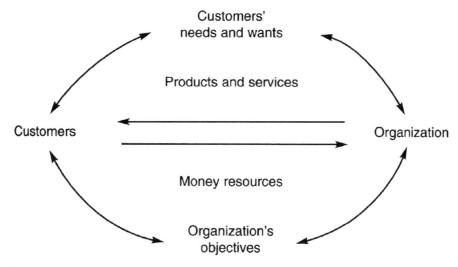

Figure 1.2 *The marketing process*

We can see from Figure 1.2 how the marketing process facilitates an 'exchange' process between customers and company. According to Dibb, Simkin, Pride and Ferrell, for an exchange to take place, a number of conditions need to exist. First, two or more parties must participate. Each party must possess something of value that the other party desires, and second each party must be willing to give up its 'something of value' to receive the 'something of value' held by the other party. In our diagram the exchange is shown as goods/service (to the customer) in exchange for money/resources (to the company). The system only works if both parties (customer and supplier) receive something of value. As stated, in Figure 1.2 the exchange is based on goods/ services for money/resources, but those are not the only types of exchange between organizations and their customers. Clearly, the nature of the exchange process depends on the type of organization and its customers. Above all, though, we must be careful not to think of exchange processes (and hence marketing) as only being relevant to profit making organizations. As already mentioned, it is now increasingly recognized that the need for a marketing culture, accompanied by the application of marketing principles and techniques, applies to any organization which wishes to undertake an exchange process with its customers. What differs between the profit seeking and other types of organizations is not the need for an exchange process, but the nature of what is exchanged between the organization and its customers. A recognition of this is one reason why an increasing number, and more importantly, variety of organizations, are turning to marketing. Because of this, in the final part of this unit, we shall consider in more detail this changing role of marketing. In particular we shall look at the widening range of applications for marketing as it has spread from being initially applied to the marketing of fast-moving consumer-goods, through to the marketing of business-to-business products and services, followed by the adoption of marketing in service industries, and finally to the 'markets' of not-for-profit organizations such as for example, local authorities, political parties, charities and churches. Some of the key additional considerations of adopting and implementing a marketing culture in these different types of organizations are also considered and discussed, as appropriate, in later units too. Some of the main key strategic implications of adopting and implementing marketing in an organization are as follows:

- Customer orientation.
- Generic business definition.
- Information/research.
- Tailored/targeted marketing programmes.
- Integrated/co-ordinated marketing efforts.
- Long-term planning.

The changing role of marketing

Earlier in this unit we referred to the evolution of the marketing concept. In the same vein we also suggested, perhaps as one would expect, that marketing thought and practice is still evolving. In fact marketing has changed considerably over the past ten years. Clearly it would be impossible and inappropriate to detail all the significant trends and changes that have occurred, but some of the more important ones are briefly introduced below. We shall introduce them here, and then consider these trends and changes in more detail in later units of the coursebook.

A wider range of applications for marketing

As already mentioned once exclusively applied only to fast-moving consumer-goods manufacturers, marketing has spread through business markets, service markets, and finally to the 'markets' of not-for-profit organizations. We shall now briefly consider some of these markets.

Business-to-business markets

These are markets where customers are primarily distinguished from those in fast-moving consumer-goods markets by the fact that they are purchasing in order to further the objectives of their organizations, rather than for personal motives and use.

These days there are plenty of examples of organizations who have recognized and used the concepts and techniques of marketing in their business-to-business markets to good effect.

Hewlett Packard, the multi-national computer and electronics company, for example, has long utilized many of the tools once associated only with fast-moving consumer-goods marketers to help build a successful company. Tools such as focus group research, global media advertising and effective public relations are used together with other key marketing tools and concepts to help build a strong market position.

These markets account for a substantial amount of economic activity in most economies and they include, for example, producers (manufacturers) and distributors/intermediaries. The importance of a marketing culture and the general principles of marketing apply to just the same extent and often in the same manner in these markets as in consumer goods markets. However, there are some quite important differences for the marketer in these markets which stem, in essence, from the different nature of the buyers and the buying process encountered in these markets. There are many implications for the marketer because of this essential difference, but a major implication is in the design and use of the elements of the marketing mix. We shall therefore be considering some of these differences in business-to-business markets in Unit 9 'Marketing in context'.

Services marketing

Already several times we have touched on the growth of service markets. The growth of service markets has, in many countries, been phenomenal in recent years. Indeed, in many developed economies such as those found in, say, the USA or United Kingdom, service industries (as opposed to manufacturing industries) now predominate. Service industries of course include a myriad of different types of markets ranging from, for example, financial services such as banks, building societies, insurance companies, and so on through to holidays, fast food, management consultancy, cleaning services, etc. It is now recognized that service products have, compared to their physical product counterparts, a number of characteristics which are different. We shall consider some of these differences and their implications in more detail in later units, but for example, services marketing differs because service products are largely intangible compared to physical products. This, in turn, has implications, for example, for how they are promoted by the marketer. Service benefits are much more difficult for the marketer to communicate to customers. Similarly, intangibility gives rise to additional considerations with respect to, for example, branding and packaging. Having said this, like business-to-business markets, the essential nature of the underpinning exchange process between service organizations and their customers is as shown in Figure 1.2 with services being exchanged for money.

Asked to name an effective services marketer, many would put McDonalds, the fast food marketer, at the top of their list. Certainly McDonalds were one of the first service companies to fully appreciate and utilize the concepts and tools of modern marketing and they continue to do so. However, many services marketers are now just as effective as their FMCG marketer counterparts. Examples of effective service marketers include Accenture, Interbrand Newell and Sorrell, Holiday Inns, Singapore Airlines and Starbucks coffee shops.

As regards the marketing concept in a service organization it is important to consider the characteristics of services as intangible, inseparable, perishable. We will consider these special characteristics of services in more detail in the Unit 'Combining the marketing mix', together with some other important characteristics of services, such as inseparability and non-ownership. At this stage it is sufficient to note that these characteristics will mean a need to ensure that a marketing orientation is managed well.

In the service organization in particular, regular customer audits will need to identify the consumers' expectations of the service quality and delivery. This means that the service quality must be managed well, and includes the tangibles, reliability, responsiveness, assurance and empathy of the organization. Again as we shall see in Unit 9 'Marketing in context' and as we have already mentioned earlier in this unit, marketers need to consider an extended marketing mix for services to include the additional elements of 'people', 'processes' and 'physical evidence'.

Developing a marketing oriented service organization has implications for the management style used, the structure of the organization, and its marketing strategy. Information systems, staff attitudes and skills, and shared values in the organization may all need to be considered to ensure a marketing-oriented service organization.

Not-for-profit organizations

Sometimes also referred to as 'non-business markets', these are organizations which are essentially established for reasons other than to earn profits for their shareholders. As in business-to-business and service markets, non-profit organizations and markets encompass a wide variety of types of organization and marketing practices. For example, they include institutions such as local authorities, hospitals, governments, universities and churches. Charities and social causes include, for example, Oxfam, famine relief and the Countryside Trust. With such a wide variety of types of not-for-profit organizations and markets it is difficult and perhaps even dangerous to try and encompass the differences in the application of the marketing culture and practices in such organizations in just a few sentences. However, so long as we recognize this danger of over generalizing it is possible to highlight a number of key differences in the application of the marketing concept and tools in these organizations. In particular,

- Such organizations often operate within a much tighter regulatory framework with regard to if, and how, they apply the concepts and tools of marketing.

- Many of the characteristics of service products, which we will introduce in later units, such as intangibility, also apply to many not-for-profit organizations.

- The marketing mix elements and their application often differ in these organizations and markets. Again, we shall consider some of these differences in more detail in Unit 9 'Marketing in context'. But, for example, it is not difficult to appreciate that the 'price' element of the marketing mix is different in this setting. Indeed, often no price is set by the marketer or paid by the customer. If we take, say, a political party marketing itself for an election then as an example, customers (voters) are not asked to pay a financial price for the 'product', but rather are being asked to 'pay' with their vote. Essentially, this example illustrates differences in the nature of the 'exchange process' between not-for-profit organizations and their customers and it is to this difference that we now turn our attention.

- In overviewing the marketing process earlier in this unit, Figure 1.2 illustrated the centrality of the concept of exchange to this process. Although the essence of this process is the same for any market, and indeed underpins the very concept of a market, and although the related concept of 'value' in this process is just as relevant, as already hinted at, the notion of what is exchanged, and what constitutes value, between not-for-profit organizations and their customers differs from profit-seeking organizations. Figure 1.3 shows in simplified form some examples of exchanges which might take place between different types of not-for-profit organizations and their customers.

- The final major difference, or certainly complication, in considering marketing in not-for-profit organizations is the fact that 'the customer' can comprise several different, and often potentially conflicting groups. So, for example, if we take a university, its 'customers' could be viewed as including: the students; potential employers/industry; local government; the local community; and national government. Because of this, often in not-for-profit organizations and marketing a distinction is made between 'customers' and 'publics', the latter term being used to denote any party to which the organization will, from time to time, need to address with its marketing efforts.

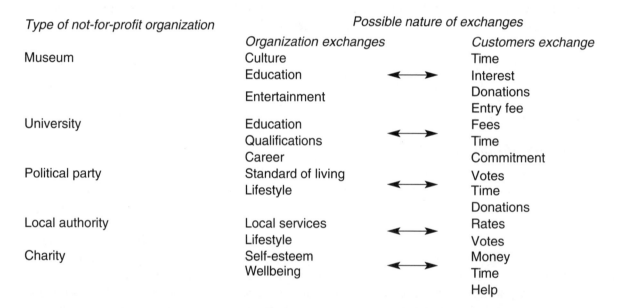

Figure 1.3 The marketing process and exchange in not-for-profit organizations

---

Activity 1.8

Select a not-for-profit organization of your choice, e.g. a church, a charity, a political party, and find out as much as you can about how it 'markets' its 'products'/services.

An increased recognition of environmental and social marketing: ethical and social responsibilities

Once exclusively concerned with satisfying 'wants' and profitability, marketers now increasingly are being called upon to balance these against the need to protect the environment and indeed the interest of consumers and society as a whole.

At one time the Xerox company would not have dreamed of producing and marketing recycled paper for their office paper products. Like many companies however, Xerox have moved with the times with specific regard to an increased concern about the environment, and in this case particularly the depletion of one of the world's scarcest resources; namely its forests. These days the Xerox company have a well-established range of paper products which utilize recycled paper. Like Xerox many companies have become much 'greener' in their marketing activities. Green marketing is discussed shortly.

In all fairness this recognition of the social and environmental impacts of marketing through the promotion of consumption has to some extent been forced upon the marketer by social attitudes and pressure groups. Social attitudes have changed over the past 10 years in many developed economies. Society as a whole is now much more concerned about factors such as the environment and the welfare and safety of customers, and the effect which consumption and marketing of products can have upon these. Of particular importance among these social trends have been the growth of 'consumerism' and 'green marketing'. We should look at each of these major developments a little more closely.

Exam hint

Although consumerism and green issues are relatively new for many marketers, and although in some parts of the world they are seen as being much less important, owing to factors such as the level of economic development, they are popular areas for questions on the Fundamentals paper. Because they might be less relevant issues in your own environment, do not be tempted to ignore them as topics for examination revision.

Question 1.1

What were President Kennedy's four consumer rights, which he proposed in his now famous speech in 1962.

Activity 1.9

List as many examples as you can think of where marketers have responded to the need to protect the environment, e.g. The development of lead-free petrol.

Activity 1.10

Take some time to research any organizations or bodies that have been established in your own country specifically to augment the rights and power of buyers in relation to sellers. These can be formal organizations or bodies established by government, or informal ones. In addition to finding out the names/titles of any such organizations, try to establish what it is they do, i.e. their aims and activities.

Green marketing

Our second and related development associated with the social based marketing concept is an increase in environmentally friendly products and services. Not only are customers more concerned to protect their rights as consumers, but an increasing number are also concerned to protect the environment. Specifically they are concerned about the potential effects of the marketing of products on the environment.

Clearly the examples shown in the Activity debrief are indicative only. You can probably think of many other green issues for the marketer. Like the consumer movement in some countries, the Green movement, too, has increased in importance and become more powerful and influential. In several European countries this movement has become political, with representatives being elected to voice the opinions and attitudes of the members of the Green movement. The Greens are a minority group no longer, and even non-Green members of society have become more aware of the potential polluting effects associated with the production and consumption of products and services.

Like the consumer movement, the Green movement, too, has resulted in legislation designed to protect the environment from pollution. Even where there is no such legislation, we are increasingly seeing voluntary codes of practice to reduce pollution. Again, the most far-sighted marketers have responded positively to the Green movement, not only conforming to legislation but also taking proactive steps to produce and market 'greener' products. In some countries environmental groups have combined to produce guides to products that are environmentally safe, giving them a seal of approval. This seal of approval can then be used by marketers in their advertising, packaging and promotion.

It is important to stress that the impact of green issues does differ between different parts of the world, with marketers in Europe and America perhaps seeing the largest impact. There is little doubt, however, that this importance and this impact are growing and spreading and will affect most marketers in the future. It is relatively easy to find examples of how green issues have affected marketing programmes already from the materials used in some products and services, to how they are manufactured, how they are promoted, and how they are designed to be used and disposed of.

Although consumerism and green issues are perhaps the best examples of some of the trends and changes that have given rise to a change in the underpinning concept, philosophy, and activities of marketing, there are several forces and factors that have caused the need for a more society-based marketing concept. Increasingly the marketer of the future will have to resolve the potential for conflict between meeting profit and commercial objectives, customer needs, customer interests, and the wider interests of society as a whole.

An increased emphasis on quality, service and customer care

As markets have continued to become increasingly competitive, marketers have recognized that customers now demand and expect consistent quality. This applies not only to product quality but delivery, after-sales service and so on. In turn customers also expect a high degree of service and customer care from the suppliers of the goods and services they select.

Research has shown that quality is one of the major factors accounting for differences in profitability. Companies which produce consistent quality products tend to be more profitable than their inconsistent quality counterparts. In part, the demand for high quality products reflects increasing affluence and disposable incomes in developed economies. We should not forget, however, that in some parts of the world high-quality products are not necessarily what is wanted, and in many cases are unaffordable. The marketer therefore must be careful to ensure that quality, and hence price levels are not beyond the reach of the customer in a particular market.

Quality, and particularly consistency of quality, again has also become more important due to changes in manufacturing processes throughout the world. Although the Japanese were the first to use Just in Time and Kanban systems in their manufacturing, these systems are now widespread throughout the world. The Just in Time approach in particular means that suppliers to companies operating a JIT system must ensure and be able to guarantee zero defects. Because components and raw materials are incorporated immediately into the production process with most JIT systems without inspection it is vital that quality can be relied on. Quality and related aspects such as customer service and care are considered in more detail in Unit 8 'The marketing mix: people, service and customer care', but related to an increased emphasis on quality and customer care is one of the most significant developments in the marketing culture, namely the growth in the concept and application of relationship marketing.

The growth of relationship marketing

Related to the growth in the importance of customer care has been the recognition on the part of many marketers that it perhaps often makes more sense to try and build long-term relationships with customers, and in particular build company and brand loyalty, than to treat each purchase a customer makes as a one-off transaction. Relationship marketing is the term that is used to describe this process of building long-term commitment and loyalty from customers. Relationship marketing itself can be defined as all of the activities which an organization can use to build, maintain, and develop customer relations. The concept of relationship marketing is perhaps one of the most fundamental changes in recent years with regard to how marketers look at marketing and practice their marketing activities. However, relationship marketing is still underpinned by the concept of exchange. Remember, during the exchange process both buyer and seller exchange something of value in return for something. Relationship marketing aims to maximize such value to both buyer and seller and to ensure that both customer and company are truly satisfied. In a way, then, relationship marketing is simply a heightening of the acceptance and application of the marketing concept. But it is also much more than this, relationship marketing requires a building of trust between the organization and its customers. It also demands long-term loyalty between both parties to the exchange. Initially, practised principally in business-to-business markets, relationship marketing has now grown in consumer markets too. So, for example, many of the UK supermarket grocer retailers have developed so-called loyalty schemes designed to reward customers for continuing patronage. In the United Kingdom examples include Tesco and Sainsburys. In the USA, Walmart and in France Mamouth.

Again, we cannot emphasize enough that the relationship marketing approach in marketing is based on a fundamentally different approach to customers even though it is still underpinned by the concept of exchange. Although conventional marketing, as we have seen, is based upon identifying and satisfying customer needs, it is essentially also based upon the premise that once these needs have been satisfied through an effective exchange between the two parties, then the process of marketing is complete. This concept in traditional marketing is therefore based upon the idea of effecting a transaction with the customer. So for example, the emphasis on completing an individual sale is the measure of the success of the exchange. Not surprisingly, this approach is often now referred to as a 'transaction marketing' approach. It is increasingly recognized that this is in effect a very short term and potentially ineffective way of dealing with customers. Relationship marketing, then, is aimed at developing a long-term series of mutually beneficial exchange processes between buyer and seller.

Under a relationship marketing approach, all the activities of an organization are used to build, maintain and develop customer relations, the objective being to build customer loyalty, thereby leading to customer retention. Relationship management is concerned with getting and keeping customers by ensuring that an appropriate combination of marketing, customer service and quality is provided. In order for relationship marketing to work, however, it is important to recognize that both parties must feel that they can benefit from long-term relationships rather than one-off transactions. A key element of relationship marketing, then, is the development of such mutually beneficial long-term relationships between customers and suppliers. With relationship marketing therefore, we see a shift towards a much more interactive, two-way set of relationships between suppliers and customers. This leads for example, therefore, to two-way communications together with the development of much more personalized marketing strategies to ensure a unique sustained competitive advantage. Relationship marketing also widens the concept of exchange to consider all of the parties involved. So, for example, relationship marketing also considers all of the organizations partnerships – suppliers, lateral, internal – as well as the buyer/consumer.

Relationship marketing requires a fundamentally different approach to that found in transaction marketing. To ensure successful relationship marketing there needs to be an appropriate supportive organizational culture and everyone in the company must be concerned with generating customer satisfaction. Hence, internal marketing is necessary in companies that are to successfully develop a relationship marketing approach. The growth of relationship marketing is linked to developments in information and databases by enabling the marketer to develop much more detailed understanding of customers, their expectations and needs. Customer databases help the marketer to listen to customers and interpret their problems. The use of customer databases has become so important in the contemporary marketing culture that the role and use of database marketing is considered in several of the later units. An outline of some of the most important developments in information and database marketing and developments in new technology in marketing are outlined below.

An increase in information and data-based marketing

As already mentioned throughout the units in this coursebook we shall see that, increasingly, information technology is being used by the marketer. There is no doubt that we shall continue to see an increase in the application of technology in marketing. Information, and particularly data-based marketing has allowed ever-more powerful and cost-effective marketing. Examples of areas where we shall see indications of this power include the growth of direct marketing and areas such as segmentation and market targeting. If we consider this last area, for example, improved information and databases are allowing marketers to identify and target smaller and smaller groups of customers but with great accuracy. This is helped by the proliferation of media channels now available to reach these smaller, more fragmented target segments. As a result, we have seen the growth of fragmented marketing approaches with a marketer being able to target more and more accurately specific groups of, or even individual customers. Information and database marketing then is having a major impact on the application of marketing. More broadly however, new technology in general is impacting marketing and marketing management.

Study tip

Because marketing is such a dynamic area of business and society it is constantly changing and evolving. Although we have introduced some of the more important trends and developments recently in marketing, it is impossible to cover all of the changes and trends which have taken place, and obviously we cannot cover those that are yet to do so. Other developments and trends which we could have mentioned include, for example, the growth in the importance of branding, the increasing fragmentation of markets and media, and the growth of network marketing. Although the examiner will not realistically expect you to be an expert in all the areas of marketing which are evolving and changing, it is important that you try and keep as up to date as possible with developments and trends. In addition to the text books, for the Fundamentals paper then, you should also try to read as widely as possible in the marketing press and journals. The CIM itself of course is a good source of information on trends and developments in marketing.

Growth of new technology in marketing

Technology, of any kind, helps to facilitate and, hopefully, improve the way we do things. Without technology many of the things we do – and often take for granted – would be at best difficult, and often impossible.

Think for a moment how different your life would be without, say, the telephone, or without access to penicillin and other modern medical treatments. What would the lives of some of us be like without the technology to, say, purify water or deliver electricity and power to our homes?

Perhaps less dramatically, but in context perhaps no less importantly, technology also affects and helps facilitate marketing and the marketing process. So much so that some areas of marketing and marketing techniques are almost totally underpinned by technology and its application. So, for example, much of advertising relies on communications technology; effective distribution and logistics relies on transport technologies; marketing research and analysis increasingly relies upon computing technology. Admittedly, this reliance on and use of technology in marketing is not new. After all, for example, trade and marketing between the Egyptians and Phoenicians was dependent on and affected by the technology of boat-building at the time. More recently, however, business in general and certainly marketing in particular, has become more and more affected by, and reliant upon, technology. Moreover, technology itself is changing at an ever-increasing rate. We shall explore some of the more important of these changes and advances in technology as they affect the marketer in more detail shortly in this unit. Suffice it to say at this stage, that advances in technology are now beginning to fundamentally change the nature of marketing and other business and commercial activities. So much so that many believe that in as little as ten years the process of exchange around which marketing is, of course, based would be changed beyond recognition compared to today. Certainly, at the very least, the contemporary marketer needs to be familiar with the key advances in technology which are currently affecting the marketing process. A summary of the reasons for this, which captures the importance of technological advances for marketers, are listed below:

- Competitive success increasingly is based on the application of advances in technology.
- Technology is increasingly being used by companies to both differentiate their products and reduce their costs.
- Many of the advances in technology allow the marketer to be much more customer and marketing oriented with, for example, much speedier and flexible responses to customer needs.
- Technological advances have led to the emergence of new critical success factors for organizations as a result of new ways of doing business.
- Advances in technology enable the marketing process to be carried out not only more effectively but more efficiently.
- New technology increasingly facilitates the ease with which information, so vital to effective marketing planning and decision making, can be collected and analysed.
- Advances in technology often underpin the growth of the global company and a move towards the global market and consumer.

Another way of illustrating the importance of some of the technological advances which are now taking place in marketing is to consider some of the effects that such technology is having, or will have in the future.

Some of these effects will be considered in more detail in later units but some of the key areas of marketing thinking and practice where technological advances have had a major effect include:

- Fundamental changes to retailing and shopping, for example in the future many customers will shop predominantly from home.
- Much greater price competition as customers are able to 'shop around' on, say, their computers.
- The potential demise of whole markets and their replacement by entirely new products and industries.
- Entirely new relationships between members of the value chain and particularly between customers and suppliers.
- Related to the above, the growth of new entrepreneurial companies such as the dotcom companies.

Needless to say, marketers have not been slow to grasp the advantages of the growing sophistication and application of advances in technology. Information and communication technology (ICT) in particular has assisted in the management of a customer-oriented culture in the following ways:

- The sophisticated use of current databases to understand consumer behaviour.
- Using the Internet as a marketing information system, e.g. for gathering competitor intelligence information.
- Using the World Wide Web to make products more accessible for consumers, i.e. the use of on-line shopping, offering more information about the company or product, etc.

- Building customer care systems for customers/clients using e-mail and webcasting.
- Considering segmentation and global niches, from the observation of the use of current, or specifically designed, Internet pages.

Together, the factors described above mean that today's marketer must not only be aware of, but understand, the advances in technology which are taking place. Moreover, the marketer must also be sensitive to, and be prepared for, tomorrow's advances in technology. This in turn means that the marketer must also have the necessary skills to use the new technologies of today and tomorrow to help facilitate the marketing process. The marketer who does not possess these skills will increasingly become a dinosaur – with probably the same fate as these unfortunate creatures! Similarly, those organizations whose management and marketers are unaware of, or unable to, utilize advances in technology will become increasingly uncompetitive. The new markets and marketing of today and tomorrow is very much technology's child.

Activity 1.14

Try to recall a purchase where you felt that you did not receive an adequate level of customer care.

- Describe what was inadequate/unsatisfactory about the level of care you received.
- Write down your feelings about the supplier/company you dealt with.
- What could/should the company/supplier do to improve levels of customer care?

Summary

In this unit we have seen that:

- Marketing is first and foremost a way of thinking that puts the customer at the centre of all organizational decisions. In doing so, marketing is a form of competition which serves as the means of creating customer value.
- Marketing orientation is the result of an evolution from a production-oriented through a sales-oriented era.
- A marketing culture must be developed throughout the organization, but this takes time and resources.

Marketing is also a management function encompassing the key tasks of analysis, planning, implementation and control and involves the co-ordination of organizational resources both within and outside the marketing function. The major tools of the marketer are the elements of the marketing mix, which in turn are allied to the processes of market segmentation and targeting.

- The marketing concept is still evolving and now embraces business-to-business marketing, services marketing and marketing in not-for-profit organizations.
- Marketing has responded to an increased awareness of environmental issues and an interest in total quality.
- Increasingly, marketers are recognizing the importance of treating customers as partners and in developing long-term, customer loyalty through the development of improved relationships with customers.
- As in many areas of management, developments in information technology are having, and will continue to have, a major impact on marketing practices.
- Database marketing is becoming increasingly important in the contemporary marketing culture.

Further study and examination preparation

Now do these questions:

Question 1.2

Identify and explain what is meant by a marketing concept by referring to at least three definitions from different theorists.

Question 1.3

What are the main differences between the following terms – production concept, selling concept and marketing concept?

Question 1.4

Identify a number of organizations which in your opinion have not adopted a marketing concept. Try to explain why you feel that this is the case.

Question 1.5

Identify the steps for introducing a marketing-oriented concept within an organization.

Question 1.6

Why might it be difficult to manage the introduction of a customer-oriented culture within an organization?

Question 1.7

How might the use of information technology assist in the management of a customer-oriented culture.

Question 1.8

What are the main differences in the exchange relationship for not-for-profit organizations such as charities?

Question 1.9

Discuss the implications of a marketing concept in a service organization.

Question 1.10

What are the main barriers when introducing a customer-oriented culture within an organization?

Question 1.11

Discuss the concept of social responsibility and comment on the implications of social responsibility from a marketing perspective relating to consumers and the marketing mix.

Question 1.12

Explain what relationship marketing means

Previous examination question

Study tip

This question is taken from Fundamentals of Marketing paper June 2000 question 6. Remember, you can access the full specimen answer for this question on the following website addresses: www.marketingonline.co.uk or www.bh.com/marketing.

Question E1

a. Identify both:

    i. A business-to-business organization

    ii. A non-profit organization

    which, in your opinion, have been successful in the adoption of the marketing concept. Give specific reasons to justify your choices.

(12 marks)

b. Explain how the use of Information Technology could assist in the management of a customer oriented culture within one of the above organizations

(8 marks)
(20 marks in total)

Bibliography

G. Lancaster, L. Massingham, R. Ashford, *Essentials of Marketing: 4th Edn,* Chaps 1 and 13, McGraw-Hill, 2002.

F. Brassington, S. Pettitt, *Principles of Marketing: 2nd Edn,* Prentice Hall, 2000, Chaps 1 & 21.

Kotler, *Marketing Management: 10th Edn,* Prentice-Hall, 2001, Chap 1.

Further reading

S. Dibb, L. Simpkin, W. Pride, O. C. Ferrell, *Marketing Concepts and Strategies: 4th European Edn*, Chaps 1 and 22, Houghton, Mifflin, 2000.

Objectives

By the end of this unit you will:

- Understand the importance of the marketing planning process, the structure and components of the marketing plan, and where it fits into the corporate or organizational planning framework (2.1, 2.8).

- Understand the models that describe the various stages of the marketing planning process (2.2).

- Understand the concept of the marketing audit and the various analytical tools used in the marketing auditing process (2.3, 2.4).

- Understand the value of marketing research and information in developing marketing plans (2.5).

- Understand the importance and approaches to objective setting (2.6).

- Understand the importance and process of segmentation, targeting and positioning (2.7, 3.1), market segmentation, targeting and positioning (2.6, 2.7).

- Appreciate the range of tools and techniques available to satisfy customer requirements and compete (3.2).

- Understand the process of setting marketing budgets (2.10).

- Understand the various management structures for implementing marketing plans and the importance of monitoring and control of marketing activities (2.9, 2.11, 3.16).

Study guide

In many ways this unit serves as an overview and framework for the rest of the units in the coursebook in as much as it encompasses the whole of the marketing process from the perspective of the steps and issues in marketing planning and budgeting. We shall be looking at the nature and the importance of the marketing planning process working through each of the various stages and introducing the relevant tools and concepts appropriate to each stage. Some central areas of marketing will be considered in this unit including areas such as the marketing audit and the related areas of so-called SWOT and PEST analysis. In addition we shall be looking at the concept of market segmentation and how this relates to the essential elements of targeting and positioning and the creation of an integrated and coherent marketing mix. The nature of marketing objectives is considered and the various marketing strategies to achieve these. Finally we shall look at implementation and control issues together with the role of marketing research and information in developing marketing plans. We would expect you to take about 5 hours to work through this unit and suggest you allow a further 4–5 hours to undertake the various activities suggested. Other than your notebook and writing equipment, you will not need anything further to complete this unit.

The nature and importance of marketing planning

In Unit 1 we suggested that there are four key elements of the marketing manager's task. You will recall that these are: analysis, planning, implementation and control. We also suggested that of these planning accounts for the major part of the marketing manager's responsibilities and activities. Having said this, effective plans must be built on, and reflect, careful analysis and as we shall see, implementation and control themselves can rightly be considered as part of the overall planning process. Put another way, then, the marketing manager's job is planning.

Not too many years ago, much of marketing was characterized by a lack of systematic and structured planning. Marketing managers often acted on hunch or intuition, or if you like, a feel for the market. Marketing activities were often unstructured and not set in a coherent and integrated framework. Often different marketing activities in different parts of the organization were uncoordinated with sometimes, for example, the sales function and the marketing function pulling in different directions. Similarly, the important coordinating role of marketing with respect to other functions in the business referred to in Unit 1 was often neglected. Increasingly, however, marketing is characterized by much more systematic and structured marketing planning using a variety of powerful and sometimes sophisticated planning tools and techniques. Contemporary marketing is now imbued with a planning culture. The reasons for this move towards a planning culture are numerous, but amongst some of the more important reasons for this move are the following:

- A more competitive marketing environment.
- A more dynamic marketing environment.
- High levels of investment required to develop new products and markets and hence high risk.
- More sophisticated and powerful planning tools and models.
- Better trained marketing managers.
- Access to marketing data and information.
- A recognition of the need for improved coordination and integration of marketing and other plans.

As a result of these and other factors then, many companies now have effective and sophisticated marketing planning systems. In addition to the move towards planning cultures in organizations, the perspective on the nature of plans has also changed in recent years. Specifically planning, including marketing planning has become more strategic in nature and as a result, so too has marketing itself. Strategic, as opposed to tactical marketing planning has the following characteristics:

- Strategic marketing planning involves longer term planning horizons.
- Strategic marketing planning involves major commitments of company resources.
- Strategic marketing planning determines the nature of what an organization is and what it is to be.
- Strategic marketing planning affects and involves all levels, functions and activities of a business.
- Strategic marketing planning reflects both internal (company) and external considerations.

There are probably as many different definitions of strategic marketing is there are different marketing textbooks. Perhaps one of the most comprehensive and yet easy to understand definitions of strategic marketing is that proposed by Cravens:

> **Definition**
>
> **Strategic marketing**
>
> It is a process of: strategically analysing environmental, competitive and business factors affecting business units and forecasting future trends in business areas of interest to the enterprise. Participating in setting objectives and formulating corporate and business unit strategies. Selecting target market strategies for the product markets in each business unit, establishing marketing objectives, and developing, implementing and managing programme positioning strategies for meeting target market needs.

The advantages of adopting a planning culture, coupled with a more strategic approach to marketing planning are many, but amongst the most important are the following:

- More structured analyses of the marketing environment.
- Objectives and strategies based on exploiting company strengths and marketing assets.
- An awareness of key marketing trends and possible future developments.
- Proactive rather than reactive approaches to marketing activities.
- An increased customer focus/customer orientation.
- Integrated marketing programmes involving cross functional activities.

Overall, these advantages have been shown to generate higher profits and more effective organizations. Let us now turn then to our basic model of the marketing planning process which you were introduced to in Unit 1 and consider the steps and stages in this process in more detail.

The marketing planning process

In Unit 1 you were introduced to a basic model of the marketing planning process. We can now examine the stages and steps in planning in more detail and see how the various stages of the marketing planning process fit together and relate to the overall corporate or organizational planning framework. Remembering again that there are many variations on the elements of the marketing planning process and their sequence, below is outlined again our basic model of the planning process showing each of the key stages and steps. This is shown in Figure 2.1.

Business mission/corporate objectives

↓

Marketing audit

↓

SWOT analysis

↓

Business objectives

↓

Marketing objectives

↓

Marketing strategies

↓

Marketing tactics/marketing mix decisions

↓

Implementation

↓

Monitoring and control

Figure 2.1 *Key steps in marketing planning*

We shall now take you through each of these steps again in more detail.

Business Mission/Corporate objectives

The start part of the marketing planning process is to determine the overall business mission and corporate objectives of the organization. It is sometimes easy to forget that marketing is only one function in an organization, albeit a central one. Marketing objectives and strategies, therefore, must be reflective and supportive of this overall business mission and corporate objectives. The business mission is the determination of what the company intends to be; if you like, its general culture and operating philosophies. An example of a business mission might be, say:

> *'To be the leading provider of technological solutions in the information technology market using the greenest technologies available and with a commitment to developing community and customer relations'.*

Corporate objectives may encompass several areas relating to, for example, growth, financial performance, innovation, corporate reputation, contributions to community and society, etc. and are more specific and quantified than the business mission statement. Before starting the marketing planning process, then, the marketing function must ascertain, and possibly help shape, the overall objectives of the organization. These in turn will then serve to feed into and shape marketing objectives and strategies and the individual elements of the marketing mix.

There is often confusion about the differences and/or relationships between corporate objectives and strategies and marketing objectives and strategies. The main differences between the two are that corporate objectives and strategies relate to objectives and strategies for the organization as a whole and encompass and affect every functional area of the business. Corporate objectives relate to broad objectives concerned, as we have seen, for example with growth, financial performance etc. as outlined above. Corporate strategies for achieving these will relate to the major routes or paths for achieving these, such as for example, growth through mergers, acquisitions, expansion, etc. Within these broad corporate objectives and strategies each functional area of the business, including marketing then, will need to develop a set of objectives and strategies which are consistent with, and supportive of, overall corporate and organizational objectives and strategies. We must stress again however, that of all the functional areas of business it is the marketing function, and therefore marketing management which will probably have most input to, and effect on, the identification and selection of overall corporate and organizational strategies.

In many organizations, and particularly the multi-product/market organization, the basic unit of marketing planning, i.e. the organizational element around which individual marketing strategies are planned, is increasingly the strategic business unit.

Definition

A strategic business unit (SBU)

It is a part of a business or organization which has its own customers/markets and its own competitors against which it is competing. It has its own management team who collectively are responsible for determining objectives, strategies and plans for this part of the business and who are responsible for the performance of the business. A strategic business unit can operate to all extent and purposes as an independent business.

Whilst a key role of marketing management then is indeed to help shape overall corporate objectives and strategies, detailed marketing plans and the sequence of steps shown in our Figure 2.1 are carried out at the level of the individual strategic business unit. Obviously, where a company has multiple strategic business units then the activities of these individual business units including, for example, the resources they will be allocated and the related aspect of which business units are to figure most strongly in the future plans of the organization, need to be assessed and coordinated. In particular, although each strategic business unit will have its own marketing objectives and strategies, the collection of business units have to be managed so as to ensure an effective balance of business units which will serve to meet the current corporate objectives and perhaps more importantly, will serve to meet future corporate objectives. A number of techniques and models for managing the collection of strategic business units have been developed. Collectively these techniques and models are often referred to as the techniques of '**portfolio analysis**'. The more important and useful of the techniques of portfolio analysis are discussed in your Unit 4 on Product Management.

Study tip

It is debatable whether the techniques of portfolio analysis are tools of strategic marketing planning or more specifically tools of product management. In fact, although the different portfolio models vary, most of the portfolio analysis techniques encompass and relate to both strategic marketing planning and managing the product mix. Although we have chosen to include these tools then in our unit on product management and new product development, they can also legitimately be classed as tools of marketing planning. Their use in this context would be as part of the marketing auditing process and hence they relate to element 2.4 of the CIM's syllabus for this subject.

Marketing audit

The second step in the marketing planning process involves the marketer in assessing the situation which faces the organization. The first half of the marketing audit will encompass the internal situation of the organization and its performance. The second half of the marketing audit involves analysing the external situation facing the organization. It is extremely important that marketing managers are able to understand the environment in which they are operating. This means that a systematic so-called PEST analysis will need to be undertaken on a regular basis.

The initials PEST are widely used and understood by marketers and they represent some of the major factors in the wider marketing environment which the marketer must assess. The PEST initials stand for:

- *Political factors* such as government regulations, policies and strategies, tax, education, business and industry.
- *Economic factors* such as movements in the trade cycle, levels of disposable income, interest rates and inflation.
- *Social/cultural factors* such as the ageing consumer, increases in one-parent families, changing values, attitudes and beliefs.
- *Technological factors* such as the increased rate of computer capability, developments in IT and production methods.

In addition to these PEST factors, the marketing audit of the environment should also encompass factors such as competitors, suppliers and distributors, which also must be taken into account in planning marketing decisions.

With regard to the internal half of the audit the marketer must regularly and systematically assess the resources, systems and procedures and skills of the organization. The internal marketing audit should examine these from the perspective of the extent to which they can be used to generate competitive advantage through customer satisfaction. In other words, resources, procedures and skills should be assessed from the point of view of a customer/marketing orientation. Obviously in carrying out the internal audit the marketing planner must decide what resources activities and skills of the organization should be included. Many companies use standard checklists for this process encompassing, and including, the following areas or aspects of the organization:

- Financial.
- Marketing.
- Manufacturing.
- Physical resources.
- Personnel.
- Research and development.

You will note, and may initially be surprised, that the internal audit encompasses not just the marketing area of the business. This relates to our earlier discussion regarding the coordinating function of marketing and the need to look at all of the business activities from a marketing/customer perspective. The internal audit is seeking to establish bases for competing in the market place. Certainly, often these bases will be primarily marketing in nature, e.g. effective advertising or packaging, say, but often companies compete using skills and resources in other functional areas of the business, so for example, research and development, admittedly through new products, may be a major means of achieving competitive success. What the marketer must do, therefore, in conducting the internal audit is to establish what are critical resources, skills and processes in the context of the particular markets the company operates in and the objectives it wishes to achieve in these. Once the marketer has done this, then we can move from a straight forward assessment of internal factors into an interpretation of these together with the external factors in the form of a SWOT analysis.

SWOT analysis

The internal and external audit allows the marketer to produce a systematic SWOT analysis. Widely known and used in marketing planning, these initial letters stand for:

- Strengths.
- Weaknesses.
- Opportunities.
- Threats.

The strengths and weaknesses part of the SWOT analysis come from the internal half of the marketing audit.

In conducting the internal marketing audit referred to above, the objective is to assess company resources, activities and skills with regard to establishing the extent to which the company is strong or weak. So when, for example, the marketer audits, say, the financial, managerial, marketing, production and research and development etc. elements of the business it is from the perspective of assessing strengths and weaknesses.

Completing the strengths and weaknesses part of the SWOT analysis helps to point out what is possible in terms of marketing objectives and strategies. For example, it would be pointless to pursue a marketing strategy in which innovatory products feature strongly if we were not ourselves strong in this area.

The opportunities and threats half of the SWOT analysis is derived, needless to say, from the analysis of the marketing environment including the PEST factors. It is relatively easy to find examples of how the marketing environment might give rise to opportunities and threats. For example:

- A downturn in disposable income may threaten the demand for, say, luxury products.
- A change in government policy may give rise to opportunities for more environmentally friendly products.
- A decline in the birth rate may threaten the baby food manufacturer. Developments information technology may provide opportunities for direct marketing.

Activity 2.1

Try to find your own real life examples of where a trend/change in each of our PEST factors has resulted in an opportunity or threat to a company.

One of the main aims of a SWOT analysis is, having identified the company's weaknesses, to look at ways in which these can be converted into strengths; and similarly to convert the threats into opportunities. Decision makers can then decide which are the best ways through which these conversion processes can be achieved.

A good way of representing the outcome of a SWOT analysis is to use a matrix approach as shown in Figure 2.2 which also shows the notion of conversion referred to.

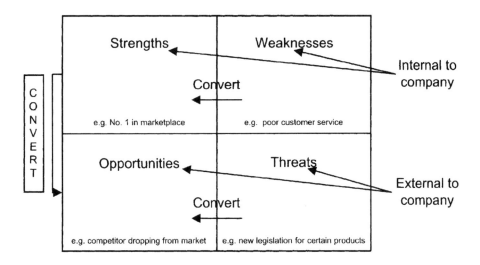

Figure 2.2 A SWOT Analysis

Marketing objectives

The marketing audit and SWOT analysis enables the marketer to determine the overall marketing objectives for the organization. Marketing objectives encompass long-, medium- and short-term marketing objectives. Marketing objectives may relate to, for example, market share, sales, growth and so on. It is important that these objectives are specific, measurable, actionable, realistic, and timely. In addition, remember that marketing objectives must reflect and be integrated with the company's overall corporate objectives.

Marketing strategies

Marketing strategies represent the overall thrust of a company's marketing activities. There are a number of components to marketing strategies as follows.

Growth strategies: the Ansoff Matrix

It is widely accepted that most companies want to grow. However, there are a number of strategies which a company may use to achieve growth. You may recall that in Unit 'The marketing culture' we suggested that one of the most useful and therefore most widely used models for identifying alternative product market growth strategies is the so-called Ansoff matrix. We shall now consider this matrix. This is shown in Figure 2.3.

	Current products	New products
Current markets	Market penetration strategy	Product development strategy
New markets	Market development strategy	Diversification strategy

Figure 2.3 *Ansoff's Product Market Growth Grid*

This framework for delineating alternative growth strategies is based on a framework comprising 'markets' on one axis and 'products' on the other. Each of the strategies delineated in the matrix are briefly explained below.

- *Market penetration* This strategy is based on expanding sales from existing products in existing markets. There are a number of ways in which this can be achieved, for example, the company may attempt to encourage customers to use the product more frequently or more heavily. Alternatively, market penetration can be achieved through attacking competitors' market share through, for example, heavy promotion and price discounts.

- *Market development* This strategy for growth involves entering new markets with existing products, for example, a company may achieve growth by attacking new market segments by export marketing. With this strategy it is essential that proposed new markets are carefully assessed with respect to, say, attractiveness, and in particular the extent to which the company can match the requirements for success in the new markets.

- *Product development* This strategy for growth involves developing and launching new products for sale in existing markets. Sometimes these may be extensions to the existing product range, such as additional features or different packaging, but also may involve entirely new products for the market. In the case of entirely new products this can be an extremely risky, if potentially profitable strategy. As we shall see in a later unit, it is essential to have systematic procedures for developing and launching new products where this strategy for growth is being pursued.

- *Diversification* This strategy is probably the highest risk of all the four strategic options for growth, involving as it does both new products and new markets for the organization. Diversification can take a number of forms ranging from moving into related products and markets through to entirely new products and markets. Again, this can be a very profitable route to growth but needs to be carefully planned if it is to succeed.

Overall competitive strategies

Having identified strategies for growth, a second facet of overall marketing strategy is to determine how a company will compete. We can distinguish between:

1. Cost leadership strategies.
2. Differentiation strategies.
3. Focus strategies.

Which generic strategy is selected as a basis for competing will obviously have major implications for the selection of marketing tactics, i.e. the design of the marketing mix.

Activity 2.2

Try to find out what is meant by each of Porter's three alternative generic strategies. When you have done this, briefly, and in your own words, describe the possible implications of each strategy for the marketing mix.

Segmentation, targeting and positioning strategies

Many would argue that one of the most important elements of marketing plans is what is known as target marketing. This in turn comprises of the sub-elements of market segmentation, targeting, and positioning.

Target marketing is central to contemporary marketing planning. The notion of target marketing is, in fact, an extension of the basic concept of marketing discussed in Unit 1. In essence it is a recognition that the marketer needs to meet the specific requirements and needs of customers as closely as possible. This is especially true in today's markets, where competition for customers is intense and where customers are better informed and more demanding. Put simply, the company that comes closest to meeting the precise needs of customers through the marketing mix will get the business.

In any given market, however, different customers will have different needs. This means that rarely these days can a company succeed by mass-producing a standardized product aimed at the whole market. Put another way, a modern-day Henry Ford offering customers 'any colour so long as it was black' would find difficulty marketing the product.

The fact that customers have different needs within a market means that the marketer must break down the market by identifying what these different needs are and the customer groups with which these different needs are associated. This first stage of target marketing is known as 'market segmentation'.

Having identified the different market segments, the marketer can then evaluate these various segments and decide which of them to cater for and on what basis. This second step is the 'targeting' step.

Finally, the marketer must decide the 'product positioning' strategy to be used in serving selected target markets. This final stage is where we see the impact of the process of target marketing on the marketing mix. In positioning products and services within selected target markets the marketing mix is designed to meet the specific needs of the target market identified in the market segmentation stage so as to secure a competitive advantage.

We shall now discuss the elements of target marketing beginning with market segmentation.

Market segmentation

At this stage of target marketing the marketer assesses the extent to which there are different customer groups in the market with different requirements and needs. The marketer must also determine the bases on which the market segments.

In fact virtually all markets for products and services, both consumer and industrial, usually segment into clusters of customers on some basis. You probably already have a good idea of the variety of bases on which different markets might be segmented. Some of the major categories of segmentation bases used by marketers are shown in the activity that follows.

Activity 2.3

In this activity we have listed the main categories of segmentation bases used to segment markets. We have distinguished between bases commonly used in consumer markets and those commonly used in industrial markets. To make sure you understand each of these main categories for segmentation you should write down examples of variables used to segment markets within each major category. So in the case of the 'demographic' bases an example of a variable would be 'age'.

- **Consumer bases**
  Demographics, e.g. 'Age'
  Socio-economic, e.g.
  Geographic, e.g.
  Personality and lifestyle, e.g.
  Purchase occasion, e.g.
  User status, e.g.
  Usage rate, e.g.
  Benefits sought, e.g.

We can see from this activity that there are many potential bases for segmenting markets and that at least some of these are common to both 'consumer', and 'industrial'. Very often the marketer will combine bases for segmentation purposes. But how do we know which bases to use in segmenting a market? The answer to this is to use bases that enable us to identify distinct and different clusters of customers with respect to the product or market in question. So, for example, we know that in segmenting the market for, say, clothing the variables of sex, income, social class, and age are all related to differences in purchase requirements.

In fact there is no one right way to segment a market. Ideally segmentation bases should allow us to reveal segments that have the following characteristics:

- Measurable – the segments revealed should be easy to measure.

- Substantial – the segments revealed should be large enough to serve.

- Accessible – the marketer should be able to reach the segments revealed.

Activity 2.4

Remembering that there is no one right way to segment a market, can you suggest what might be appropriate basis/bases for segmenting the markets shown below.

1. Holidays.
2. Cars.
3. Cigarettes.
4. Industrial abrasives.
5. Office-cleaning services.

Targeting strategies

Having identified market segments, the marketer must now decide which of these segments to target, (i.e. market to, and on what basis). This decision will be affected by a number of factors, but the marketer will need mainly to evaluate the relative attractiveness of the different segments in the market and the company's ability to serve the different segments. Ideally we are looking for attractive segments we can serve well. There are three broad alternative targeting strategies – undifferentiated targeting, differentiated targeting, and concentrated targeting. We have defined each of these below.

Definition

Undifferentiated targeting

Undifferentiated targeting is targeting the whole market with one marketing mix.

Definition

Differentiated targeting

Differentiated targeting is targeting several market segments with a different marketing mix for each segment.

Definition

Concentrated targeting

Concentrated targeting is targeting just one segment within the total market. There are advantages and disadvantages to each targeting strategy, with, again, the choice being dependent upon many factors such as company size and resources, market risks, competitors and so on. Even if you are relatively unfamiliar with these three alternative targeting strategies, you should be able to assess some of the advantages and disadvantages of each.

Activity 2.5

For each of the targeting strategies see if you can assess what might be some of the advantages and disadvantages.

Complete the following:

- Undifferentiated targeting
    1. Advantages, e.g.
    2. Disadvantages, e.g.
- Differentiated targeting
    1. Advantages, e.g.
    2. Disadvantages, e.g.
- Concentrated targeting
    1. Advantages, e.g.
    2. Disadvantages, e.g.

Positioning strategies

You will have noted in our discussion of targeting strategies, however, that we are beginning to see the influence of target marketing in planning the marketing mix. We said earlier that it is in the positioning step that this influence can be seen most directly. Having segmented the market, and decided on the targeting strategy, the marketer must ensure that the targeted segment is reached and its needs served by designing the marketing mix so as to position it in the segment against the competition.

So, for example, if we are targeting the higher income segment of a market that is looking for high quality products, can pay premium prices, reads up-market magazines and shops at exclusive outlets, to a large extent our marketing mix decisions are made for us. This is the advantage of solving the positioning problem, and this is why positioning, though only the final step in target marketing, is so important to planning the marketing mix.

Activity 2.6

Look out for examples of brands that are clearly targeting different market segments within the same product market, e.g. different soap powders, different cigarettes, different cars, etc. Take note of how they are positioning themselves in the market place against competition and in particular how the brands differ in terms of their marketing mix.

Exam hint

In collecting your examples of positioning of brands it can be useful to use 'positioning maps' to illustrate the relative position of brands in a market. The use of such 'maps' to illustrate the relative position of brands in a market can also be very useful in the examination to make your points quickly and visually. An example of a simple positioning map with two brands is shown in Figure 2.4. You will note that it is only possible, of course, to show two dimensions or elements of the marketing mix.

Figure 2.4 A Simple Positioning Map

Marketing tactics/marketing mix decisions

Having determined the key elements of marketing strategy, we are now in a position to develop the more detailed marketing tactics. Essentially, this involves planning how the different marketing tools will be used in the marketing plan. It is therefore concerned with planning a co-ordinated marketing mix for each target market. By this stage of the planning process the previous steps will effectively now dictate these marketing mix decisions. It is in this stage of the marketing plan that these elements are brought together to form an integrated and cohesive whole.

You were introduced to the notion of the marketing mix and the elements which this includes in Unit 1. To remind you, the marketing mix represents those controllable factors or tools which the marketer can make decisions about with a view to developing effective marketing programmes. The basic marketing mix comprises of the Four Ps of Product, Price, Place (Distribution) and Promotion. Increasingly, marketers now think about an additional three elements comprising of People, Process and Physical evidence. Within each of these major tools of the marketing mix however, there are any number of variations and ways in which the marketer may use each tool to satisfy customer requirements and compete effectively. So, for example, taking the promotional element of the mix, we can identify the following sub-elements within this marketing mix tool:

- Advertising.
- Sales promotion.
- Personal selling.
- Publicity and PR.
- Sponsorship and exhibitions etc.

Further, each of these tools can be used in a wide range of ways. So, for example, when it comes to advertising the marketer can aim advertising at, say, distributors or consumers or both. Similarly, advertising programmes and spends may be run over an extended period of time with short bursts of advertising spend or with large advertising spends concentrated in short bursts. The content of the advertising itself can be factual, emotional, or informative. Media use for advertising could be one or a combination of press, television, trade publications, magazines, newspapers, etc. Put simply, then, each of the marketing mix tools encompasses an extremely wide range of tools, techniques and approaches which are available to marketers.

The context for the marketing mix

Planning the marketing mix, as we have already seen, stems from the earlier stages and decisions in our planning process shown in Figure 2.1. A major consideration, however, in marketing mix decisions in addition to the ones already outlined as part of the normal planning process, such as targeting and positioning decisions, is the contextual setting for marketing mix decisions. According to the context, then marketers will apply the marketing mix tools and techniques in different ways. A key element affecting the marketing mix tools are the different stages in the life of a product and market which we shall consider in the Unit 'The Marketing Mix: Product decisions'. In addition however, contextual factors also relate to different organizations with respect to, for example, whether they are profit seeking or not, or perhaps the size and resources of the organization and differences between markets and customers such as, for example, marketing to consumers and marketing to businesses. To a large extent these different contextual settings will determine the appropriateness or otherwise of the different mix elements and how they are combined. Understanding the context for marketing mix decisions, then, is vital.

Before we move on from the marketing mix however, in this unit, we need to discuss the importance of creating an integrated and coherent marketing mix.

The importance of combining and co-ordinating the marketing mix: the concept of synergy

A key distinguishing characteristic of effective as opposed to ineffective marketing is the extent to which the individual elements of the marketing mix are coordinated and combined so as to give a consistent and planned approach to the market.

As we have seen, each of the individual tools of the marketing mix calls for wide-ranging and complex decisions. Often other functions would input to these decisions. For example, in the case of pricing decisions we saw that a key input is information on costs from the accountancy function. Similarly, new product development decisions may require the expertise and inputs from research and development, design, and production. Because of this, it is vitally important that someone, or at least some function, takes responsibility for ensuring that these individual decisions hang together in a coordinated manner. That someone, or function, is marketing.

Effective marketing planning requires that all activities that impinge on the satisfaction of customer needs must be co-ordinated by marketing. This means coordinating activities in functions outside the marketing function in the organization, and includes the coordination of external organizations such as market-research and advertising agencies.

If marketing does not take responsibility for this coordination, then it is almost inevitable that decisions about the marketing mix, such as, for example, product, price, will be taken unilaterally. If this happens, there will be little consistency between the elements of the marketing mix. We know that if the marketing mix elements are coordinated we are much more likely to achieve something which has been referred to as 'synergy'.

Definition

Synergy

Synergy is where the outcome of combining individual elements together is greater than the simple sum total of each of the elements. It is often expressed as 2 + 2 = 5.

An example of synergy is, say, where the marketer ensures that a high price is set to reflect a quality product sold through exclusive distribution outlets with costly and quality sales promotion. Each of the marketing mix elements acts in concert to give a marketing presence which is consistent and where each element serves to support and enhance the other elements in the marketing mix.

One could also appreciate the importance of consistency, and hence synergy, in planning the combination of the marketing mix elements by reflecting on the problems that marketers can have where this consistency is lacking. For example, one sometimes comes across examples of prestige/quality products being retailed in down-market outlets. Similarly, we see examples of marketers trying to charge premium prices for basic products. Thirdly, we sometimes see examples of where, although there is some consistency in the mix itself, the mix as a whole is inappropriate for the target market, e.g. top quality and premium priced products being targeted at lower income groups.

Finally, we can find examples of where the mix is consistent and was initially targeted at appropriate customer groups; but over time customers and their needs can change and competitors are always looking for new ways to compete. What this means is that planning the marketing mix is a continuous activity in what are dynamic markets.

Activity 2.7

Try to find examples yourself of marketing programmes exhibiting one or more of the problems just outlined.

Obviously then, the marketer has to try and ensure that the mix elements are combined and coordinated in an effective manner. In part this involves no more than simple common sense, so for example, it would not make sense to product a luxury top end product distributed through exclusive outlets with bargain basement prices. Perhaps the most important aspect in coordinating the marketing mix, however, is to ensure that it is consistent with the intended target market and the positioning strategies determined earlier in the process for these. In addition, remember though we have already suggested that one of the most important factors affecting how the marketing mix elements are utilized and combined is what is termed in the syllabus for marketing fundamentals the 'contextual setting' in which the marketing mix tools are used. As already explained, contextual here means the different types of market and marketing settings in which marketers operate. These different contexts encompass fast-moving consumer goods settings, business-to-business settings, large or capital project based settings, services settings, voluntary and not-for-profit settings, and finally, small to medium enterprise settings such as those for example found in sales support organizations. These different contexts have such an important influence on the selection and emphasis given to the marketing mix tools and how they are coordinated and combined that we shall consider the effect of these different contexts in more detail in our Unit 'Marketing in Context'. But let us now return to our final stage of the marketing planning process, namely the implementation, monitoring and control of the marketing mix and programmes.

Implementation, monitoring and control of the marketing mix and programmes

Plans are nothing unless they degenerate into action. Implementation is the steps and activities required to bring plans to life. Implementation involves the detailed scheduling for planning activities and involves areas such as budgets, staffing, detailed timetables and so on. In addition, organizational structures and systems must be designed in order to ensure that plans are effectively implemented. The marketer must therefore act in order to ensure that the necessary structures, people, budgets, and processes are in place in order to effectively implement marketing plans.

In this section of the unit we shall consider in particular the budgeting element of implementing marketing plans together with the alternative management structures available for implementing marketing plans. We shall then consider the key area of monitoring and control.

Marketing budgets and the marketing plan

As already mentioned broad objectives and strategies must eventually be translated into detailed action programs in order to bring the plan to life. These detailed action programs will encompass the activities to be performed, by whom, when and most importantly at what cost. It is this final detail of action programs that raises the issue of marketing budgets. Obviously without the necessary supporting financial resources then marketing programs and plans will never be implemented. Budgeting then is a key aspect of implementing marketing plans. But what exactly is a marketing budget?

Definition

Marketing budget

A marketing budget represents the amount of resources allocated to support marketing activities over a period of time.

Within this seemingly straightforward definition, in fact we have several potentially complicating issues when we consider marketing budgets and budgeting further.

First of all resources of course could include manpower, facilities, time, and so on. Here, we shall discuss resource allocation in a budgeting context with specific regard to financial resources, i.e. monetary budgets, but we should not forget that budgets encompass more than simply financial resources.

Secondly, there are two related sub-facets when it comes to marketing budgets. The first of these concerns how decisions are made with regard to the determination of the overall marketing budget covering all marketing activities in the marketing plan. The second concerns how that overall budget will be allocated between the different elements of marketing activity within the marketing plan. So, for example, we have to determine how much of the budget will be allocated to, say, sales or selling activities, how much to branding and packaging, how much to distribution and so on. We shall be considering both overall budget determination and the issue of allocating budgets to the different elements of marketing activity in this section.

Finally, there are different time horizons with regard to all budgets including therefore, marketing budgets. In general terms we can distinguish between annual and longer term budgets in marketing. Both are necessary in order to encompass of course, different planning horizons within the marketing plans themselves. Long term marketing strategies aimed at pursuing long term marketing objectives require long term budgeting procedures. Here, we shall confine ourselves principally to annual marketing budgets required to support the annual marketing plan.

With these considerations in mind then, we can now consider the annual marketing financial budgeting process. We shall start by considering the alternative approaches to determining the overall annual marketing plan budget.

Alternative approaches to determining annual marketing plan overall financial budgets

There are a number of approaches to determining the overall amount to be allocated to the marketing activities in the annual marketing plan.

Affordable method

The first and perhaps the simplest way of determining the overall annual marketing budget is to base the budget on what the company can afford. You will immediately recognize of course that although a simple approach, there is relatively little or no real merit in adopting this approach to setting the annual marketing budget. Admittedly it does ensure that the company does not 'overspend' with regard to its financial resources but it means that, for example, in the case of a company which is making little profit it will allocate relatively little to its annual marketing budget and hence remain at the very best stuck in its low profit situation.

Percentage of profits

In a sense, a variation on the affordable method. This approach to setting the overall marketing budget is based on setting the budget according to some percentage of the company profits. Sometimes the profits used are the previous year's profits, or in other cases can be based on forecast profits. Either way, however, the problem with this approach is that it assumes that budgets are a function of profits and not the other way around. In addition, as with our affordable method therefore, it can condemn the low profit or low profit forecast organization to remaining in the marketing wilderness. Finally, even if we accept that this method is simple and is at least related to some objective measure, it does not of itself tell us what percentage of profits is an appropriate one to allocate for the marketing budgets.

Percentage of sales

This is probably the most widely used method for setting budgets in organizations including marketing budgets. The budgeting process in this approach starts usually with a sales forecast which is then used to determine what activities will be needed to support the sales levels forecast which in turn results in not just marketing budgets but production budgets, manpower budgets, and so on. Again, one can see why this is a widely used method of budgeting. It does appear to have an inherent logic and indeed many activities and costs in a company stem from and are directly related to the level of sales achieved. However, like the percentage of profits approach, this is essentially a negative way to determine the overall marketing budget. If sales are forecast to decrease, for example, then so are marketing budgets. This in turn of course can lead to a further drop in sales ad infinitum.

Objective and tasks

This approach to setting the overall annual marketing budget is in fact the most rational and defendable approach. In this approach, the budgets are determined by establishing what tasks need to be performed, in this case with regard to marketing tasks, in order to achieve the marketing objectives set out in the marketing plan. These activities can then be costed and the total of these costs represents the required total budget to support the marketing plan. The downside to this approach to setting the overall marketing budget is of course that it does require substantial effort, time and information. It requires, for example, detailed costings for the marketing activities in the marketing plan, or in some cases detailed estimates. The major advantage, however, is that it forces the marketing planner to think about the costs of the various marketing activities in the marketing plan, how these costs relate to the achievement of marketing objectives and therefore if they are cost effective, and how costs might be controlled.

Allocating budgets to marketing activities

Outlined, then, are the major alternative ways of determining the annual financial budget for the marketing plan. In addition, decisions must be made with regard to the allocations of this overall budget to the various marketing activities in the plan. In the multi product company, these allocation decisions must also be made with respect to the different products or brands of the business and, where appropriate, to the different strategic business units. All three methods above can be used to allocate the budget between products, brands and businesses. So, for example, we can allocate the budget between different products on the basis of forecast sales for each. Often, however, these allocation decisions are made on the basis of which brand or product manager in the organization shouts loudest, is most persuasive, is friendly with the marketing director, and so on. In fact, as with the overall budget allocation to support the marketing plan, the objective and task method is the only defendable way of allocating the budget between the various marketing activities. So, for example, in determining the promotional budget the marketing manager must assess what tasks the promotional element of the marketing mix will be required to perform in the context of the overall marketing objectives in the plan. These can then be costed and the budget allocation to this element of the mix determined.

In principle, determining and allocating marketing budgets is straight forward. In practice, it can be complex. In addition to ensuring that the necessary financial and other resources have been allocated for the effective implementation of marketing plans, there must be suitable organizational and management structures in place for their effective implementation.

Management and organizational structures for implementing marketing plans

Plans are implemented by people, and particularly by managers, and in turn require suitable and appropriate organizational structures for their implementation. Companies use a myriad of different management and organizational structures to implement their marketing plans. Management structures include, for example, product manager systems where marketing plans are organized and implemented around products. Structures which are based on brands and utilize brand manager systems therefore. Structures which are based around customers or markets. So, for example, organizations have management structures for, say, business-to-business customers and separate management structures for marketing their fast moving consumer goods. These are just some of the dimensions for distinguishing and identifying between different management and organizational structures for implementing marketing plans. With variations on a theme, there are literally dozens of possible alternatives. The reason for such a myriad of alternative approaches is that, in fact, there is no one method of organizing for the implementation of marketing plans which is always and inevitably superior. In some circumstances, organizing around products for example with product managers is the most effective method. In other circumstances organizing around markets is the most appropriate and effective. Many factors affect what is an appropriate management and organizational structure for implementing plans including, for example:

- Organizational size, and complexity.
- Organizational resources.
- Spread/diversity of product markets.
- Speed of market and technological change.
- Competition and competitive market structure.
- Geographical spread of organization and markets.
- Organizational culture.
- Managerial skills and expertise.
- Requirements for control etc.

It is impossible and downright dangerous to be prescriptive about the form which management and organizational structures should take in implementing marketing plans. Having said this, irrespective of the precise management and organizational structures and systems, these should be selected and designed so as to ideally provide the following:

- Company-wide customer orientation.
- Organizational flexibility and speed of response.
- Innovation.
- Co-ordination and integration between different functional areas of the business and outside organization.
- Effective communication.
- Motivation and leadership.

In practice, most management and organizational systems and structures are a compromise between the above ideals, but if organizational and management structures are not appropriate and supportive of marketing plans and activities, this can be a major problem for an organization and indeed management and organizational structural problems and weaknesses are a major contributory cause of marketing and organizational poor performance and even failure.

These, then, are the important budgeting and management/organizational issues in implementing marketing plans. Our final element of the marketing planning process involves the monitoring and control of marketing plans.

The importance of monitoring and control

Essentially the process of monitoring and control comprises comparing actual performance against required or desired performance objectives and then taking any necessary action to correct differences between actual and required. Because of this, the control process in marketing stems from the marketing objectives and strategies of the company.

Without monitoring and control it is impossible to assess the extent to which marketing objectives have been achieved and the strategies have been effective. Given the potentially large costs and use of resources in implementing the elements of the marketing mix, it would be inadvisable not to assess how well these resources have been used.

In addition, we know that markets are dynamic. The environment changes, customers change, competitors change, even the company itself can change over time. This means, therefore, that the marketing mix needs also to change to reflect and cope with these outside changes. Monitoring and control of the marketing mix facilitates the planning of such changes. Without monitoring and control there is a danger that marketing strategies become outmoded and no longer fit the market situation.

Types of control in marketing

The major types of control used in marketing include the following:

1. Customer feedback/customer tracking, e.g.

   - Customer surveys.
   - Customer complaints.
   - Sales-force reports.
   - Customer panels.

2. Sales analysis and control, e.g.

   - Sales volume/value.
   - Sales trends.
   - Breakdown of sales by product, customer, sales person, etc.

3. Market share analysis and control, e.g.

   - As per sales analysis above, but based on percentage of market.

4. Profitability analysis and control, e.g.

   - Analysis of costs and margins.
   - Net profits.
   - Return on capital.

5. Strategic control. This is the most wide-ranging and comprehensive of control techniques used in marketing, covering the control of the strategic planning process itself. Two main tools are used in strategic control, and both call for a wide-ranging review of the effectiveness of marketing activities, namely:

   - Marketing-effectiveness rating reviews.
   - The marketing audit.

Extending knowledge

If you are unfamiliar with some of these tools of control in marketing you should consult a basic text such as G. A. Lancaster and L. Massingham & R Ashford (2002) *Marketing Management*, 4th Edition, Chapter 16.

Activity 2.8

If you can, try to arrange an interview with a senior marketing manager (this could be in your own company of course) and try to establish what types of controls are being used to evaluate marketing performance.

The outcome of the marketing planning process: The marketing plan

We have covered all of the major steps in the marketing planning process but remember, this is the process and not the marketing plan itself. The marketing plan represents the outcome of this process, so what does a marketing plan look like and what are the main contents of a marketing plan? Below we have listed the main content areas of a 'typical' annual marketing plan illustrating the structure and outline content of an annual marketing plan. Although the structure and contents of the plan would probably not vary all that much for longer term plans, it is important to remember that the specific layout and structure of a marketing plan can vary slightly according to the situation and the company.

Management summary

This part of the plan summarizes the main points of the plan covering key objectives, major strategies and outline marketing mix programs.

Product market situation

This part of the plan covers the analysis of the market for the product(s)/services; included in here would be, for example, data on target market, market size, market trends and projections. This section will often include information on customer needs and buying behaviour. The product part of this section of the plan should contain information on prices, contributions and net profits for each of the major product lines encompassed by the plan. The competitive and distribution situation should also be included.

Strengths, weaknesses, opportunities and threats analysis

This section of the plan encompasses the external marketing audit encompassing our so-called PEST factors, forecast changes which will give rise to opportunities and threats. This part of the marketing plan should also contain the internal marketing audit encompassing company strengths and weaknesses.

Marketing objectives

This element of the plan details broad sets of objectives which the plan is intended to achieve. Remember, these objectives will stem not only from the analysis encompassed in the first sections of the plan but also should reflect corporate objectives. Objectives should be stated, remember, in SMART terms and should encompass financial, marketing and any other objectives pertaining to stakeholder and social responsibilities, etc.

Marketing strategies

The marketing strategies element of the plan encompasses decisions regarding core target markets, decisions regarding product market expansion plans, (the Ansoff matrix) the basis for competing, i.e. the competitive advantage, and the desired product/brand positioning.

Action programs

The action programs part of the plan involves the preparation of detailed programs for each of the marketing mix elements encompassing as a minimum the four conventional Ps of the marketing mix, but increasingly in almost every company the additional 'People' element of the mix, and in the case of service industries and markets, the further two Ps of 'Process' and 'Physical Evidence'. The action programs should contain plans for implementing these including the allocation of tasks and responsibilities, and required marketing structures and systems.

Budgets/financial implications

This part of the plan should encompass a delineation of costs and required budgets for marketing programs. These budgets should be allocated to the various marketing activities as appropriate. This part of the plan should also contain projected sales which will enable, in turn, projected profit and loss statements.

Controls and evaluation

This part of the plan contains information on expected standards of performance as the basis of control, it should also contain information on how results will be measured and the control mechanisms to be used.

Contingencies

The contingencies part of the plan detail what actions will be taken should there be any problems. So, for example, if the marketing plan is based on a set of assumptions, say regarding levels of inflation/interest rates etc, and should these materially alter during the period of time that the plan is in operation, requiring changes in elements of the plan, then this contingency section is aimed at encompassing any potential changes in plans of action.

Appendices

The appendices part of the plan should contain most of the detailed background analyses carried out in the production of the marketing plan. The plan itself should be as brief and focused as possible and therefore the appendices provide an opportunity to include the more detailed background analysis and information in a separate part of the plan for those who wish to examine this detail.

Further issues in marketing planning and budgeting

In this final part of the unit we consider two further issues with respect to marketing planning and budgeting. First of all we consider the important issue of the use of marketing research and information in marketing planning. Secondly we look at some of the ways in which marketers are making use of technological advances and new technology in the marketing planning process.

Marketing research and information in marketing planning

At virtually every stage of the marketing process, and certainly in every stage of marketing planning, the marketer must make use of the most accurate and up to date information available within the time and cost constraints pertaining. A way of illustrating how marketing research and information can help in this respect is to examine the most common areas or problems given by marketers as the focus for marketing research activities. These are as follows:

- Market share analysis.
- Market size potential analysis.
- Sales analysis.
- Business and market trends.
- Short and long range forecasting.
- Competitor analysis.
- Pricing analysis.
- Analysis of products.
- Communication analysis.
- Distribution and logistics analysis.

We can see that many of these areas of analysis relate to areas or aspects of the marketing plan and the marketing planning process. In addition, implicit in the areas of research listed above is the analysis of customer and market segments. A key part of marketing research activities, therefore, in marketing planning, is this analysis and understanding of customers and market segments. Marketing research and information has several uses and advantages in the context of marketing planning. Amongst some of the main advantages and uses are the following:

- It improves the marketer's ability to make decisions.
- The changing values and behaviour of customers can be monitored.
- Competitors' development of their strategies can be identified.
- It can be used to continuously evaluate the current effectiveness of an organization's strategies and tactics such as, for example, a television advertising campaign.
- Research in the form of environmental scanning can help to identify the changes in social, legal, political and technological advancements.

Marketers therefore must, and do, make use of the tools and techniques of marketing research in preparing marketing plans. Sometimes this marketing research will be one off ad hoc research aimed at addressing a specific and identified research problem and objective such as, for example, establishing the potential market size for, say, a new product. In addition, however, and increasingly, the marketing planning process is aided and abetted through marketing information systems in the organization.

Marketing information systems and marketing planning

Increasingly, often supported through improved information technology, (some of which we shall consider shortly in the unit) marketers have extended their concept of the scope and uses of information for marketing decisions. Marketing research is now seen in many companies as just one, though important, element of a total system of marketing information. Traditionally, marketing research is carried out to solve specific marketing problems. In this sense to a large degree it is *ad hoc*. As mentioned earlier it is now realized that information is needed on a continuous basis. The marketing information system is designed to generate and disseminate a flow of information to marketing managers. The collection of data to solve one-off marketing problems through marketing research is, as just mentioned, one element in this system. The three other elements in a marketing information system are:

- A marketing intelligence sub-system.
- An internal information sub-system.
- A decision support sub-system.

The marketing research and marketing intelligence subsystems feed into the marketing information database, which in turn feeds into the analysis and decision support system part of the marketing information framework. All of these elements combine to provide information for marketing decision making. These key elements of a marketing information system, and how they interlink, are illustrated in Figure 2.5

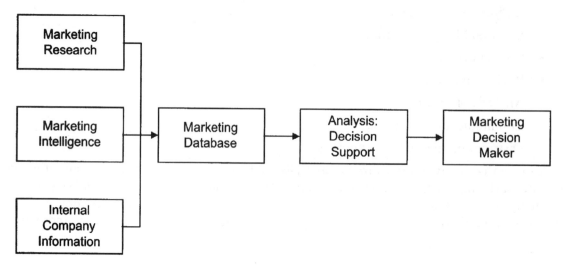

Figure 2.5 *Elements of the Marketing Information System*

Data brought into the organization through marketing research becomes just one element in a company's marketing databank. This is a file of data collected through both the marketing information system and marketing research projects. The marketing databank allows researchers to retrieve information and this is useful for addressing problems quite different from those that prompted the original data collection. Often a research study developed for one purpose provides valuable information for developing a research method for further studies.

The marketing information system (MKIS) should be designed around the marketers' decision-making needs and should produce only the information required to take more cost-effective marketing decisions.

Activity 2.9

Try to make an assessment of the current information provided for marketing decisions internally in your organization, e.g. information from accounts, etc. How could such internal information provision be improved (if at all) in your organization?

Technological developments and the marketing planning process

Needless to say, the marketing planning process has not been untouched by developments in technology. You should be at least aware of some of the ways in which the marketing planning process is being affected by these developments. Below therefore we have given an indication of just some of the ways in which the planning process is being affected.

Marketing audit

E-commerce and new technology is increasingly being used in the marketing audit. The Internet, on-line sources, and internal databases all help in analysing and investigating the economic environment, competitors, customer requirements and dynamics.

Marketing objectives

Again, both internal and external analysis using databases and on-line sources can be used in this area. For example, using databases to identify current rates of loyalty and retention of current customers may help to formulate objectives.

Marketing strategy

Databases are particularly useful in identifying and analysing market segments. In addition technology can be used as a driver to underpin marketing strategy in terms of differentiation from competitors.

Marketing tactics

E-commerce and advances in technology are affecting every element of the marketing mix, e.g.:

- Product – computer aided design (CAD) systems for product design and packaging.
- Pricing – the analysis of current database of customers and reaction to pricing variations.
- Place – the use of the Internet as a direct channel of distribution such as home shopping and e-tailing.
- Promotion – the use of DRTV, databases and direct mail and websites as a promotional driver to link with current sales promotions and advertising. The website can also be used as a communication tool for crisis management and media relations.
- Process – improved communications with sophisticated databases and automated customer-handling operations.
- People – interactive CD-Roms, Internet-based company training for staff, use of the intranet for internal communications.
- Physical evidence – the website as a 'window' of the organization to allow the customer to enter the organization and delve into areas which they would otherwise not have access to (e.g. a virtual tour of the factory).

Evaluation and control

Analysing the effectiveness of the marketing plan by identifying the number of web 'hits', interrogation of the database to check the effectiveness of direct campaigns, etc. We can see, then, that e-commerce and e-technology is affecting every facet of marketing. Let us now consider some of the areas mentioned above in even more detail with regard to uses and applications of the new technologies.

Summary

- In this unit we have looked at the central key activity in marketing, namely marketing planning.
- We have examined in turn each of the steps in the planning process beginning with the identification and formulation of overall business and corporate objectives through to the evaluation and control of marketing plans.
- We have in looking at the marketing planning process introduced some of the key models that describe the various stages of this process and the various analytical tools including the marketing audit, PEST and SWOT analysis, the Ansoff matrix and the notion of generic strategies.
- The importance of objectives and influences on these has been explored.
- We have looked at the concept of market segmentation and how this relates to the essential elements of targeting and positioning and the notion of creating an integrated and coherent marketing mix.
- Key issues in implementing marketing plans have been examined including the various management structures available and the setting of marketing budgets.
- We have described the structure of an outline marketing plan and identified its various components.
- We have seen the need for monitoring and controlling marketing activities and the way in which marketing plans make use of marketing research and information.
- Finally, we have seen that like every other area of marketing activity marketing planning too is being influenced by developments in technology.

Further study and examination preparation

Question 2.1

Identify the elements of a PEST and SWOT analysis and explain their importance for marketing planning purposes.

Question 2.2

Briefly identify the steps involved in the marketing planning process.

Question 2.3

What are Porter's three generic marketing strategies and how could these be implemented?

Question 2.4

Explain the relevance of the Ansoff Product Market Expansion Grid in identifying opportunities for growth.

Previous examination question

Study tip

This question is taken from Fundamentals of Marketing paper June 2000 question 2. Remember, you can access the full specimen answer for this question on the following website addresses: www.marketingonline.co.uk or www.bh.com/marketing.

Question E.2

a. What is a SWOT analysis and how does it lead to an understanding of realistic market opportunities?

(8 marks)

b. Explain the importance of marketing planning for a new consumer product to be launched in your country.

(4 marks)

c. Using examples, identify the main steps involved in the marketing planning process.

(8 marks)
(20 marks in total)

Bibliography

G. Lancaster, L. Massingham, R. Ashford, *Essentials of Marketing: 4th Edn,* Chaps 1 and 13, McGraw-Hill, 2002.

F. Brassington, S. Pettitt, *Principles of Marketing: 2nd Edn*, Prentice-Hall, 2000, Chaps 1 and 21.

Kotler, *Marketing Management: 10th Edn*, Prentice-Hall, 2001, Chap 1.

D.W. Cravens, *Strategic Marketing: 6th Edn*, Irwin, 1999, Chap 1.

Further reading

S. Dibb, L. Simpkin, W. Pride, O. C. Ferrell, *Marketing Concepts and Strategies: 4th European Edn.* Chaps 1 and 22, Houghton, Mifflin, 2000.

M. McDonald, *Marketing Plans: How to prepare them, how to use them: 4th* Edn, Butterworth-Heinemann, 1999

S. Dibb, and L. Simkin, *The Marketing Planning Workbook: 1994,* Routledge.

Unit 3
The marketing mix: product

Objectives

By the end of this unit you will:

- Understand the role of the product in satisfying customer requirements (3.2).

- Understand the notion of products as bundles of benefits that deliver customer value and have different characteristics (3.4).

- Understand the notion of the different levels of a product (3.4).

- Understand the product lifecycle concept and recognize its effects on marketing mix decisions (3.5).

- Understand the principles of product policy: branding, product lines, packaging and service support (3.6).

Study guide

This unit covers the first of the elements of the so-called 'marketing mix', a phrase coined by Neil Borden in the USA. Product is of course one of the core four Ps of the marketing mix – an expression introduced by another American academic, E. Jerome McCarthy.

The unit introduces what many consider to be the most critical element in the marketing mix, for without products there would be nothing to market and hence no need for other marketing mix decisions. You will consequently learn about different categories of products and the notion of the product mix. We examine the notion of products and bundles of benefits that deliver customer value together with the related notion of different levels of product, from the core product through to the potential product. One of the most vaunted and widely used concepts used in marketing is introduced in this unit, namely the so-called Product Lifecycle Concept underpinned as it is by the product adoption process. The important areas of branding and packaging in product management are considered, together with the increasingly important augmented product level element of service support. We would expect you to take about 4 hours to work through this unit plus about the same amount of time on the exercises. However, you must go back to ensure that you have fully understood the various ideas that have been introduced, as they will come up again and again throughout your life both as a student and as a practitioner of marketing.

Introduction

We have started our discussion of the tools of the marketing mix with the product element. As mentioned in the study guide for this unit there are those who believe that product decisions are the most important decisions in the marketing mix. Admittedly it is possible to have the most effective product decisions and management and yet fail to price, distribute or promote these products effectively and the likely outcome would therefore still be marketing failure. However, in one sense all the rest of the marketing mix elements stem from, and are affected by, the core decision of products.

Figure 3.1 explains more fully the tangible and intangible attributes that relate to a product.

Figure 3.1 Product dimensions

Marketing people should consider this broad view of the product or service in order to present customers with satisfactions that have been identified as being appropriate to their needs. The marketing mix creates the product or service in this broader sense, and marketing efforts should be devoted to delivering something that matches defined customer needs and wants. These needs and wants are determined through the medium of marketing research, which was the subject of the Unit 'Tools of marketing: marketing research – analysing and understanding buyer behaviour'.

What we have just explained relates to the product or service in its broadest context, and this is sometimes referred to as the extended product. In effect it considers the product as all marketing effort and not merely a single physical object. Services too can be regarded as products, e.g. a special non-interest-bearing bank account for young persons who receive full time education. To consumers, products or services represent need satisfactions.

The five levels of product

In addition to considering the tangible and intangible attributes that relate to a product, it is useful for the marketer to think of the product as comprising a number of levels. These different levels are shown in Figure 3.2 and discussed below.

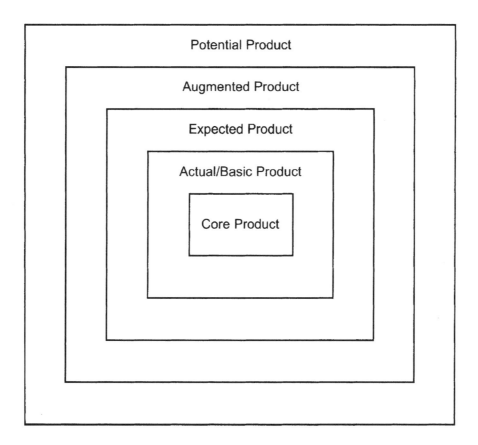

Figure 3.2 *The Five Levels of the Product*

Extended knowledge

For further information on the basic anatomy of a product see, for example, Brassington, F., and Pettitt, S., *Principles of Marketing*, 2nd Edition, Prentice-Hall 2000, Chapter 7.

Level 1 – the core product

This level of product is the most fundamental level and consists of the core benefit(s) which the product or service provides. So, for example, in the case of a car this might be, say, transport.

Level 2 – the actual or basic product

This level of product comprises the features offered in a product. It could include, for example, the design of the product, its packaging, its quality levels and so on.

Level 3 – the expected product

This level of product is a set of attributes that the buyers normally accept and agree to when they purchase the product. Clearly where these attributes exceed the buyers' expectations we have satisfied customers, where they do not come up to the customers' expectations we have dissatisfied customers.

So, for example, when a customer purchases a car he expects it to start, accelerate, steer, stop, etc. Much less obvious, however, are the 'psychological expectations' of buyers, such as, for example, expectations with regard to the extent to which a product will confer, say, status or credibility for the purchaser.

Level 4 – the augmented product

The augmented product are those aspects or elements of a product which support the core and actual product features, so, for example, we could include customer service, delivery and credit, after-sales support, and so on. In many ways this is where a product can meet and exceed the customers' desires beyond their expectations referred to in Level 3. Today's competition mainly takes place at the augmented product level. Product augmentation requires the marketer to look at the buyers' total consumption system. On the other hand the marketer has to realize that the product augmentation strategy will inevitably cost money, and the augmented benefits can soon become expected benefits by the customer.

Many products are essentially marketed at the augmented product level. In other words, it is this level of the product which is used to distinguish the offering from that of competitors, thereby bestowing a competitive edge. So, for example, many computer companies distinguish their product offerings on the basis of, say, the level of after sales service including on-site and off-site warranties. It can be these aspects of the product offering which are most influential in customer choice of supplier.

Level 5 – the potential product

The fifth level of the product is the potential product, which encompasses all the augmentations and transformations that the product might ultimately undergo in the future. This level is important because it raises the possibility of future product improvements in order to keep the product competitive.

Some products have much more potential than others. For example, products which embody developing technologies where constant improvements are being made. However, all products have some further potential and the marketer must be creative in looking for and seeking to develop such further potential for products and brands.

Functional, physical and symbolic Issues

Another useful concept in looking at the anatomy of a product is to consider the product/ service portfolio from the point of view of the benefits related to functional, physical and symbolic issues.

It is important to think of products from the consumer point of view as comprising a bundle of benefits which the customer is seeking to obtain from purchase of a product or service. So, for example, in purchasing a car the customer is seeking the benefit of convenient transport. In addition however, the customer may also be looking for psychological benefits of status or perhaps a feeling of safety from choosing a particular model. Marketers have long known about the importance of distinguishing between features and benefits when marketing and selling products. So, for example, if we are marketing a two-speed drill for use in the home, the marketer needs to sell the benefits of, say, a wide range of possible applications and uses which stem from this feature of having a two-speed motor. Advertising and promotion in particular needs to identify and stress the benefits of the product or service rather than the features. We would go so far as to suggest that the distinction between features and benefits with regard to the product or service underpins the marketing concept and the idea of looking at the business through the eyes of the customers and their needs. We can, however, take this distinction between features and benefits of the product/service portfolio and identify the functional, physical and symbolic issues associated with benefits related to products.

The functional benefits related to the product/service portfolio relate to the core and actual product levels in our earlier discussion of the five levels of the product. As we pointed out, the product must be functional and fill the essential core needs with regard to what the customer is actually looking for when they buy the product or service. So, for example, nobody would buy a camera that did not reproduce images. Similarly, no one would buy a toothpaste which did not care for one's teeth. It is essential, therefore, that first and foremost the product or service fulfil these functional needs.

In fulfilling functional needs, the physical attributes of the product are important, so, for example, decisions with regard to the appearance of the product, the materials it is made from and the design and packaging all need to relate to the functional benefits desired from the product. In addition to these physical attributes, however, it is important for the marketer to understand the symbolic issues of the product. Symbolic issues may derive from and be related to many aspects of the product. Ultimately, as you would expect, given the marketing concept, symbolic issues, their nature and importance derive from the perceptions and needs of the customer. Symbolic issues are essentially socially or psychologically driven. So for example, alcoholic products such as drinks have strong symbolic connotations associated with aspects such as hedonism, excess, virility, sexual attractiveness, and so on and so forth. In other words, a product is much more than its physical and functional attributes. A lot of marketing, and again particularly as evidenced in the promotional element of the marketing mix, centres on symbolic issues of the product. These symbolic issues can be linked to brand attributes in order to position products and brands in markets. The marketer needs to be aware of the symbolic connotations of products and brands and in particular needs to understand the customer's perception of these symbolic issues. Understanding of these can provide the marketer with important insights into the behaviour and perceptions of customers which can in turn be used to develop more effective marketing programmes. These symbolic issues of the product are considered in more detail later in this unit when we turn our attention to branding.

Activity 3.2

Consider the following products and services and then write down what you consider to be the need satisfactions to the buyers of each:

- A housewife who has ordered some made-to-measure curtains for the living room.
- A buyer for a large multiple grocery chain who has just placed a long-term order with a yoghurt producer to manufacture and supply a range of products under the grocery chain's own label.
- An 8-year-old child who has just purchased an ice cream cornet from the ice cream delivery van.
- A 17-year-old who has just purchased his first motorcycle.
- A newly married couple who have just purchased their first home.
- A couple who have just completed their weekly shop at the local supermarket.

Compare your answers with those shown in the debriefing.

Product and service classifications

Now that we know that products and services have many intangible as well as tangible attributes, we can consider products and services in identifiable groups. We can use a formal classification system whereby we can ascribe to each group a customer view of products and thereby assess why and how they might be purchased.

We can distinguish between consumer and industrial goods and services. Industrial goods and services are those purchased by manufacturers, who use them to make products and services that are in turn sold to make other products or services. Consumer goods and services are sold to the ultimate user. We shall now examine each category in turn.

Consumer goods

These goods are split into a number of categories and sub-categories.

Convenience goods are our first category here. These are simple items whose purchase requires little effort on the part of the purchaser, e.g. routine items like bread, detergents, toothpaste, shampoo, etc. A primary aim of manufacturers of such goods is to attempt to predetermine the purchase decision by promoting it as a branded product, so the consumer looks for a certain brand rather than merely going for a generic (non-branded) product.

Convenience goods are further classified into **staple** and **impulse** purchases. Staple goods are those consumed by most people every day, e.g. fruit and vegetables, and here product differentiation tends to be minimal. Impulse purchases, on the other hand, mean that there is no pre-planning in their purchase, and here supermarket displays (or merchandising) are often designed to promote such sales.

Activity 3.3

List three examples each of staple and impulse purchase convenience goods.

Shopping goods include major durable or semi-durable items. They are generally more expensive than convenience goods and their purchase is less frequent. Much pre-planning goes into their choice in terms of searching for information and price comparisons. For instance, the purchase of a new bedroom suite will call for extensive consideration of the relative merits of different bedroom suites on offer, and consumers will consider price along perhaps with credit terms, delivery arrangements and guarantees. The quality of sales staff in stores is basic to the success of marketing shopping goods. Promotional strategies aim to simplify the decision process for consumers by ensuring that they have a high level of brand awareness even before purchase planning begins.

Shopping goods can be further classified as **homogeneous** or **heterogeneous**. This rather technical terminology simply means that homogeneous goods are not really exclusive. In terms of their market appeal they are broadly similar to each other in both their technical performance and in price, examples being refrigerators and washing machines. Certain brands in this category attempt to differentiate themselves from other brands through image or technical or design superiority. Heterogeneous goods, on the other hand, tend to be non-standard, and price is often of secondary importance to the customer after image. Here behavioural factors play an important role in the purchasing decision.

Speciality goods are the next category, and their purchase is characterized by an extensive market search and a reluctance to accept substitutes once the purchase choice has been made. Consumers of such goods are usually prepared to pay a premium price for the prestige associated with the product or service, and it is important that companies marketing such products create and preserve the correct image. Examples of such products are expensive perfume brands, designer label clothes, expensive 'West End' type restaurants and exotic cars.

Unsought goods are those the customer has not considered buying before being made aware of them, and the promotion of such goods is often done through the so called 'hard sell', which has served to dent the image of marketing in general and selling in particular. Unsought goods often satisfy a genuine need that the consumer did not recognize existed, and it might be said that double glazing is sometimes an example of this in that it helps to obviate condensation and assists in insulating the home from heat loss. However, consumers rarely recognize this until they have been approached by someone selling double glazing.

Industrial goods

Only certain goods within this classification are directly essential to the manufacturing process, as will be seen in the classifications that follow.

Installations are critical and usually expensive items. They are the major items of plant and machinery required for the production of an organization's products. Their purchase is often critical to the economic well-being of the company, for it often commits the company for a long time into the future. Purchase is often the result of a very extensive search process, and although price must be viewed as important in such a decision, it is rarely the single deciding factor. Much emphasis is placed on the quality of sales support and advice, and subsequent technical support and after-sales service.

Accessories are goods that are usually less expensive than installations, and their depreciation is normally over fewer years. Although their purchase is important, it is not as critical as for installations. Accessories include ancillary plant and machinery, office equipment and office furniture.

Raw materials account for most of the time and work of a typical purchasing department. Quality, consistency of supply, service and price are important considerations here.

Activity 3.8

List three examples of raw materials.

Component parts and materials include replacement and maintenance items for manufacturing machinery. They should not be confused with 'accessories', because they include those products that facilitate or are essential in the manufacturing process but do not form part of the finished products. Examples are adhesives and packaging materials.

Activity 3.9

List three examples of component parts and materials.

Supplies are sometimes called the convenience goods of industrial requirements. They include such items as office stationery and cleaning materials. Their purchase is often routine and undertaken by less than senior employees. Most supplies tend to be homogeneous in nature, and price is usually the major factor in purchasing decisions.

Activity 3.10

List three examples of supplies.

Industrial services have grown considerably over recent years. Many companies now find that it is less expensive to employ outside agencies, with their attendant specialist expertise, than attempting to carry out these functions themselves. As long as suppliers can match the standards required by the company, this makes sense, as the company can then concentrate upon its own areas of expertise in producing and marketing its products. Maintenance and catering are examples of such specialist services. Management consultancy, which is often required on an *ad hoc* basis, is also an example of such a service.

Activity 3.11

List three examples of industrial services.

The product mix

The product mix is sometimes called the product assortment, and it consists of all the products or services that a company offers to its customers.

The three considerations under this heading are:

- Length of product mix.
- Breadth or width of product mix.
- Depth of product mix.

Before we consider each of these headings, we should understand that consistency among different products in the product mix is a prerequisite to successful marketing. In other words, decisions upon one product should not be taken without having due regard to other products in the product assortment. For instance, it would be unlikely that Rolls-Royce Cars would consider producing a family saloon car, because of the detrimental effect this would have upon their image as producers of one of the most prestigious makes of car in the world.

Length of product mix

The length of a company's product mix is the total number of individual products or services in the entire product mix. The length can be stretched downwards or upwards (depending upon where the company's products are located in the eyes of customers in terms of being up-market or down-market) or the stretch can be in both directions (termed a two-way stretch). Such line stretching happens when the company decides to increase its present product line.

Activity 3.12

Consider why a company might engage in:

1. downwards line stretching,
2. upwards line stretching,
3. two-way line stretching.

Breadth of product mix

The breadth or width of a company's product mix relates to the number of product lines that the company possesses. For instance, a company producing coffee might have ground coffee in one product line, instant coffee in another and coffee beans in a third.

Depth of product mix

The depth of a company's product mix refers to the number of products in each product line. In the coffee producer example it might be that the instant coffee line consists of powdered coffee, granulated coffee, premium blend granulated coffee and Brazilian blend granulated coffee.

In considering the structures that have been described, their organization is sometimes referred to as the product manager type of structure where a product (or products) manager is in charge of a product line and a brand manager is in charge of a specific product (or brand) in that line.

However, the terms are not altogether clear because quite often the term product manager is interchangeable with the term brand manager. In industrial goods marketing the term product manager is more prevalent, whereas in the marketing of fast-moving consumer goods (FMCG) the term brand manager is more common.

Product life cycle

This concept is based on the idea that a new product enters a life cycle once it is launched on the market. It has a birth (introduction) and a death (decline). By thinking of product in this manner it is possible to devise different marketing strategies for relevant stages in the product's life.

This theory is perhaps an oversimplification, because in reality very few products will fit into the theoretical curve, so there is a danger of taking the concept too literally.

Figure 3.3 shows the course of the product life cycle from the developmental pre-introduction stage to decline. A profit (and loss) curve is superimposed on this figure.

During the development phase there are of course no sales, but the product is picking up costs of development, including marketing-research costs. The introduction phase witnesses a slow growth as the product 'catches on'. Once it has caught on, sales grow rapidly and the product becomes profitable. The product then matures as the market reaches saturation. In fact the terms 'maturity' and 'saturation' are sometimes used interchangeably, although some authors say that saturation follows maturity. This phase tends to be longer than Figure 3.3 infers. Decline is the final phase, when the product eventually drops out of the market, usually at the point when losses begin to be incurred.

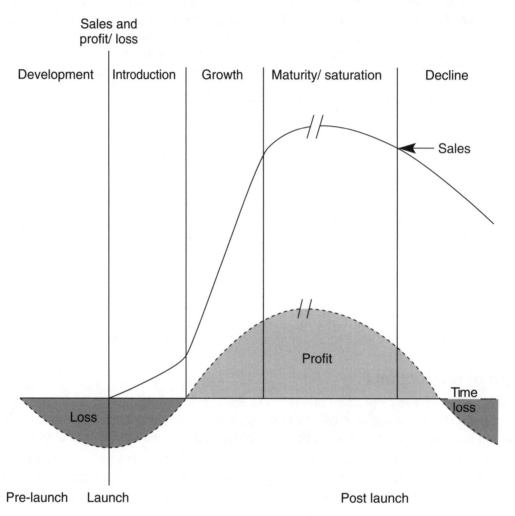

Figure 3.3 *The product life cycle*

The product life cycle is influenced by the nature of the product itself, changes in the macro environment, i.e. outside the control of the company, and changes in consumer preferences and competitive actions. These factors also influence the time span of the life cycle, which can range from a few weeks to many decades.

Characteristics of the different product life-cycle stages

It can be useful to the marketer to understand the essential characteristics of each stage of the product life cycle. Kotler has usefully summarized the characteristics for each stage and these are shown in Table 3.1.

Table 3.1 *Characteristics of each product life-cycle stage*

Development	Introduction	Growth	Maturity	Decline
No sales	Low sales	Rapidly rising sales	High sales	Declining sales
High cost of R&D	Negative profits	Rising profits	High profits	Declining profits
Test market	Innovator customers	Early adopters	Middle majority customers	Laggard customers
	Few competitors	More competitors	Competitors start to decline	Smaller number of competitors

Understanding these characteristics is useful because it helps the marketer to develop strategies for the different life-cycle stages. These different strategies are now discussed.

Strategies at different life-cycle stages

Development of course takes place before the product launch and here marketing research in the form of testing out the product's acceptance takes place. Some companies attempt to ensure secrecy during this phase in order that competitors cannot pre-empt the product's launch, while others use this period as a time for informing the public that the new product is forthcoming.

Introduction is when the new product is launched, and the goal here is to create awareness. This usually calls for a disproportionate level of marketing expenditure relative to sales revenue, and it must be regarded as an investment in the product's future. Promotion tends to be informative at this stage, and the principal aim of selling is to communicate the product's benefits to customers. Pricing is considered later, but for innovative products a skimming strategy is often employed at this stage. These pricing implications are dealt with in the Unit 'Tools of marketing: price'. If indeed the product is innovative, then it is likely that it will be only available in a limited number of outlets at this early stage (termed 'selective distribution', which is dealt with in more detail in the Unit 'Tools of marketing: place').

Activity 3.13

Think of a new product that has not been long on the market that you feel is in the introductory phase of its product life cycle.

Growth is where competitive products usually enter the market and there is less product distinctiveness. Rising sales generally mean more profitable returns, and company or product acquisitions sometimes feature at this stage. Promotional expenditure still features highly, but the type of promotion moves from informative advertising to advertising to achieve brand superiority. In FMCG examples finding shelf space is important, and every effort is made to persuade retailers to stock. In non-FMCG examples suppliers are often in competition with each other to acquire dealerships and distributive outlets. During the growth period a company must attempt to optimize the product's price. At the end of the growth period prices are sometimes reduced because the full effect of economies of scale can be passed on to customers. As the growth period tends towards maturity, market shares will begin to stabilize and a hierarchy of brand or market leaders will probably have emerged.

Maturity is where most products are situated, and much marketing activity is devoted to this stage. The major characteristics here are that sales continue to grow, but at a much decreased rate; attempts are made to differentiate and redifferentiate products; and there is increased brand and inventory rationalization among retailers and distributors.

Promotion tends to reinforce brand loyalty, and there is a need for sustained promotional activity, even if only to retain existing customers. Distribution strategies too are designed to retain outlets. 'Price wars' are common, and the aim of price-cutting is usually to attempt to increase purchases sufficiently to offset any revenue losses.

Saturation follows maturity, and this period sees some marginal manufacturers retiring from the market when faced with severe competition and reduced margins. As prices begin to fall in battles to retain market share, profits begin to fall correspondingly. In some cases the major thrust of promotional effort moves away from consumers to distributive intermediaries in that maximum display at point of sales is regarded as being important to support brands, so 'below the line' activity features more strongly than 'above the line' (dealt with in detail in the Unit 'Tools of marketing: Promotion'). Many marketing writers do not recognize this as a separate phase and simply view it as the tail end of the maturity phase.

Again remember that products may be at different stages according to country, but three products that are in the maturity or saturation phases of the product lifecycle, at least in the United Kingdom, would be mobile phones, video cassette recorders, and microwave ovens.

Decline is where consumer preferences may have changed or innovative products may have displaced existing products. Characteristics of this period are intensified price-cutting and producers deciding to abandon the market. Some firms find it worth extending the product's life cycle well into decline, while the number of competitors is falling. During this period the attention of management is likely to move from active marketing to strict cost control as the main means of maintaining profitability.

Examples of products that are at the decline stage of their lifecycles, again in the context of the United Kingdom would include cassette recorders, heated hair rollers, black and white televisions.

Applications of the product life cycle

The ability to accurately identify the transition from one stage of the product life cycle to another is a key issue for marketing management. Such prediction requires the use of marketing research and market intelligence. Once these are in place, marketing management has the basis for long-term marketing planning, with appropriate strategies duly budgeted to meet changing conditions.

Normally an extension of the product life cycle can be found by finding new uses for the product or by finding new markets, but such extensions should not call for too many product modifications. It should also be remembered that although Figure 3.3 shows the maturity/saturation as a short continuum, in fact this period can last for months, years or decades, depending upon the nature of the product being considered.

The product lifecycle stages and the marketing mix

We have already considered the fact that marketing strategies and hence by implication, the marketing mix will need to be modified in each stage of a product's lifecycle. We can now consider this in a little more detail. Below is outlined in indicative terms the likely focus and thrust of the combination of the marketing mix elements in each of the stages of the product lifecycle.

In the introductory stage

Spending on the promotional element of the mix will be high compared to sales. This is necessary to create awareness and interest. (See the Unit 'Tools of marketing: promotion'.)

Within the promotional mix the emphasis will tend to be on advertising backed by special sales promotions to the trade. Selling will emphasize missionary selling.

The product element of the mix is likely to be basic, with few (if any) variations or added features.

Distribution and logistics (place) will centre on securing initial channels of distribution and ensuring that products are in stock to coincide with the launch plans.

Price may be set either to skim or to penetrate the market according to circumstances. (See the Unit 'Tools of marketing: price'.)

In the growth stage

Spending on promotion will still be heavy to expand the market and strengthen competitive position.

Product quality may be improved, together with the addition of special features, styling, etc. The product mix may be widened.

The emphasis in place will be on securing new channels of distribution. If price skimming has been used in the introductory stage, prices will be reduced to bring in the next price-sensitive layer of the market.

In the maturity stage

Promotion will be aimed at trying to maintain market share. The emphasis is likely to be on sales promotions aimed at both trade and consumer. Advertising is likely to take the form of reminder advertising.

Further product modifications may take place to try and maintain sales. Further features and alternative product variations may be added.

Distribution decisions will stress the importance of ensuring that costs are kept to a minimum compatible with desired levels of customer service.

Price, although needing to be competitive, may be less price-elastic, owing to brand loyalty.

In the decline stage

At this stage of the product life cycle both the total market and for many brands their market share will gradually be eroded. Those customers still buying the product will tend to be core customers that have bought the product or brand for a long time and still remain loyal. Any new customers buying at this stage will come from the laggards group of adopters, i.e. those who do not seek market innovation and older members of the community who tend to be behind in current developments. Competition will be intense but will gradually reduce as companies leave the market. Some competitors may attempt to re-grow the market and/or capture market share by introducing product improvements or technological advances.

Promotion will tend to be reduced to minimum levels. Emphasis within the promotional mix will again tend to be on sales promotion.

Unprofitable products in the range will be phased out. Similarly, unprofitable/marginal outlets will be phased out. Price elasticity will be high, so that prices and company margins may be cut to maintain sales and dealer loyalty. Trying to maintain sales as long as possible is essential. The organization may seem to cut costs by, for example, reducing the number of product features. Price should be carefully monitored but remember at this stage the product may be a cash cow and prices should be kept steady if possible so as to maximize this cash flow.

Activity 3.17

Reflect on the examples of products and services in different stages of the life cycle which we have asked you to consider so far in this Unit. Try to establish the extent to which the marketing mix for these different products and services corresponds to the indicative use of the mix suggested in this unit for each stage of the life cycle.

Criticisms of the product life cycle

Needless to say, the concept of the product life cycle, particularly as a planning tool for marketers, is not without its limitations. Indeed, the concept of the product life cycle has many critics. The main criticisms of the product life cycle have been as follows:

- The stages are not always easily defined. Identifying where one stage ends and another begins, therefore, is often difficult and dangerous in terms of basing marketing plans upon the identification of each stage.

- As we shall see shortly, not all products go through each stage. For example, fad products such as 'cyberpets' the children's toy. We shall consider different possible shapes for the product life cycle in the next part of the unit.

- The life cycle is not inevitable or a given, but rather strategic decisions can change the cycle. In other words, product life cycles may be a function of strategies and not the other way around. For example, the re-positioning of a product can have an impact on the length of the stages.

- The length of life cycles differs enormously and therefore makes the concept difficult to use. So, for example, the life cycle varies between different industries. In electronics, for example, life cycles are relatively short. Whereas in more traditional industries such as, for example, ship-building life cycles can be extremely long.

Product life cycle patterns

It has been suggested that the product life cycle can take a number of shapes, depending upon the type of product or market being considered. Certain patterns are suggested in Figure 3.4.

In example (*a*) sales grow rapidly after the initial launch, followed by a sharp drop as the novelty wears off. Eventually this decline will be arrested and the product will enter a relatively long period of sales stability as late adopters (see next section on the product adoption process) purchase and early buyers purchase again and become replacement buyers. A good example of a product that has evidenced this shape of life cycle, being at the maturity stage for many years without disappearing from the market is the 'mini' car first produced by Austin.

In example (*b*) we see a truncated pattern, which shows that sales grow steeply from the start. Here we find products for which there is a large market appeal and for which there is little perceived risk. A good example of a product with this truncated pattern would be the video recorder market in the United Kingdom.

Example (*c*) shows a rapid growth followed by a rapid decline, with little maturity. In this category we see fad products. The 'cyberpet' was given earlier as an example of a fad-type product. And indeed many children's toys fall into this category. Having said this, some children's toys such as the Barbie doll exhibit product life-cycle patterns similar to those shown in Figure 3.4(b).

Example (*d*) shows a pattern with a relatively short introduction followed by rapid sales growth, a short maturity and then decline, only to be followed by a repeated process once the product goes so far down the decline curve. This type of cycle is typical for seasonal or fashion products. Skiing holidays would be a good example of this type of life-cycle pattern, or sales of Christmas cards.

In example (*e*) we see a scalloped pattern as sales pass through a number of mini life cycles. Such mini life cycles might be new adaptations of the original product that add value or represent an updating in styling. A good example of a product exhibiting this type of life-cycle shape is the market for televisions, where manufacturers and marketers are continually adapting the product with new features in order to extend the life-cycle curve.

Activity 3.18

Consider each of the five life cycles suggested in Figure 3.4. Think of a product or service example that equates to each one.

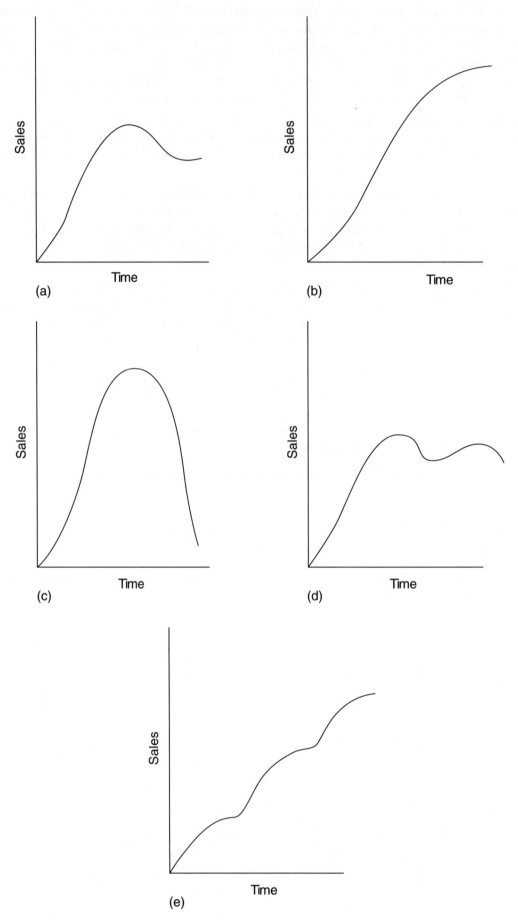

Figure 3.4 *Different patterns of the product life cycle*

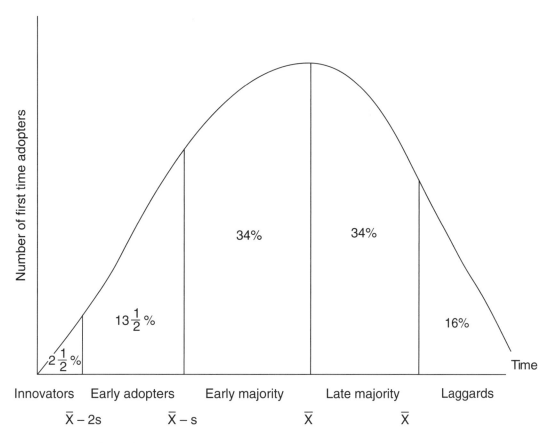

Innovators   Early adopters   Early majority   Late majority   Laggards

$\overline{X} - 2s$ $\overline{X} - s$ $\overline{X}$ $\overline{X}$

Figure 3.5 *The product adoption process*

The product adoption process

It is essential to consider the product life-cycle concept in conjunction with the product adoption process. From the product adoption process we can learn something about the users or consumers who are the targets of marketing efforts. Its nature is described in Figure 3.5.

The rate at which the product moves through the adoption categories is the function of a process called the diffusion of innovations. It should be specifically noted that this measure is for first-time adopters only; once the product has been purchased, successive purchases do not count in this theory. In other words, what we are looking at is the extent to which each adopter category successively influences another towards adoption. Each of the adopter categories is now discussed in turn.

Innovators are likely to be younger, better educated and relatively affluent, with a higher social status than other customers. In terms of personal characteristics they are likely to be broad-minded, receptive people, with a wide range of social relationships. Their product knowledge relies more upon their own efforts to gather objective information than on company literature or sales people.

Early adopters possess many of the characteristics of innovators, but tend to belong to more 'local' systems. Although their social relationships are less broadly based, they tend to be opinion leaders and are highly influential within their particular group. As such, they are a major target for marketers, whose aim is to have their product accepted as quickly as possible.

The **early majority** group is slightly above average in socio-economic terms. They rely heavily on the marketing effort for information and are clearly influenced by the opinion leaders of the early adopter category.

Late majority adopters are more likely to adopt innovations because those innovations have become generally accepted by previous groups. Social pressure or economic considerations are more influential in this group than innate personal characteristics.

Laggards make up the cautious group. They tend to be older, with a relatively low socio-economic status. The innovator group may be considering another newer product before laggards have entirely adopted the original innovation.

Needless to say, innovators and early adopters are extremely important to the success or failure of new products. The marketer, therefore, needs to understand who are the innovators and early adopters in a market, how to reach these categories of customers, and how to influence them. Fortunately, we actually know a lot about the characteristics of these groups of adopters.

For example, with regard to the characteristics of innovators and early adopters we know that they tend to come from higher income and socio-economic groups: that they tend to be more extrovert and cosmopolitan in their personalities and lifestyles and their behaviour involves more risk taking than their later adopter counterparts.

Innovators and early adopters actually seek out new products and part of their consumption pleasure is involved with being amongst the first to try out new products and services. There is a high degree of symbolic element attached to the consumption of new products and innovations for this group. They desire to be seen as being innovators in the market and essentially wear new products as social badges which serve to confer status and importance in their eyes.

We also know something about the characteristics of new products and services which affect the speed and extent of their take up in the market. In particular the following characteristics are known to affect the diffusion and adoption process for new products and services.

- **Communicability**. The easier it is for the potential benefits of a new product or service to be communicated to the market, the more likely the product is to be adopted. So, for example, if a new product can be shown to, say, reduce costs to the customer substantially, and where these cost savings can be readily communicated and understood, then the quicker and more extensive would be the acceptance of the new product. With many products however, the potential benefits are sometimes difficult to communicate to the customer because, for example, they are technical in nature or perhaps entirely new benefits which the customer has therefore to be educated about. In some respects, the relatively slow take up of DVD products so far in the United Kingdom is partly because of the difficulties of communicating the relative benefits of this new technology.

- **Trialability**. The easier it is for a customer to try a new product either on a limited basis and/or before making a major commitment to purchase, again the more likely that product is to be adopted. Adopting a new product or service after all can represent a substantial risk to a customer. So, for example, the customer risks whether the product will be satisfactory or not, or perhaps whether the new supplier will continue to be in business etc. Anything the marketer can do, therefore, to reduce such perceived risks by making it easier to trial the product before making a purchase or long term commitment is likely to help adoption. Allowing customers to use a vehicle through an extended test drive period when launching a new car is an example of making it easier to trial a product. Similarly, the use of samples through, say, direct mail shots is another good way for the marketer to make it easier for the customer to try out a new product.

- **Relative advantage**. Remember that customers are buying benefits when they purchase products or services. In the case of encouraging the adoption of new products, the marketer must ensure that the target market understand and appreciate the relative advantages of the new product compared to existing/established products available in the market. Remember there is a risk element for the consumer with regard to adopting new products, therefore the consumer must feel, or rather the marketer must be able to persuade the customer to feel, that the relative advantages offered by the new product are enough to overcome these risks and the inbuilt inertia which is normal for customers.

We know therefore that new products which only offer marginal extra advantages to customers and certainly those which are essentially 'me too' products which offer no advantages are unlikely to be adopted.

Activity 3.19

Consider the 'home personal computer'. Analyse how this product has spread through a market with which you are familiar and the different groups of consumers who have adopted it at varying stages of diffusion.

Activity 3.20

Consider Figures 3.3 (The product life cycle) and 3.5 (The product adoption process). They are quite similar in shape. Do you feel that there is a relationship between the two?

As marketers we are also interested in consumer behaviour as it relates to new products. Figure 3.6 shows a sequential model of the adoption process for an innovative new product. We shall use this model again in the Unit 'Tools of marketing: Promotion' when we look into promotion tools. First, let us consider the elements of the model and its relationship to the product life cycle.

It is the task of the marketer to create awareness and then to guide the consumer through subsequent stages of the process. Without awareness, consumers cannot even begin to consider it as a solution to need-related problems. To be worthwhile, innovative products should always be problem-solving in nature as far as the consumer is concerned.

Awareness (Figure 3.6) can come about by word of mouth communication or from the marketing efforts of the company. The individual is exposed to the innovation and becomes aware of its existence.

Interest is aroused and information will be sought.

At the **evaluation** stage the consumer weighs the relative advantages of the new product against those of existing products and perhaps against directly competing products if these have been launched.

The consumer decides to make a trial through a test run or purchasing a small amount. For this reason many new FMCG products are sold initially in 'trial sizes' or are distributed as free samples. If a trial cannot be made, the likelihood of adoption will decrease.

At the **adoption** stage the consumer decides whether or not to adopt, i.e. begin to buy and use, the product on a regular basis.

Post-adoption confirmation comes when the product has been adopted and the consumer is seeking assurance and reassurance (unconsciously) that a sensible decision has been made. New information has been accepted and prior information has been rejected. Often, after an important purchase, a phenomenon called 'post-purchase dissonance' is present; this is a feeling of unease that the goods purchased may not represent good value. The product itself may be perfectly acceptable, yet the consumer may feel that the purchase was not as good as it could have been. Despite these uneasy feelings, consumers frequently rationalize and reinforce their purchase decisions and will not voice dissatisfaction and thus appear poor judges to their peer group colleagues. With this in mind, companies should attach as much importance to after-sales service and general customer care as they do to making the sale in the first place.

Figure 3.6 *The adoption process*

Activity 3.21

Think of a major product you have purchased. Remember how you purchased this product and the formal and informal information sources you consulted. Now try to match your various stages of purchasing behaviour to the elements of the adoption process in Figure 3.6. Did you have any feeling of post-purchase dissonance afterwards?

Packaging

It is open to discussion whether packaging should come under the product heading or under promotion. That it is an inseparable sub-component of the marketing mix is without doubt. If it is viewed in terms of product protection, then it is considered as part of the product, but if it forms part of a product's display on, say, the shelves of a supermarket, then its function must be regarded as coming under promotion.

It is increasingly recognized that packaging has now become so important in competitive marketing and customer choice that it is often referred to as being the fifth 'P' of the marketing mix. There is no doubt that recently packaging has become a very effective and potent marketing tool, especially as an increasing number of products are sold on a self-selection basis at supermarkets. We have also seen the growth of so-called 'copy cat' packaging where, often, unscrupulous companies attempt to mislead customers by making their packaging similar to the market leaders.

The first consideration under packaging is 'outers' or outer containers. Industrial products are usually packed in plain simple boxes, principally for protection while the goods are in transit. However, for consumer products, outers can sometimes form part of a product's display, especially when it is sold in small shops or other convenience outlets. The example of potato crisps comes to mind here, where the outer has a serrated round hole. The retailer then presses the serration through and sells individual packets of crisps from the bulk box.

For consumer goods in particular, the package around the goods themselves forms part of the communications process. This is most important for goods that are sold in self-service outlets.

Here the goods themselves must form part of the selling process, and if the goods in the package are not prone to attractive display, e.g. canned foodstuffs, then the package must attempt to 'sell' the goods. Sometimes the packaging is referred to as the 'silent salesman' in this respect. A fuller discussion upon the implications of this comes in the Unit 'Tools of marketing: Promotion', which deals with promotion.

Exam hint

Remember, the examiners will often ask for, and will almost certainly be looking for even where they do not specify, the use of relevant examples to show that you understand and can apply the fundamentals of marketing. In the case of packaging, it is relatively easy to collect examples for potential use in the examination in the process of your everyday shopping and consumption behaviour. This is because packaging is so easy to observe and experience. Keep your eyes open then for examples of new/innovative packaging. In particular look out for packaging which you feel is particularly good and packaging which is particularly bad. In terms of good packaging you are looking for packaging which, for example, makes the product stand out, easy to handle and use, or has some other consumer benefits such as storage, re-use etc. In terms of bad packaging you are looking for packaging which, for example, does not stand out, is not easy to handle and use, or is in some other way inconvenient or dysfunctional.

The principal considerations under the heading of packaging are:

- Size and range of sizes.
- Protection and preservation.
- Convenience for the customer.
- Information in terms of instructions for use or contents.
- The relationship between packaging (it is sometimes termed the 'silent salesperson') and promotion.
- Ease of handling for the intermediary.
- Innovation opportunities.

Activity 3.22

Think of an industrial product. Consider the functions of packaging in relation to this example. Then think of a non-food consumer product and consider again the functions of its packaging. Finally, think of a processed food item for sale in a typical supermarket and consider its packaging functions.

Developments in Packaging Design

Packaging has in recent years been one of the most innovative areas of marketing. The development of new packaging materials and new packaging technologies have added considerably to the armoury of tools with respect to the marketer's decisions in the use of packaging design. For example, toothpaste packaging is now much more user-friendly than it was only a few years ago. Cans are much easier to open with their ring-pull designs than their potentially dangerous can opener predecessors. In addition to these technical changes in packaging, packaging has also been one of the areas which has felt the greatest effects of an increasing concern with the environment and 'green issues'. Packaging is increasingly recyclable. Indeed in some countries there are very stringent regulations indeed concerning this aspect of packaging. In Germany, for example, all packaging must be recyclable and there are substantial fines for it not being so. Related to this, there is a movement towards 'less being more' in packaging. Consumers do not want to feel they are paying excessive amounts for packaging apart from, for example, where it is desired for, say, gift giving purposes etc.

Branding

It is a moot point whether branding and brand management is part of the product or promotional element of the mix. In fact, it is both. As we shall see, brands perform a strong communication role in marketing and are often supported by heavy spends on promotion. Most however, consider branding to be part of the product management element of the marketing mix and so we shall consider the importance of the brand and the elements of managing brands in this unit.

Irrespective of where in the mix we think branding lies, there is little doubt that building and managing successful brands is one of the most important areas and issues in contemporary marketing. There are many reasons for this but amongst some of the most important are as follows.

- Brands represent one of the most important and powerful of ways for a company to create and maintain a differential advantage.
- Brands represent ease of choice and psychological comfort for consumers.
- Related to the above, prestigious brands confer status and legitimacy for some consumers.
- Successful brands are a major company asset not only in marketing but in financial terms.
- Successful brands give the marketer substantial power and leverage when dealing with intermediaries with regard to, for example, securing shelf space.

Together, these factors have made brands and brand management one of the hottest issues in marketing over the decade of the 90s and if anything this trend is set to continue with an even greater momentum during the first decade of the new millennium. But what are some of the key issues in the brand area of product management, and in particular what makes for successful management of this element of the product. First we need to establish what a brand is.

What is a brand?

In its most prosaic sense a brand, or perhaps more accurately branding is an approach to distinguishing one supplier's product(s) from another supplier's products in the market place. This is best illustrated by the fact that one of the decisions regarding building and managing brands relates to the basis of such distinctions. Again, in its simplest sense a brand is often distinguished through its name. So, for example, in the Cola market we have of course Coca Cola, Pepsi Cola, Virgin Cola and so on. In addition, or alternatively, brands may be distinguished through for example their appearance such as, say, their packaging. Finally a brand may be distinguished through, for example, their image which in turn may comprise of a combination of factors including for example, design, after-sales service, company reputation and so on. Certainly brands are often and usually physically distinguished from their competitor brand counterparts, but actually a brand is much more than simply the physical characteristics of a product. In essence a brand represents a product which has a set of values that meet certain of the customer's psychological needs leading to a perception of added values and feelings of confidence on the part of customers. It is these added values and the psychological and perceptual effects they have on customer choice that constitute the essence of what a brand is.

The importance of brands in customer choice

It is now recognized that in many markets, and not just as initially felt in the market for fast moving consumer goods, brands and brand values are amongst the most important influences on buying decisions and customer choice. There are many reasons for this but Peter Doyle has suggested the following are amongst two of the major reasons.

Firstly, Doyle believes that in markets now characterized by a wealth of alternative offerings, the task of choosing between competing products has simply become too difficult, time consuming and expensive for most buyers. In addition, the customer is subjected to an enormous variety of competing claims and advertising and selling messages. Reputable brands allow the customer to choose with confidence and reduce the risks, therefore, associated with choice and the complexities thereof.

The second reason according to Doyle we have already touched on and that is that brands are strongly associated with, and bought, for emotional, psychological and status reasons as well as function. It is in fact the brand and the brand image which conveys as much functionality, in a psychological sense, as the product itself. Most Colas refresh so why is Coca Cola the world's leading brand in this market? Most watches tell the time accurately so why do some choose a Rolex or a Tag Hauer? As we have moved into the 21st century of course these psychological and emotional reasons associated with brand values reflect the fact that in many societies consumers have moved from merely buying products and services to fulfil basic physical needs and requirements to buying products to satisfy higher needs such as self-actualization and esteem.

We can see then the importance and relevance of branding in customer choice and company success, but what are the elements of developing and managing successful brand and in particular what are some of the key decisions that the marketer must consider?

Elements of branding and brand management

Amongst the major elements of branding and brand management decisions are the following:

- **Branding versus no branding.** Perhaps an obvious decision but the marketer must decide whether or not to brand the organization's products and services. The alternative is to market products unbranded and therefore essentially as commodity items. As you would expect from our discussion above, increasingly marketers are opting to brand their products hoping to build better value and hence stronger market positions. However, some products are difficult to brand in the sense of being difficult to distinguish in any way from their competitive counterparts. Examples would include: many raw materials, industrial commodities, and so on. Even here, however, an element of branding can be introduced through developing a corporate approach to branding establishing a corporate image. Some marketers of course do not brand their own products but rather leave the branding element to their distributors. So, for example, in many markets we have retailer brands as opposed to company brands.

- **Brand names.** If a marketer decides that branding is the best option, then brand names must be selected. Brand naming is in fact a quite surprisingly complex and technical area of brand management. There are, for example, legal issues to be considered with regard to ensuring that no other manufacturers brand names are infringed; there are language problems and issues when it comes to international marketing; and finally, related to language issues there can be cultural issues associated with the choice of brand names. Although some of the mistakes made by brand namers in the past are potentially amusing or perhaps insulting depending on your view, such as the Slovakian pasta brand 'Kuk & Fuk', for the marketer such brand naming mistakes are horrendous. In choosing a brand name, ideally, the name should have the following characteristics:

  1. It should be distinctive.
  2. It should be legal.
  3. It should be protectable.

4. It should be user-friendly.

5. It should match the desired image of the company and the positioning of the brand.

When it comes to naming there are also strategic aspects to consider. In particular the extent to which individual as opposed to company branding will be used. So, for example some organizations rely principally on company brand name establishing this as the dominant brand identity across the range of their products. Examples would include Heinz and Mercedes Benz. At the other extreme companies such as Unilever and Proctor and Gamble prefer a strategy of individual brand names and identities for each of their products. Other companies adopt a middle ground approach either using both company and individual brands such as, for example, Kelloggs, and yet others using range branding where groups of products, for example, product lines are marketed under their own brand family names.

Establishing and supporting successful brands

Although decisions regarding whether or not to brand, naming brands and generic or individual naming brand strategies are important, perhaps the most important element of branding and brand management is how to establish, build and support successful brands. Needless to say, this is not an easy process and will often require considerable skill, investment and patience on the part of the marketer. The following, however, are some of the key steps in building and supporting successful brands.

- Establish target market and customer needs with respect to what constitutes important aspects of brand choice and values.

- Determine the brand values to be established in relation to these needs and considering competitor offerings and brand perceptions.

- Position brands so as to occupy important value positions in the market with regard to customer needs and perceptions which can be defended.

- Ensure that brand values are communicated to customers.

- Ensure that brand values are supported over time.

- Monitor changes in company and competitor brand positions and update brands as appropriate.

As already mentioned it is not easy to build successful brands from scratch. Many of the market leading brands today have taken many, many years to develop to this position. Moreover, the often dominant position of the leading brands in a market place can make it very difficult and often impossible to displace them. This may seem surprising given our earlier discussion of the product lifecycle in this unit. After all, the lifecycle concept seems to suggest that brands in particular have finite lives. In fact, the lesson here is that the effective marketer can, through careful attention to re-vitalizing, re-positoining and rationalizing brands keep even the longest established brands fresh and exciting.

Activity 3.23

Try to find a good example of a brand which has been long established and yet is still successful in today's market place. In what ways have the marketers of this brand maintained its successful position in its market.

Service support

Alongside branding, perhaps the other major emerging issue with regard to consumer choice has been that of the service support element of the product part of the marketing mix. In some ways, in fact, many of the reasons for the emergence of brands as an important element in customer choice also underpin the growth in importance of service support. As with branding, customers are now looking for more than simply basic functional products to satisfy their needs and requirements. They are looking for value in the product over and above its basic functional performance. They are looking then for additional elements of back-up and service from the marketer which adds value to the product and generates higher levels of customer satisfaction, generating brand loyalty and leading to long term relationships with customers.

Service support, of course, lies at the augmented, and to some extent, potential levels of the product outlined earlier in this unit. Some products of course comprise of services only, but even here, additional levels of service support over and above that of, say, competitors can be a primary reason for customer choice and loyalty. The marketer therefore must consider whether or not to offer additional levels of service support, what these service support elements will comprise of and how to distinguish service support offerings from competitors.

Service support can be provided in a number of ways. Examples would include:

- Technical support.

- Marketing support (for example in the case of supplying to intermediaries).

- After sales support.

Within these general approaches to offering service support there are any number of specific examples of ways in which product support can be provided. So, for example, technical support can be offered through technical sales support staff or through perhaps a telephone enquiries service. Marketing support can be provided through, for example, promotional tools or perhaps even through financial support systems such as the provision of credit facilities to customers. Finally, after sales support again can be provided through, say, customer help lines or even through support systems such as return and exchange policies.

Service support, then, is an important element in customer choice in contemporary markets. We shall return to service support in our Unit 8 when we consider the role of people, customer care and service as an element of the marketing mix in its own right.

Summary

In this unit you have seen that:

- Product decisions lie at the heart of the marketing mix tools.

- Products can be usefully viewed as a collection of tangible and intangible attributes that combine to provide bundles of benefits underpinning customer satisfaction.

- It is useful to distinguish between the different levels of a product ranging from the inner-most core product or basic benefits through to the augmented and potential product levels.

- Another useful concept of the anatomy of a product is to consider the functional physical and symbolic issues associated with product benefits.

- Useful concepts in managing products include the notion of the product mix which in turn is based on product lines and individual product items.

- The product lifecycle suggests that products have finite lives and pass through definitive and identifiable product lifecycle stages.

- Different strategies exist for different phases of the product life cycle, and the curve of the product life cycle itself can assume a variety of shapes.
- The product adoption process consists of a number of discrete adopter categories that each behave in a different way to a new product offering.
- Packaging, branding and service support elements have become very important elements of the product area of the marketing mix.

Further study and examination preparation

Now do these questions:

Question 3.1

Explain what is meant by the augmented product.

Question 3.2

Outline the different adopter categories in the product adoption process.

Question 3.3

Define the role of packaging.

Question 3.4

Explain the characteristics of the different phases of the product life cycle.

Question 3.5

How could the product life cycle concept be criticized?

Previous examination question

Study tip

This question is taken from Fundamentals of Marketing paper December 1999 question 3. Remember, you can access the full specimen answer for this question on the following website addresses: www.marketingonline.co.uk or www.bh.com/marketing.

Question E3

A publisher identifies that one of their products – a special interest photography magazine – is in the decline stage of its product lifecycle after enjoying many years with high sales in a growth market. You have been asked to submit a report that:

    a.   discusses the likely characteristics of the magazine during the decline stage

(8 marks)

    b.   advises the company on the marketing mix strategy to be adopted for the magazine

(12 marks)
(20 marks in total)

Bibliography

F. Brassington, S. Pettitt, *Principles of Marketing: 2nd Edn,* Chaps 7, 8 and 9, 2000.

Further reading

G. Lancaster, L. Massingham, R. Ashford, *Essentials of Marketing: 4th Edn,* Chap 8, McGraw-Hill, 2001.

S. Dibb, L. Simpkin, W. Pride, O. C. Ferrell, *Marketing Concepts and Strategies: 4th European Edn,* Chaps 8, 9 and 10, Houghton, Mifflin, 2000.

P. Kotler, G. Armstrong, J. A. Saunders, V. Wong, *Principles of Marketing: 2nd European Edn,* Chaps 11 and 12, Prentice-Hall, 1999.

Objectives

By the end of this unit you will:

- Understand the importance of introducing new products and describe the processes involved in the development and launch (3.7).
- Understand the relationship between portfolio analysis and the principles of product policy and management (3.6).

Study guide

This unit is an extension of the previous one and you should expect that it will take you 3 hours to complete, plus a similar amount of time on the exercises. It develops the notions of product portfolio analysis and new product development and, once you have completed it, you will have covered the most important areas of this element of the marketing mix.

When you have completed this unit, go through this and the previous unit to ensure that you have fully understood this important element of marketing.

The importance of new product development

Activity 4.1

Think about the product concepts and tools you have covered already. Consider how useful these are in planning marketing activity:

- in the short tactical term (say 3 months),
- in the longer strategic term (say one year or more).

Although, as we have seen, it is possible to extend the life cycle of products, the very concept of the life cycle suggests that eventually many products will mature and decline. Innovation through new product development, therefore, is important to the survival of an organization. There are many examples of organizations that have suffered with not keeping up with the times. With new technological advances changing the way we live and the sophistication of consumer requirements, products can quickly become obsolete and services can become unnecessary. Recent examples of these include Betamax videos and 45 rpm records.

As a company's products progress along the life cycle, it is important that new products are developed to keep the company profitable.

As already stated then, new products are the key to a company's survival, but this is probably the most risk-laden area of a company's activity. Not only can large sums of money be lost, but product failure can also damage a company's reputation. Needless to say, the prime objective of new product development strategy is to launch a successful product, but it is also essential that any strategy is also designed to reduce risk throughout the stages of development.

In consumer markets new products appear on a regular basis.

Activity 4.2

Think of four new consumer products that have appeared over the last 12 months.

Exam hint

The fact that you have developed these examples here will help you to remember them in the examination. Remember that examiners like to see real examples quoted in examination answers, as it demonstrates that you can apply what you are writing about through a practical illustration.

There are a number of definitions for various types of new products or services.

Innovative products

Innovative products are by definition new to the market. They provide completely different alternatives to existing products in existing markets. To a certain extent 'technological break-throughs' are less common now than, say, when the first television was developed. Nowadays it tends to be more a matter of refinement of existing products. However, in the field of medicine and the development of drugs, breakthrough products still appear from time to time.

Replacement products

Replacement products are new to consumers, but replace existing products rather than providing a total innovation. This type of product is more common nowadays because research teams tend to be commissioned to work upon product refinements rather than upon 'blockbuster' innovations. Even the digital audio tape (DAT) is a replacement product, although its development could be regarded as a breakthrough.

Imitative products

Imitative products is the category in which most new products fall. Once a firm has successfully launched an innovative or replacement product or service, others will follow. They are sometimes termed 'me too' products. Not all companies have the resources to develop new product ideas and they are happy to let others complete costly market development before launching their new product. If the innovative company is able to secure some kind of patent or copyright, then imitators will have to seek permission from the innovator before they can copy the product or idea. This is known as licensing. However, not all innovations are patentable and new products will quickly find imitators.

Relaunched products

Relaunched products are the final category, and this is where a product can be successfully relaunched via a different marketing strategy (perhaps by changing the emphasis of the product benefits). It is then categorized as a new product even through its physical characteristics may not have substantially altered.

Activity 4.3

Think of a product that fits each of the categories just described.

For new product development to be successful it should be managed effectively. In practice there are a number of ways in which this is done.

Product managers

Product managers emerge where a company assigns the task of new product development to product (or brand) managers. This has already been discussed in the Unit 'Tools of marketing: product', but the problem is that such people are normally so taken up managing their existing products that they do not have the inclination to produce more than simple modifications to the brands under their control.

New product managers

New product managers report to a senior products manager. This is perhaps a better method than the first one, but the problem, again, is that such managers tend to relate more to line extensions and modifications of products than to totally new products.

New product committees

New product committees exist in most large companies. They change in terms of their membership structure and meet on an *ad hoc* basis. Their function is to review new product ideas and approve or reject them.

New product departments

New product departments exist in some large companies, usually under a manager who has authority across other line managers. The function of such departments is to generate and screen new ideas and to work with the research and development department through to conducting final product testing and commercialization. Sometimes individuals who work on specific products and see them through from inception to implementation are called 'product champions'.

New product venture teams

Such teams are brought together from a number of different parts of an organization's operations. They tend to be found in large, high-technology, multinational companies. Their sole responsibility is to develop a specific product or business within a predetermined time and budget allocation.

The process of new product development

The product or service is of course central to all marketing activity. Without it no other marketing activity would take place. The sale of the product or service provides revenue, and it is the medium through which a company fulfils the marketing concept. It is therefore essential that any new product development programme should be conducted in a professional manner.

The first attempt at formalizing a theory about the process of product development was done by the American firm of management consultants Booz, Allen & Hamilton. In 1968, after they had conducted a study, they concluded that it took fifty-eight new product ideas to produce one successful product. They repeated the study in 1981 and found that companies had in general found out how to handle the product prescreening and planning processes more effectively, because it was found that it then took only seven new product ideas to produce a successful product.

From their findings we now have a generalized formal product development programme that incorporates a number of stages. Not all stages will be relevant for all products, but as a general guide it is useful.

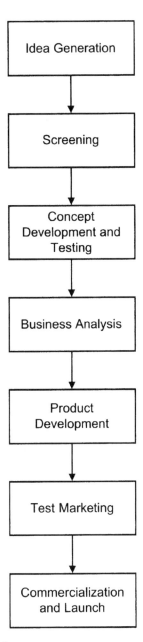

Figure 4.1 *Stages in New Product Development*

Idea generation

Idea generation can spring from formal research and development departments, or from production departments, which might see ways of modifying and improving the product. Marketing is of course important as a source of ideas through the marketing research process and indeed from the company's sales people, who are in constant touch with the market place. It is the task of senior management to create an idea-oriented environment in the company and create a climate that encourages the generation of new product ideas.

Screening

Screening is meant to reduce the pool of ideas to a manageable number through the identification of the most potentially worthwhile ideas, and a number of questions must be answered:

- Is there a real consumer need?
- Does the company have the resources and technical competence to market and manufacture the product?
- Is the potential market large enough to generate profits that correspond to what the company expects?

Concept development and testing

If the product idea passes the initial screening then the company can begin to refine and develop the product concept for testing with potential consumers. At this stage the product or service will still be only an idea and so it can be difficult, particularly with service products, to assess possible customer reaction. However, concept testing is now well developed and refined. It is possible to produce descriptions of products indicating what the product is and the central benefits that it would bestow. It is also possible to use pictorial descriptions of physical products so that the concept may be assessed.

If the answer to any of the screening questions is 'no', then no further work need be done. It is a fact that many new products fail because in a company's enthusiasm to develop such products, these very obvious questions have not been asked.

In order to develop an effective screening technique, the company must isolate a series of factors research has shown to be desirable in the market place. The firm should of course develop products that make the best use of its own production and marketing strengths. An internal appraisal of the company's strengths and weaknesses, together with input from marketing research, should establish what these criteria should be. Products that best satisfy the various screening criteria should then be selected for further development.

Business analysis

'Business analysis' is the next stage, and this is concerned with financial rather than with practical matters. Demand is estimated, together with costs and profitability. All costs should be taken into account here, including marketing as well as costs of production. It is at this pragmatic stage that a number of seemingly good new product ideas are discarded.

Product development

'Product development' is the stage when costs can rise phenomenally. Up to now time and energy will have been expended perhaps commissioning a market-research survey, but these are likely to be small by comparison with this stage. By this stage the company should have tried to minimize the risk and isolate potentially valuable new product ideas. During this product development stage the company develops a prototype product in order to confirm its potential. Once this is satisfactory, the company must again turn to the market place to obtain feedback on the product's suitability in terms of performance and customer attitude. Prototypes should correspond as closely as possible to the envisaged production model so as to obtain accurate customer reaction.

At this stage it is now a matter of 'fine tuning'. It is also an opportunity to abandon the product if market reaction is negative. It is important that correct decisions are taken now, because, although it may be frustrating and appear wasteful to abandon a product at this stage, the costs and potential damage to the company's reputation will be greater if the product is launched and subsequently fails.

If this stage is successful, the firm should then have the confidence to go ahead with the product launch. This decision is critical and requires considerable business analytical skills, because if full-scale production is undertaken, then costs of setting up production facilities will greatly add to the final cost. Many companies go to this final full-scale production phase, depending upon the nature of the product to be marketed. Many fast-moving consumer goods (FMCGs) go through the next screening process.

Test marketing

Test marketing is the final check on whether or not the new product can be marketed appropriately. When a company enters a test market, it is fairly well committed to launching the product, and the test's real purpose is to look at the product's appropriateness in a geographically controlled situation. The objective of a test market is to investigate the appropriateness of proposed marketing strategy and tactics, to refine them, and then predict the effects of such strategies in terms of market potential.

In the United Kingdom test marketing is made a little easier by the existence of Independent Television areas that divide the United Kingdom conveniently into well defined regions that can be used as test market areas. They are appropriate when television advertising is a component of marketing strategy. In other parts of the world there are not such discrete independent television areas with well defined regions and hence test marketing in other countries can be more difficult with respect to the selection of test areas. The chosen area for a test market should be as closely representative of the final total market as possible, and if this was not to be the case, the whole objective of testing would be lost. Sometimes companies run two test markets at the same time, which offers opportunities for experimentation by varying the marketing mix in the two markets simultaneously to try to find the best balance within an optimum budget.

Test marketing is obviously an attempt to establish whether or not a new product is viable. For this reason, test marketing is principally used to gauge the response to a proposed new product, and in particular to try and forecast potential sales and profits. However, test marketing can be used to specifically assess a particular part of a proposed or amended element of the marketing mix such as, for example, new or improved packaging, different pricing levels, special promotional deals etc.

Figure 4.2 *Decay rate of new product ideas*

In industrial markets, where the number of customers might be quite small, testing can be done by initially marketing to a few co-operating customers, who will provide feedback before full-scale production is commenced. This is more correctly termed a 'product placement test'.

It has been known for competitive companies to attempt to 'sabotage' a test marketing programme by creating artificial conditions in the test area for the duration of the test, e.g. they might conduct an intensive promotional programme of their own with a view to depressing sales of the product being test-marketed. For this reason, test markets should be as unobtrusive as possible, which is why many FMCG manufacturers confine their activities to test towns rather than television areas. Such towns are in concentrated areas of population, with their own newspaper, and tend to be separated geographically from other urban conurbations.

Commercialization and launch

Commercialization is the final stage, where many ideas have been filtered out and a viable proposition has been selected. Production, financial and other commercial criteria have been examined and a suitable product, acceptable to the market place, is ready to launch. Even after all the preceding stages, success cannot be guaranteed at this stage, and a facet of the earlier Booz, Allen and Hamilton study found that even at this juncture only one in two products would be successful. All that can be said is that with a sequential examination of the criteria just described, then the risk of ultimate product failure is reduced.

Figure 4.2 describes the decay curve as the stages are passed through as first put forward by Booz, Allen and Hamilton, and Figure 4.3 shows the relationship between costs and the steps outlined before.

Information and communication technology and new product development

Obviously much new product development in itself is underpinned by developments in, and the applications of new technology, in as much as new products often incorporate new technology. In addition to this aspect of technology and new product development, however, developments in ICT are also affecting the new product development process.

The interactive nature of the Internet allows the marketer to involve and encourage customer participation in product design and also speed-up the design commitment. In particular, net technology allows a much more flexible approach to the process of new product development whilst at the same time involving the customer in the process. The following represent some of the ways in which this flexibility and customer involvement are achieved.

- The customer can be involved in very early stages of product specification and design. The database can be used to identify key customers and their requirements. This can then be followed up with communication to selected customers so as to gain information about their particular needs and the implications of these for the product concept.

- Product concepts and proposed technical solutions to customer needs can then be interpreted into the design process and again the design options evaluated directly and immediately with customers.

- Finally, as the product is further developed, customer needs can be integrated with technical solutions by using intranet, extranet and Internet communications to integrate tasks, synchronize design changes and capture customer response as the projects evolve. Applications of new technology to flexible product development include motor vehicle design, software product development and specific 'one-off' products.

Portfolio analysis

Portfolio analysis comprises of a collection of techniques which is aimed at managing a company's collection or portfolio of products and/or strategic business units. As we shall see, there are several techniques and approaches in this family of analysis techniques, but essentially they share the objective of attempting to manage more effectively in the multi-product business. The first technique of portfolio analysis we shall consider was itself one of the first to be developed and used by marketers, namely the so-called Boston Consulting Group portfolio analysis method.

The Boston Consulting Group (BCG) portfolio analysis

The technique of portfolio analysis was pioneered in the USA by the management consultants Boston Consulting Group (BCG). The methods proposed identified the company's strategic business units (SBUs) or product groups, and represented these on a matrix that considers market growth and relative market share. These are positioned in the matrix as circles with a diameter proportional to their sales revenue. Figure 4.4 explains this.

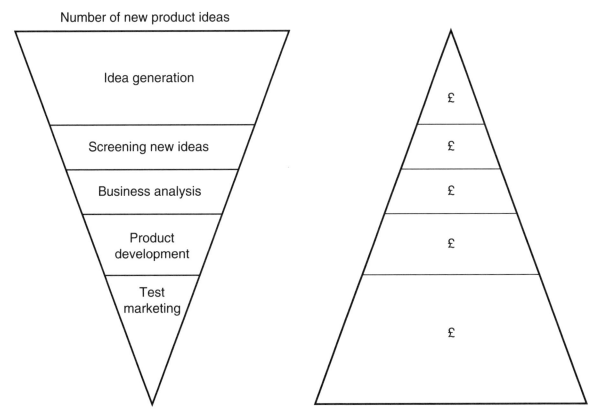

Figure 4.3 *The relationship between cost and the stages of product development*

Four boxes into which SBUs or product groups fall can be identified in Figure 4.4. In order to help you understand these we have provided examples for each category.

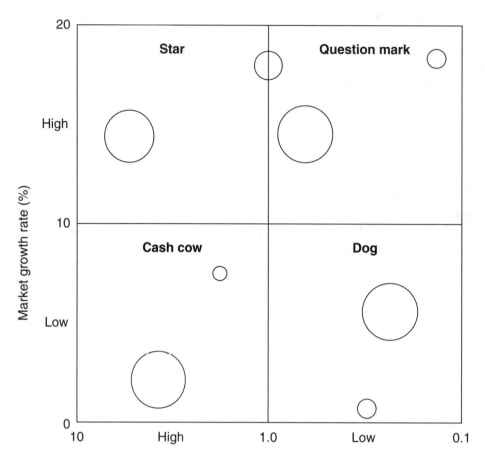

Figure 4.4 *The Boston Consulting Group (BCG) matrix*

- 'Stars' are those SBUs that have a promising future. Significant investments of cash are necessary to develop their full potential. If managed correctly, they will develop into a valuable source of revenue as the market evolves. A good example of products, which for many companies are at this stage, are the Internet products. Most are agreed that products in this area, if properly developed and managed, will represent the 'stars' of the future for many companies.

- 'Cash cows' have achieved a high market share in a mature market. They deserve the company's fullest attention, as the cash they generate can be invested in newer market areas with high growth potential. Levi jeans are a good example of a product that is probably a cash cow for the Levi Strauss company.

- 'Question marks' (or problem children or wildcats, as they are sometimes called) pose a problem to management. While market growth prospects are good, question mark SBUs have a low relative market share. If they are to be moved to the left, i.e. increase their relative market share, then substantial investment will be required. Based on the available marketing information, marketing management must use its skill to decide whether such investment could be better employed supporting other SBUs. Many smaller companies find themselves with the problem of too many question marks, because by definition these smaller companies have low market share. Some of the more specialist car producers at the top end of the market such as TVR, for example, have found themselves in this position. The Rover part of the BMW Rover Group had problems with products with low relative market share and with little or no growth potential in the market in which these products are positioned.

- 'Dogs' show no growth potential and their relative market share is low. Although they may not necessarily be a drain on the company's resources, they are unable to make a positive contribution to profits. Many small textile companies in the UK, for example, have brands which are in markets where there is little or no growth potential and where, due to the company size, their relative market share is low. Companies like this, therefore, tend to have an unhealthy predominance of dogs in their portfolio.

Although this model was developed for multi-industry companies, it can be used by single industry operations; this is where the SBU is represented by a single product or product line, and it is this latter application that is now becoming more popular in use. In reality, little can be done by a single company to change the market growth rate that defines an SBU's position on the vertical axis. The options are therefore to eliminate SBUs from the portfolio, or to move them from the right to the left along the horizontal axis, i.e. to increase their market share. Increased sales will increase the size of the SBUs themselves and remember the size of the circles represents the value of sales. Forecast sales figures can also be plotted for each product which will help indicate the potential movement of the product in the matrix.

The accuracy of any model is only as good as the information upon which it is based. Marketing should ensure that decisions are not based on partial or misleading information. A BCG matrix-type model requires a great deal of accurate market and company information before it can be used as a meaningful management tool. In addition to presenting strategic alternatives, a well prepared BCG matrix is valuable because it forces objective consideration of the elements of the portfolio in relation to each other.

Activity 4.4

If you have the practical resources and appropriate information at your disposal, place each of the products your company makes or the services it supplies in what you consider to be their appropriate positions within the BCG matrix. Justify your criteria in respect of each entry.

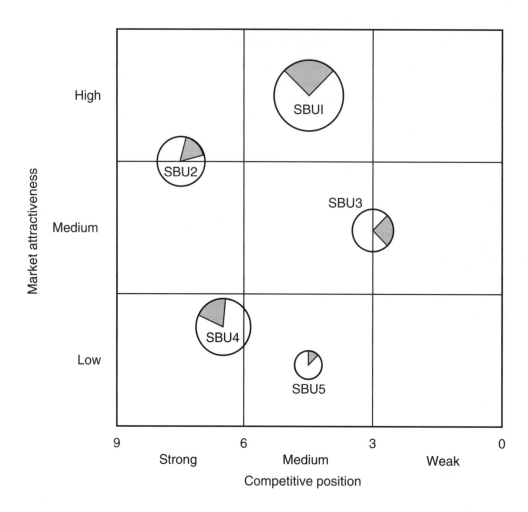

Figure 4.5 *GE matrix*

Essentially, only two criteria are used with respect to positioning products in the different cells of the BCG portfolio analysis matrix, namely, relative market share and market growth rate. However, cash flow too can give an indication of where a product is likely to be in the matrix. Perhaps as you would expect, products in the cash cow area of the matrix have strong positive cash flows whereas stars and dogs often have high negative cash flows. Question marks too are likely to be net users of cash rather than contributors, though perhaps to a lesser extent than star classified products.

GE Business Screen matrix

General Electric (USA) and McKinsey & Co (management consultants) developed a business screen matrix that attempted to overcome some of the criticisms of the BCG matrix. It is now known as the GE matrix and it is described in Figure 4.5.

SBUs or product lines are considered, with the two dimensions of competitive position and market attractiveness. These two criteria are good in evaluating a business or group of products in that they will be seen to be successful to the extent that they go into attractive markets and have the requisite competitive business strength to succeed in those markets. The two complement each other, for a weak company operating in an attractive market will not do well, and neither will a strong company operating in an unattractive market.

Each of the two dimensions is further analysed into a number of factors that underpin each dimension. In order to use this technique, the strategic marketing planner must first determine these various factors that contribute to market attractiveness and business position.

The following factors are used to assess product/market attractiveness:

- Size.
- Growth rate.
- Competitive diversity and structure.
- Historical profit margin.
- Technological requirements.
- Social impact.
- Environmental impact.
- Legal impact.
- Energy requirements.

For assessing competitive position, the following factors can be used:

- Market share.
- Share growth rate.
- Product quality.
- Brand reputation.
- Distribution network.
- Promotional effectiveness.
- Productive capacity.
- Productive efficiency.
- Unit costs.
- Research & development performance.
- Managerial personnel.

The list can be modified according to each company's requirements and circumstances.

The GE matrix is compiled in five steps:

1. Identify strategic business units (or product groups).
2. Determine factors contributing to market attractiveness.
3. Determine factors contributing to business position.
4. Establish ways of measuring market attractiveness and business position.
5. Rank each SBU high, medium or low on business strength, and high, medium or low on market attractiveness.

Some kind of numerical rating should be given to the relative importance of the last two factors. Multiplying these together and totalling them for each SBU gives a composite score that enables the matrix to be compiled. In addition, the total market size for each SBU can be represented by the area of the circle with the company's SBU share of that total market represented as a segment in the circle. Thus a visual portfolio can be shown, as in Figure 4.5, and a complicated analysis can be presented in a more digestible form.

Having completed the matrix, the marketing planner can then assess the balances of SBUs or product groups within the organization, and determine future strategies for each.

According to an SBU or product group's position within the matrix, we can distinguish between three broad strategic alternatives and these are detailed in Figure 4.6.

SBUs that score high or medium on competitive position and market attractiveness are those in which a company should seek to maintain an investment and possibly grow. SBUs that score a combination of low/low or low/medium on competitive position and market attractiveness should be considered for no more investment, and as much cash as possible should be harvested from them. SBUs scoring either high/low or medium/medium combinations on competitive position/market attractiveness should be examined to see if some degree of selective investment is possible to maintain or increase earnings.

If we take the example of the Mercedes car company it is probable that the four-wheel drive products in the range are examples of SBUs ideal for investment and growth. In the larger executive saloon car end of the market, however, Mercedes are more likely to profit from pursuing a selectivity earning strategy. Finally, it may well be that, in some parts of the market where the company is in a weak competitive position at the moment, harvesting and divesting strategies might be necessary.

Activity 4.6

If you have the practical resources and information at your disposal, construct a GE-type matrix in relation to your own organization's product groups or SBUs. Justify your reasons for placing each entry in a particular box.

Classifying product groups or SBUs in the GE-type matrix is more complex than in the BCG one. The criteria used to assess the position of product groups or SBUs uses many more factors with regard to assessing product/market attractiveness and competitive position. Furthermore, there are a variety of ways of measuring these dimensions of the matrix which can lead to a degree of subjectivity with respect to positionings in the grid.

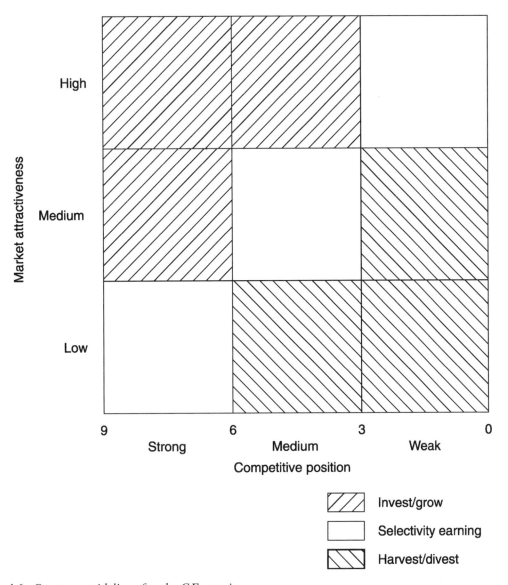

Figure 4.6 *Strategy guidelines for the GE matrix*

Activity 4.7

Consider what you feel to be the chief benefits the GE matrix offers over the BCG matrix. Then list the chief drawbacks in relation to the GE matrix approach to portfolio analysis and compare your analysis with the answer shown in the debrief.

Porter's industry/market evolution model

In 1985 Michael Porter developed a model that furthered research he had published in 1980. The work was reported in his book *Competitive Advantage: Creating and Sustaining Superior Performance* (Free Press, New York).

In summary he based his model on three broad stages in the evolution of an industry/market:

- *Emerging industry* – characterized by buyers' uncertainty over product performance, potential applications and likelihood of obsolescence, and sellers' uncertainty over customer needs, demand levels and technological developments.

- *Transition to maturity* – characterized by falling industry profits, slow-down in growth, customers knowledgeable about products and competitive offerings, less product innovation and competition upon non-product aspects of marketing.

- *Decline* – characterized by competition from substitutes, changing customer needs, and demographic and other macro-environmental forces and factors affecting the market.

He then used the characteristics of each stage to suggest a number of strategies as being appropriate to each, as shown in Figure 4.7.

Emerging industry strategies (growth column) should be developed to take account of industry competitive structure characteristics:

	Growth	Maturity	Decline
Leader	keep ahead of the field	Cost leadership; raise barriers; deter competitors	Redefine scope; divest peripherals; encourage departures
Follower	limitation at lower costs; joint ventures	Differentation; focus	Differentiation new opportunities

Strategic position (vertical axis label)

Figure 4.7   Industry life cycle and strategic position

- Threat of entry.
- Rivalry among competitors.
- Pressure from substitute products.
- Bargaining power of buyers and suppliers.

Transition to maturity strategies (maturity column) should be developed to focus upon:

- Developing new market segments.
- Focusing strategies for specific segments.
- Developing a more efficient organization.

Decline strategies should:

- Seek pockets of enduring demand.
- Divest the product or SBU.

Activity 4.8

Summarize what you consider to be the similarity between Porter's model and the product life cycle analysis and compare your answer with that suggested in the debriefing.

A D Little industry maturity/competitive position matrix

This was developed by the management consultants Arthur D Little, and its approach is similar to the one developed by Porter. 'Stage of industry maturity' (similar to the stages of the product life cycle) is on the horizontal axis and 'Competitive position' on the vertical axis, and it is shown in Figure 4.8.

Eight key descriptors to determine which stage a product group or SBU is in are then assessed:

- Rate of market growth.
- Industry potential.
- Product line.
- Number of competitors.
- Market share stability.
- Purchasing patterns.
- Ease of entry.
- Technology.

Company's competitive position	Stage of industry maturity			
	Embryonic	Growth	Maturity	Ageing
Dominant				
Strong				
Favourable				
Tentative				
Weak				

Figure 4.8   *A D Little competitive position/industry maturity matrix*

Activity 4.9

Assess the shortcomings of the A D Little matrix and then compare your answer with that shown in the debriefing.

Shell directional policy matrix

This approach was developed by Shell Chemicals (UK) in 1975. Its approach is similar to the GE Business Screen Matrix and it has two dimensions:

- The competitive capability of the company.
- Prospects for sector profitability.

The company's products are plotted into one of the nine cells and subsequently there is a suggested strategy for each cell, as shown in Figure 4.9.

Sector profitability includes the criteria of market growth rate, market quality, industry situation and environmental considerations. On each of these factors a product is given from one to five stars. The same procedure is followed for each of the other three factors, so that the score on sector profitability is the total of the ratings on all four factors.

Prospects for sector profitability

	Unattractive	Average	Attractive
Weak	Disinvest	Phased withdrawal	Double or quit
		Custodial	
Average	Phased withdrawal	Custodial	Try harder
		Growth	
Strong	Cash generation	Growth	Leader
		Leader	

Company's competitive capability

Figure 4.9 *Shell directional policy matrix*

Competitive capability uses the same approach, except that the company's capabilities are assessed on the basis of market position, product research and development, and production capability. These are further divided into sub-factors applicable to any particular industry.

The strategy recommendations contained in each of the nine cells are shown in Figure 4.9. The chief proviso, Shell maintains, is that whatever strategy is eventually selected, the aim is that it should be 'resilient' in terms of being viable in a diverse range of potential futures. Thus, each strategy should be evaluated against all future possible scenarios and the results in all cases should be acceptable in commercial terms.

Activity 4.10

What do you consider are the limitations of the Shell directional policy matrix? Compare your answer with the debriefing.

Barksdale and Harris portfolio analysis/product life cycle matrix

This was developed in 1982 by H. C. Barksdale and C. E. Harris (Jr) and reported in the *Journal of Long Range Planning*. The matrix is specifically designed to deal with the criticisms that the BCG matrix ignores new products and overlooks markets that are in decline, i.e. have a negative growth rate. The key assumptions on which the technique is based are:

- Products have finite life spans as epitomized in the product life cycle concept.

- Strategic objectives and marketing strategy should match the market growth rate changes in order to take advantage of opportunities as the product goes through the various stages.

- For most products, costs of production are closely linked to volume, and unit costs go down as volume increases.

- Capital expenditure is related to rate of growth, and products in growth markets will use more resources than products in mature markets.

- Margins and the cash generated are positively related to share of market. Products with a high relative share in their market will be more profitable than products with low shares.

- When maturity is reached, products with a high market share generate a stream of cash greater than that needed to support them in the market, and the cash generated is available for investment in other products or in research and development to create new products.

Based on these assumptions, the model highlights the additional issues that arise out of pioneering new products (labelled 'infants') and products in declining markets (labelled 'war-horses' or 'dodos'). The result is a combined product life cycle/product portfolio model, as illustrated in Figure 4.10.

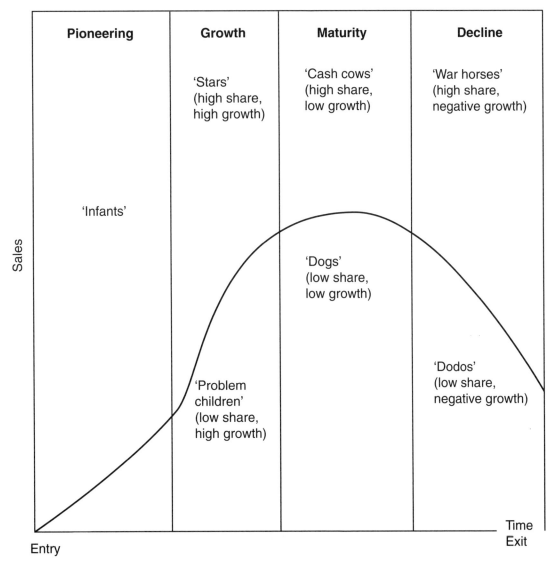

Figure 4.10 *Combined PLC/product portfolio concepts Barksdale and Harris*

The approach is based on the idea that both the initial and decline stages of the life cycle are important. It recognizes that product innovations as well as products with negative growth rates are important and should not be ignored in strategic analysis. The result is a matrix composed of the four BCG categories plus:

- 'War-horses', which are products with high market share and sustainable as cash generators, but in a market with negative growth. In other words, they were cash cows when the market was mature, but in a declining market the transition might require reduced marketing expenditure or even some kind of selective withdrawal from certain market segments or the elimination of certain models.

- 'Dodos' are products that have low shares of declining markets, with little opportunity for growth or cash generation. The appropriate strategy is to remove them from the portfolio. However, if competitors have disappeared, it might still be profitable to keep them, so timing is critical.

- 'Infants' are pioneering products that possess a high degree of risk. They do not immediately earn profits, and consume substantial cash resources. The length of the innovative, pioneering period can vary depending upon the type of product being considered.

In summary, the method produces an eight-box matrix, as shown in Figure 4.11.

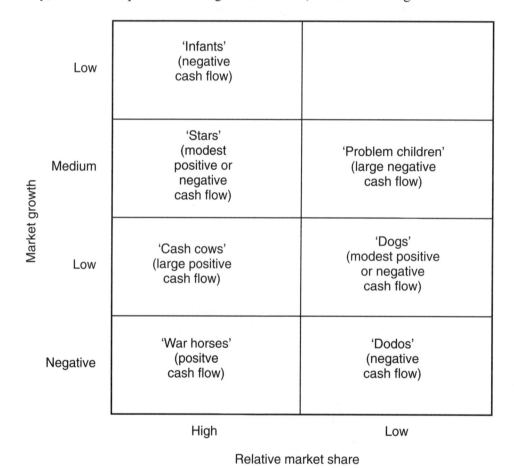

Figure 4.11 *Product life cycle portfolio matrix*

Activity 4.11

What do you feel are the advantages and the limitations of the Barksdale and Harris matrix? Check your answer with that suggested in the debriefing.

Summary

In this unit you have seen that:

- New product development is a key activity in the management of the product element of the marketing mix.
- There are a number of definitions and types of new products with regard to their degree of newness and a variety of approaches to managing new product development effectively.
- The new product development process encompasses a series of stages from idea generation to commercialization and launch which should be conducted in a systematic manner
- Portfolio analysis offers a number of models for analysing and managing the product mix and SBUs.

Further study and examination preparation

Now do these questions:

Question 4.1

Why is new product development important for all organizations?

Question 4.2

List the stages of new product development.

Question 4.3

Identify why the Boston matrix is often used in portfolio planning.

Question 4.4

Why might the Boston matrix be criticized as a marketing management tool?

Previous examination question

Question E4

Prepare notes for a presentation to general management on the importance of new product development and the stages involved in this activity.

(20 marks)

Bibliography

F. Brassington, S. Pettitt, *Principles of Marketing: 2nd Edn.* Chaps 9 and 20, 2000.

Further reading

S. Dibb, L. Simpkin, W. Pride, O. C. Ferrell, *Marketing Concepts and Strategies: 4th European Edn.* Chaps 1 and 22, Houghton, Mifflin, 2000.

G. Lancaster, L. Massingham, R. Ashford, *Essentials of Marketing: 4th Edn,* Chaps 6, 12, Appendix 1, McGraw-Hill, 2002.

Objectives

By the end of the Unit you will:

- Understand the role and importance of price in the marketing mix (3.8).
- Appreciate the process of making pricing decisions and the range of internal and external factors affecting these (3.8).
- Understand the different pricing policies, strategies and tactics (3.9).

Study guide

This unit covers the second key element of the marketing mix and the only one that generates revenue for the company.

In the profit-making organization, and perhaps surprisingly in many not-for-profit ones too, pricing decisions are central to the effectiveness of a company. For obvious reasons prices have a major impact on levels of profits. However, pricing is more than simply an accountancy exercise – indeed it is a vital element of marketing plans. For example, price helps to position a product/service in a market and ultimately in the mind of the customer.

All too often marketers shy away from attempting to understand some of the key inputs to pricing decisions and instead leave it to accountants. For example, many marketers do not understand the different types of cost in producing a product or how to conduct a breakeven analysis. Similarly some do not understand the relation between price and demand, and factors such as 'price elasticity'. Where this is the case, the marketer is unable to make informed and professional pricing decisions and instead is at the mercy of the accountant and the economist. The intention here is not to turn you into instant accountants or economists but simply to help you understand the contributions and jargon of these disciplines in helping make pricing decisions.

We would expect it to take you about 3 hours to work through this unit and suggest you allow a further 3 to 4 hours to undertake the various activities suggested. Other than your notebook and writing equipment you will not need anything further to complete this unit.

The role and importance of price in marketing

As consumers we all know what is meant by 'the price' of a product or service. In simple terms price is the monetary value placed upon a product/service by the marketer, and we must pay it in order to acquire or use the product or service. A 'price', however, can take several forms, depending upon the circumstances. For example, in the case of a credit card we pay an annual 'fee' and a monthly 'rate of interest'. At the end of the month we may pay a landlord 'rent'. An agent may charge us 'commission'. All these are variations on the word 'price'. In the case of many not-for-profit organizations there is no price as such for the product. For example, the customer may instead be required to give up his or her time, or perhaps his or her vote, as opposed to paying over a monetary sum.

Immediately, therefore, we can see that even the word 'price', which we all take for granted as knowing what it means, is more complex and varied than we might at first imagine. In addition, price plays a vital role in marketing. Some major roles of price are as follows:

- As mentioned earlier, price is the major basis for generating revenue and, where relevant, profits in an organization.
- Put simply:
    1. Revenue = price × quantity
    2. Profit = revenue − costs
- Prices connect customers and suppliers at the point of exchange.
- Prices send signals to customers about factors such as product quality, exclusiveness, etc. There are powerful behavioural and psychological aspects to the price element.
- Price is also used as a powerful competitive weapon in markets, sometimes to drive other competitors out of business, prevent new ones entering, and forcing those that remain to follow prices that have been laid down.

Activity 5.1

As we have already seen, there are various terms for the word 'price'. Using your experience and knowledge, look for as many different examples that mean the same thing as price used by different industries, for different products, etc.

A good idea would be to look through newspapers and magazines in addition to keeping your eyes open when you next go shopping.

Perspectives on pricing decisions

Broadly we can distinguish between three different approaches to pricing decisions each with its own distinct perspective and emphasis. These three approaches correspond to the three disciplines, concepts and techniques of the economist, the accountant, and the marketer. Each of these would individually suggest a different approach to pricing decisions.

Exam hint

In the past comparing and contrasting the approaches and perspectives of these three disciplines has been a popular area for questions on the Fundamentals paper. We shall therefore continue by outlining each perspective and the contributions of these three different disciplines to the pricing decision.

The economist's perspective

Pricing is viewed as the mechanism/signal whereby demand and supply are brought into equilibrium. The operation of this mechanism varies according to market structure, ranging from perfectly competitive markets to imperfect competition and monopolistic market structures.

The economist looks at price on the assumption that companies are 'profit maximizers'. The major contribution of the economist to price planning in marketing is the notion surrounding the relationships between demand and price.

The accountant's perspective

The emphasis is on recovering costs to make a profit, often expressed as a required rate of return. This emphasis on costs means that the accountant stresses the importance of identifying and classifying different costs.

The major contribution of the accountant therefore to planning pricing decisions is this analysis of costs together with techniques such as breakeven analysis. The major disadvantage of the accountant's perspective is that there is a tendency to ignore demand and market considerations.

The marketer's perspective

The emphasis is on the effect of price on competitive market position, including sales, market share, and sometimes profit levels. However, price is seen as being only one factor affecting market demand.

The marketer stresses the importance of 'value' rather than just price. The marketer's approach to pricing is essentially based on pricing 'at what the market will bear'.

Although these are three different perspectives on price, each has something to contribute to informed pricing decisions. This means therefore that the marketer can and should draw upon each of these perspectives when making pricing decisions. We can see this more clearly by examining the considerations or inputs to pricing decisions.

Activity 5.2

Before we look at inputs to pricing decisions try to find out how prices are set in your own company and who is responsible for setting them. We can use this information later in the unit when we look at pricing methods.

Inputs and information for pricing decisions

Before we look at approaches to making a pricing decision and, in particular, how to structure these and specific methods of pricing, it is important to ensure that you understand what are the key inputs or considerations in any pricing decision made by the marketer. The key considerations in most pricing decisions are now outlined and discussed. We can think of these considerations as the four C's, namely: Costs, Customers, Competition and Company considerations.

Costs and prices

As mentioned earlier, information on costs is the key contribution of the accountant to setting prices. In most companies costs determine the lower limit to the prices a company can charge. The following represent some of the information and analysis on costs that we need when setting a price on a product for the first time:

- Total costs.
- Average costs.
- Fixed costs.
- Variable costs.
- Marginal cost.
- Relation between volume and cost: 'scale economies'.
- Relations between experience and costs: 'experience curves'.

Some definitions might be useful before proceeding.

Definition

Total cost

The sum of all fixed costs and variable costs times the quantity produced.

Definition

Average cost

Average cost = Total cost divided by number of units produced.

Definition

Fixed costs

Costs that do not vary with the number of units produced or sold.

> **Definition**
>
> **Variable costs**
>
> Costs that vary directly according to the number of units produced or sold.

> **Definition**
>
> **Marginal cost**
>
> The addition to total cost of producing one additional unit of output.

> **Definition**
>
> **Scale economies**
>
> The potential reduction in average costs as a result of increasing output/sales.

> **Definition**
>
> **Experience curves**
>
> The potential reduction in average costs as a result of learning/ experience based on cumulative output.

By providing this type of analysis and information on costs the accountant plays a key role in contributing to pricing decisions. In addition, a variety of tools of analysis provided by the accountant can be useful. Perhaps the best example of such a tool is breakeven analysis. But before we look briefly at breakeven analysis you should undertake the following activity.

> **Activity 5.3**
>
> **Examples of types of cost**
>
> Preferably using your own organization, explore and list examples of various kinds of cost:
>
> 1. Fixed costs.
> 2. Variable costs.
> 3. Neither of the above.
>
> When you have completed this activity, you should look at the debriefing for examples of different types of cost.

Using this concept of different costs enables the accountant and the marketer to explore some of the relationships between costs and prices. Two of the most useful tools of cost analysis are the related notions of 'contribution' and 'breakeven'.

Contribution

Contribution is calculated in the following way:

Selling price − variable cost = contribution

As the term implies, contribution is the amount, if any, which is left after deducting variable costs from a selling price and which therefore 'contributes' to covering fixed costs. By calculating contribution, the marketer can assess if it would be worthwhile, at least in the short run, to sell a product at less than total cost. As fixed costs by definition would be incurred irrespective of how much is produced or sold, then we might decide that if we can cover variable costs, we should continue to produce the product. In the long run of course all costs must be covered.

Breakeven analysis

The breakeven point represents the level of output at any given price where total revenue is exactly equal to the total costs of production and marketing. The breakeven quantity (BEQ) can be calculated in the following way.

BEQ = Fixed costs/Contribution

Activity 5.4

Contribution and breakeven calculations
Calculate:

   i.   The contribution, and

   ii.   the breakeven point

from the following information:

      Selling price = £20.00
      Variable cost = £10.00
      Fixed costs = £100,000.00

Compare your calculations with those shown in the debriefing.

Breakeven analysis can also be done graphically. An example using the same information as in the previous activity is shown in Figure 5.1.

Not only is Figure 5.1 easy to interpret, but we can also use the chart very simply to examine the effect on breakeven quantities of different prices.

We can see then how the accountant can make a valuable contribution to pricing decisions by providing information and analyses on costs.

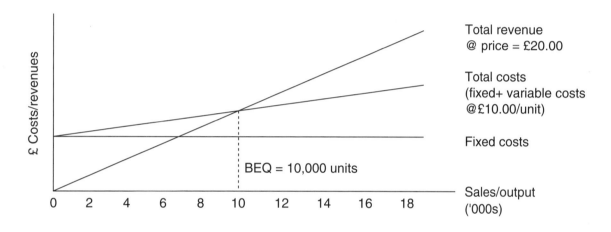

Figure 5.1 A simple breakeven chart

However, as we shall see later, it is dangerous to base pricing decisions on cost information alone. As mentioned earlier, costs set the lower limit to the prices the marketer can charge. The upper limit is determined by demand or customer considerations. We shall now turn our attention to this second input to pricing decisions.

Customers (demand) and prices

Our second key input to pricing decisions is information on customers or, more specifically, demand. Demand sets the upper limit to the prices the marketer can set. We cannot charge prices higher than the customer is willing and able to pay. The concepts and techniques of the economist are useful here. At the very least the marketer would like to know the relations between quantities demanded and different prices. Put another way, he would like to know the shape of the demand curve. A simple demand curve is shown in Figure 5.2.

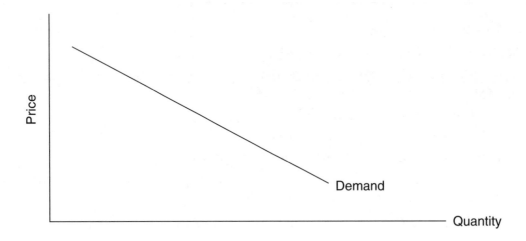

Figure 5.2 *A simple demand curve*

We can immediately see that even the simple diagram of Figure 5.2 gives the marketer valuable information for pricing. The shape of the demand curve shows how much will be demanded at any given price, and the effect on demand of changes in price. This second piece of information is referred to as 'price elasticity' and indicates how sensitive demand is to changes in price.

Definition

Price elasticity of demand

Percentage change in quantity demanded/% change in price.

In simple terms, the steeper the demand curve, the less sensitive demand is to changes in price, i.e. relatively price 'inelastic'. Similarly the flatter the demand curve, the more sensitive demand is to changes in price, i.e. relatively price elastic.

Examples of products which are relatively price inelastic are those where either the customer has no option but to purchase, such as for example car insurance, electricity and other energy forms, water, etc., or where the customer has developed a high degree of brand loyalty to a particular supplier which serves to desensitize the customer to changes in price. Incidentally, this highlights the value of effective branding in markets.

Examples of products which are relatively price elastic are those where there is considerable choice and discretion in product selection on the part of a customer and/or where brand loyalty is relatively low. Many undifferentiated products and commodities such as, for example, flour, salt, and bread, etc. fall into this category.

Information on the demand curve can be gleaned from market research including customer surveys and test marketing. You should note that the shape of the demand curve and therefore price elasticity is influenced by many factors. Three of the most important of these factors are: the marketing strategies of the company; the product life cycle; and the marketing strategies of competitors. We shall look at competitors as our third input to pricing decisions so let us briefly consider the first two factors.

Pricing and the consumer's purchase decision-making process

As we have seen, all marketing decisions should be based on an understanding of the customers and their needs. This is as true for pricing therefore as it is for any element of the marketing mix. The marketer must therefore understand the consumer's decision-making process and in particular some of the factors related to price and pricing which a customer might consider when deciding to make a purchase. Some of the more important of these factors are outlined below.

- *Competitors' prices* a consumer is likely to shop around for a product and will consider the competitors' offering and pricing structure.

- *Discounts offered* discounts offered often will have an effect on the buying decision process – an extra 10% off the price may induce trial.

- *Quality and image of the product* the consumer will consider the price in relation to the perceived quality and image of the product and packaging and often the distribution outlet. Many consumers are happy to pay a higher price for Marks & Spencer food as they believe that the quality of the product is guaranteed to be of a certain standard.

- *Disposable income and lifestyle* consumers will need to consider their disposable income and lifestyle when considering the price of a product and making purchases.

- *Personal objectives or utility* the consumer will have their own set of objectives for purchasing a product – it may be for a gift, a personal treat, a necessity, something to make them feel good, etc. These considerations will have some impact on the purchase decision related to the price. For example, a person may buy a more expensive bottle of red wine to take to a dinner party with friends and a cheaper one for a Friday night in front of the television.

- *Value for money* the perceived value of the product will often be a prime consideration, especially for essential items such as food products.

- *Personality and culture* a person's personality may have some bearing on the purchase decision related to price. A person may be more thrifty or generous which will have some bearing on their perceptions of the pricing and purchasing of products. There may be cultural differences in the perception of prices and product, for example, in certain countries a very expensive gift of jewellery is given as a wedding dowry.

- *Perceived risk* a consumer may consider the purchase of a product in relation to perceived risk. So, for example, the consumer may well prefer a higher priced security alarm for the car, considering this to be more effective than the lower priced product.

- *Previous experience and loyalty* experience about a product which has been purchased previously will inform the decision and loyalty towards that product.

We can see therefore that 'getting inside the customer's head' with respect to their purchase decision-making process and the factors which affect it can be very useful in providing insights for effective pricing decisions.

Price elasticity and marketing strategies of a company

The marketer can and does attempt to influence price elasticity through marketing strategies. Very often the marketer will try to 'desensitize' the customer to price, i.e. make the customer less sensitive to price in the purchase decision. For example, the marketer may attempt to create brand loyalty through other elements of the mix. Most marketers would like to alter the slope of the demand curve so that demand for their products is less sensitive to price.

We have already touched on the fact that price sensitivity and therefore price elasticity is lower where brand loyalty exists in a market. Similarly, and related to this, where a company has strong relationships with its customers, again, demand is less likely to be price sensitive. The marketer therefore must consider ways of decreasing the customer's sensitivity to price, and branding and relationship marketing represent two major approaches. Evidence suggests that prices can be as high as sometimes a factor of 2 compared to competitors where strong brand loyalty exists.

Pricing and the product life cycle

We discussed the product life cycle in the Unit 'Tools of marketing: product'. In general terms price elasticity varies in each stage of the life cycle.

Question 5.1

See if you can gauge how price elasticity might change in each stage of the product life cycle. Figure 5.3 has four diagrams showing different degrees of price elasticity. Examine them carefully and then write down which stage of the product life cycle – introduction, growth, maturity or decline – each diagram corresponds to. Then compare your answers to those shown in the answer.

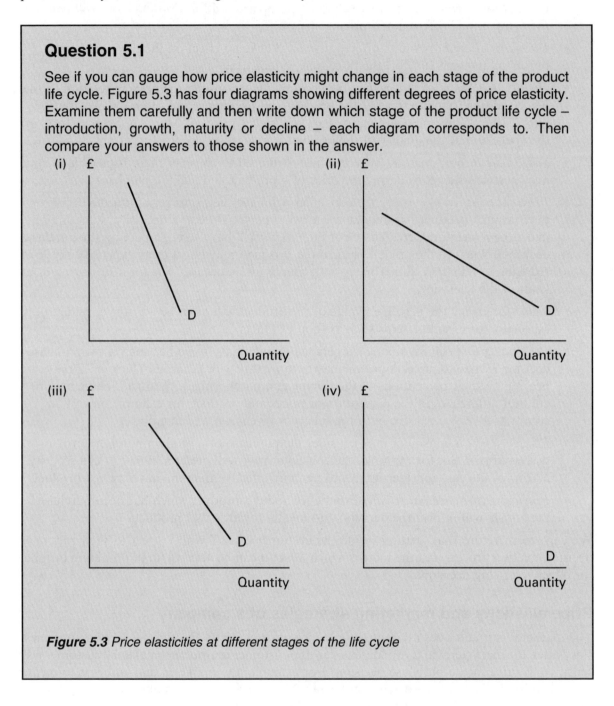

Figure 5.3 Price elasticities at different stages of the life cycle

Partly because of these differences in price elasticity at various stages in the life cycle, together with other considerations in the life-cycle stages, such as differing degrees of competition, size of market, etc. it is very often necessary to have differing pricing policies for each stage of the product life cycle. These are shown in Table 5.1.

Table 5.1 *Pricing and the product life cycle*

Introduction stage	Growth stage	Maturity stage	Decline stage
Skimming policy with high prices, but low profit margin due to high fixed costs	Reduce price to penetrate market further	Price to match or beat competitors	Cut price if not repositioning
Penetration policy to enter the market and gain a high share quickly or to prevent competitors from entering		Retain higher prices in some market segments	Some increases in prices may occur in the late decline stage

Both skimming and penetration pricing policies together with their advantages and disadvantages are discussed in more detail later in the unit.

Competitors and prices

Our third input to pricing decisions is information on competitors. In all marketing decisions it is important to assess competitors, both existing and potential. This is especially true of pricing decisions. The extent and nature of competition in a market obviously affects the prices the marketer is able to charge, and the price elasticity of demand, which we have just considered. In markets where competitors are numerous and aggressive, and where new competitors can enter easily, price competition is likely to be intense and price elasticity high. On the other hand, where the number of competitors is limited and/or where a company is much more powerful than its competitors, the marketer may enjoy some degree of monopoly power, and price elasticity will be low.

Monopoly power in a market may derive from several sources. So, for example, a company can gain a degree of monopoly power from, say, control over resources and raw material supplies in a market. Diamonds occur only in certain parts of the world and any company which controls this supply has potentially at least a degree of monopoly power. Monopoly power may also stem from government and/or regulatory restrictions. So, for example, to some extent, although recently deregulated in many countries, airlines may have some degree of monopoly power due to government protection and regulations which prevent competitors from entering markets. Finally, and many would argue, perhaps the only defensible monopoly is where the monopoly power stems from superior performance on the part of a company which in turn generates very loyal customers and makes it very difficult for other competitors to enter.

Throughout the world most countries have legislation to protect the customer from the worst excesses of monopoly power. Related to this, a number of factors have also tended to increase competition in markets throughout the world. So, for example, the World Trade Organization promotes world trade without barriers; many governments have acted to deregulate markets and in the United Kingdom, for example, we have seen a continuing trend towards privatization even in public utilities. Finally, increasing global competition and the ubiquitous Internet of course have meant more and more competition between companies.

The marketer must carefully assess the prices competitors are charging and/or are likely to charge, and how they may respond to the marketer's own pricing decisions.

Activity 5.6

Try to find examples of the following:
1. Markets characterized by intense competition between companies and brands.
2. Markets where, although competition is intense to some extent, marketers have been able to lessen the effects of competition by effective marketing, e.g. by building, say, brand loyalty.
3. Markets where there are few or no competitors and the marketer enjoys a degree of monopoly power.

Compare your findings with those shown in the debriefing.

Company considerations and prices

This fourth major input to pricing decisions encompasses a number of considerations. All marketing decisions, but again particularly pricing decisions, should reflect and be consistent with company objectives and marketing strategies. So, for example, the pricing decision will probably be different if the company objective is growth as opposed to short-term return on capital.

Similarly pricing decisions should reflect wider considerations, such as company resources, target markets and positioning, and desired company/corporate image. It is important to stress that the pricing decision must be consistent and planned in conjunction with the marketing mix. Finally, pricing strategies will obviously differ where price is used as a major element of competitive strategy as opposed to where it is used in a more passive way in the marketing strategy. Some companies decide to be price leaders, others price followers.

Activity 5.7

We have seen that pricing decisions should reflect company and marketing objectives and strategies. For each of the following indicate whether you think a higher or a lower price would generally be appropriate:

The ABC Company wishes to achieve rapid market growth.   Higher/Lower

The XYZ Company wants quick returns on capital employed.   Higher/Lower

The LPT Company wishes to promote a quality image.   Higher/Lower

The NYZ Company is targeting socio-economic groups D/E.   Higher/Lower

Communicational aspects of pricing

Another major consideration in pricing decisions is the fact that prices have an important communicational role as regards customers and potential customers. In other words, the price set for a product sends signals to customers about the company and its products. This is why we have suggested that pricing decisions must be in line with target markets and positioning, and desired company/corporate image. Pricing decisions therefore need to be closely linked, as already mentioned, to other areas of the mix, but particularly to the promotion elements. So, for example, pricing may be linked to promotional objectives so as to encourage trial of a new product.

Another area where price has a strong communicational aspect is in relation to price as an indicator of quality. Rightly or wrongly, but certainly in the absence of experience or, say, objective information about a product offering, customers will often use price as an indication of the quality of a product offering. This means then that, contrary to what many companies appear to believe and certainly practice, it is possible to price a product too low where the price acts as a deterrent to potential customers, and particularly new ones, because of suspicions regarding the quality of a product. Economists have long known about this phenomenon as it gives rise to an unusual backward-sloping demand curve.

Other considerations/information in the pricing decision

Although these are the four major considerations in pricing decisions there are often many other factors that will need to be taken into account when setting prices. The marketer will need information on these before making a decision.

Activity 5.8

Before proceeding, try to list as many other factors not already encompassed in our discussion that might need to be taken into account in pricing decisions.

Structuring pricing decisions

As with any other decision-making process, pricing decisions are likely to be most effective when they are taken in a planned and systematic way. Pricing is not something that is best done as an afterthought during the marketing of a product.

You will find different suggested frameworks for structuring the pricing decision according to the particular textbook you consult. In other words, there is no one way to structure this decision. However, Figure 5.4 represents a logical and acceptable way of structuring the process.

Extending knowledge

Because there are so many alternative ways in which the structure of the pricing decision can be described, it would be a good idea to have a look at alternatives.

One of the most useful contributions to structuring the pricing decision is that suggested by A. R. Oxenfeldt in 'A Decision-Making Structure for Price Decisions' (1973) *Journal of Marketing*, 37, January.

Figure 5.4 *A structured approach to pricing decisions*

We have already looked at some of the key steps in our structured approach to pricing decisions. In particular of course our 4Cs. We now need to look at the two remaining steps in this framework; namely selection of a pricing method and selection of specific prices. We also need to say a little more about pricing policies. We shall start by discussing pricing methods, followed by the considerations in setting specific prices, and finally look at pricing policy.

Selection of a pricing method

Earlier we looked at the perspectives and contributions of the accountant, the economist, and the marketer with respect to pricing decisions. To a certain extent the legacy of these different perspectives can be seen in the different methods of pricing. The three major categories of pricing methods are cost-based methods, competitor-based methods and demand/market-based methods. We shall now examine each of these in turn.

Cost-based methods

As you would expect, cost-based methods of pricing primarily reflect the accountant's approach to pricing. Additionally, as you would expect, these methods set prices primarily on the basis of costs. There are several alternatives for cost-based pricing but the major ones are:

- *Full cost/cost plus pricing.* One of the simplest and most widely used methods of pricing. Usually a standard percentage is added to the total cost of the product to arrive at a price.

The strengths of full cost/cost plus pricing are as follows:

- It provides a means of trying to ensure that all overheads (e.g. fixed and product costs) are met. In addition, it tries to allow for a profit return on top.

- It should be easy to calculate, as the organization is more certain about cost than demand.

- No need to have to make frequent adjustments to the price as demand changes. Where competitors are using cost plus pricing in the industry prices will tend to be similar and therefore price competition is minimized.

- It can be seen to be fairer to both buyers and sellers.

The weaknesses of full cost/cost plus pricing include:

- This approach to pricing takes no account of other elements in the marketing mix, i.e. product, place, etc.

- It does not reflect consumers' perceptions. If a consumer perceives a product as cheap, it is often associated with poor quality.
- Being a cost-based pricing strategy, it ignores other factors such as the going rate for similar products. It does not consider different segments, etc.
- It does not consider the 'needs' and 'wants' of customers. Similarly, this method does not consider competitors' prices.
- It may be difficult to identify direct costs and overheads for each item.
- It does not consider the elasticity of demand for the product.
- This method only works if the price actually brings in the expected level of sales.
- *Marginal cost pricing*. Here the distinction between the variable and fixed costs comes into play. With this pricing method the marketer assesses whether or not a contribution to fixed costs can be obtained. Hence marginal cost pricing can lead to prices that are less than full cost.

Marginal cost pricing overcomes some of the major weaknesses of full cost/cost plus pricing, for example, it allows prices to reflect demand conditions to a greater extent. However, it is still primarily of course cost based and hence is not really marketing oriented.

In general, cost-based pricing methods are inward looking and neglect marketing considerations.

Competitor-based methods

Sometimes companies base their pricing decisions largely on competitors' prices. You should note that this does not mean charging the same prices as competitors; they may be more or less than major competitors. Such pricing is predominant in oligopolistic markets. A larger company may act as the price leader, with smaller companies following this lead. This pricing method is sometimes called 'going rate pricing'.

The advantages of competitor-based pricing include the fact that it is relatively simple, and of course, takes into account competitor considerations. However, one of the disadvantages of this pricing method is that it is essentially passive in approach, especially when following rather than leading competitors on price. The major disadvantage of this approach to pricing, however, is that it does not reflect differences in company cost structures, objectives, resources, and marketing strategies.

A particularly good example of where competition and therefore competitor-based methods of pricing can come to predominate in a market is in the pricing methods used by many of the larger UK supermarkets. Although some companies do try to avoid it, competitor-based pricing is so predominant now in this market that price wars are the order of the day and margins have been severely depressed.

Demand/market-based methods

Obviously these are the most marketing-oriented methods of pricing. Predominantly prices are set with demand and market considerations in mind. There are several alternative methods available to the marketer that are demand/market-based according to circumstances. Some of the most frequently encountered methods are as follows.

When pricing new products, the marketer may choose between **market skimming prices** and **market penetration prices**.

Activity 5.9

In your own words write down what you think is meant by, first, market skimming and, second, market penetration pricing.

As you probably guessed or knew, market skimming is where the marketer charges a high or premium price for a new product, effectively skimming off the cream of demand.

Activity 5.10

Can you assess the circumstances which would tend to suggest price skimming for a new product?

The advantages of a market skimming pricing policy are as follows:

- It allows for quick recovery on investment in the new product such as R&D costs, etc.
- It may confer a prestigious/quality image to customers.
- Higher prices are likely to appeal to innovator groups.
- It allows for flexibility in reducing prices should the initial price result in too few sales. It also allows for reduced prices for later stages of the product life cycle to appeal to the mass market.

Amongst the disadvantages of a market skimming pricing policy are:

- It may encourage competitors to enter the market more quickly.
- It results in lower levels of sales and hence fewer economies of scale and experience curve effects, i.e. costs are higher.
- It may attract attention from regulatory bodies, or consumer groups where 'profiteering' is suspected.

Many marketers have used price skimming as their approach in markets and many will no doubt continue to do so. We have seen in the Unit 'Tools of marketing: portfolio management and new product development' that the innovators in markets in particular want to be amongst the first to purchase new products and are willing and able to pay higher prices to achieve this. Many new electronic consumer products are priced in this way therefore. For example, when they were first launched, CD players were extremely expensive compared to their prices today. Similarly, the new generation of DVD based players are also an example of a price skimming strategy at work.

As you also probably guessed market penetration pricing is the setting of low prices in order to gain rapid market share.

Activity 5.11

Can you assess the circumstances which would tend to suggest penetration pricing for a product?

The advantages of a market penetration pricing policy are as follows:

- It should produce larger sales volume.
- This should lead to an organization gaining a large slice of the market.
- It can prevent competitors from entering the market.

The limitations of a market penetration pricing policy include:

- It is often difficult to raise price after this policy has been used.
- It is less flexible than using a skimming policy.
- It may not be appropriate due to the costs of R&D and competitors' positions.

Recently the petrol retailers in the United Kingdom have launched their new low-sulphur petrol products, which are aimed at a cleaner environment, at penetration prices. By pricing these products at slightly lower prices than their other existing products in the range the companies are hoping to switch customers to these cleaner fuel products.

Perceived value pricing is perhaps one of the most marketing-oriented ways of setting prices. The price is set on the perceived value of the product to the customer. It is in fact a variation on 'price at what the market will bear'. The marketer uses other elements of the mix – product, promotion, etc. – to build up the perceived value of the product or service in the mind of the customer. Prices are then set to reflect this value.

Perceived value pricing also is related to our earlier price as an indicator of quality. This approach to pricing is particularly useful when pricing products for organizational markets or more expensive consumer products where the usage takes place over a long period of time, such as for example, a car. Mercedes use this approach very successfully in pricing their products. The perceived value of their products is heightened through stressing the quality and engineering aspects embodied, but in addition, Mercedes, probably with some justification, stress the lifetime value of their cars, not the least of which is affected by their claims for low depreciation costs.

Activity 5.12

Think back to a purchase you made in the past where:

1. You got 'very good value for money'.
2. You got 'very poor value for money'.

Reflect on what each of these meant for the prices you paid.

Psychological pricing has to do with the strong behavioural forces at work in the pricing of products and services. For example, we know that price is used by consumers as an indicator of quality. Similarly, high prices can bestow 'prestige' on the purchaser. Some marketers believe that ending the price with certain numbers can influence buyers, e.g. pricing a product at £9.99 instead of £10.00. This is known as 'odd' pricing. Similarly there is some evidence that rounding prices up from say £9.99 to £10.00 adds to an image of quality in the mind of the customer. This is known as 'even' pricing.

Psychological, and particularly odd pricing is used extensively in retailing with regard to consumer products. Even pricing tends to be used where connotations of quality are important in determining product and brand choice and is often used in pricing expensive restaurants or theatre tickets.

Activity 5.13

Next time you go shopping make a note of examples of 'odd' and 'even' pricing.

Promotional pricing is perhaps more of a tactical than a strategic approach to pricing, but price is potentially a very powerful tactical weapon. This approach to pricing is based on temporary changes in price, usually though not always reductions, in order to boost sales. Examples include:

- **Cash rebates**: A variety of different types of these, but as the term implies they all involve offering some cash reduction or payback to customers. They may be related to, for example, purchasing in quantity or perhaps for buying at particular times of the year. Some holiday package companies are beginning to use systems of cash rebates to tempt customers to book early

- **Special event pricing**: Again, a variety of different types, but this is where special prices are linked to one-off events. So, for example many companies offered special prices and promotional deals during the recent Sydney Olympics.

- **Loss leader pricing**: Used extensively in retail marketing settings, this approach to pricing involves setting very low prices on certain selected products as an attraction to draw customers into the store.

- **Low interest deals**: Obviously, this type of pricing weapon is particularly useful where a customer is likely to want extended credit on a product. So, for example, it is used extensively in marketing cars or other high value consumer products where payments are spread over a period of time.

- **Other promotional deals**: Many sales promotion offers are effectively price offers including some of the ones we have discussed above. But for example 'two for one' offers, 'buy one get one free' offers (bogofs), '20% extra' offers, etc. – all widely used by marketers – are in fact really promotional pricing offers.

Marketers need to be careful how they use promotional pricing. Excessive use can lead to an image of 'inferior' products, and/or customers can come to expect low prices.

Activity 5.14

When you are looking for examples for odd/even pricing also make note of any special promotional pricing you observe.

Product mix pricing. Much of our discussion of pricing to date in this unit has centred on making pricing decisions for individual products. However, most companies produce and market a mix of products, and very often there are interrelations between the products in this mix with respect, for example, to costs of production, marketing costs, or customer demand. Very often therefore the marketer must set prices that reflect these interrelations so as to maximize sales and profits.

There are many examples of such product mix pricing in marketing. Here are just two:

- Cheap razors to sell higher priced razor blades.
- The use of 'price points' in retail sales of clothing, e.g. shirts at £15.00, £20.00, and £25.00.

Activity 5.15

Complete your list of examples of pricing in practice by making note of any examples you come across exemplifying product mix pricing.

Selection of specific prices

So far we have considered what might be called pointers to setting prices. For example, we have looked at inputs to pricing, broad approaches or methods of pricing and so on. However, the outcome of all these deliberations and considerations should be the setting of a specific price on a product or service. Of course the earlier steps in pricing procedure should serve to direct and constrain the selection of the final price. This narrowing of the price range from which to select the final price is intentional and indeed is part of the process of a structured approach to pricing. But in this final stage the marketer will still have some flexibility with regard to the specific price selected. This flexibility is needed to reflect the marketer's assessment of any final considerations in setting the price. Examples would include the state of the economy at the time of pricing, any special seasonal factors, unusual competitor activity and so on. We should remember that marketing managers are also paid to use their expertise and experience in making decisions as well as following systematic frameworks.

Price adjustment policies

Having set prices, often companies will need to adjust their basic prices to account for various customer differences and changing situations. Companies therefore need to establish price adjustment policies. Three examples of price adjustment policies are as follows:

- *Discount and allowance pricing* this is where the basic price is adjusted to reward customers for responses such as early payment, large or off-season purchases. These can be in the form of cash discounts, quantity discounts for bulk purchases and seasonal discounts for products bought out of season. Trade-in allowances and promotional allowances are price reductions given to encourage purchase.

- *Segmented pricing (price discrimination)* companies will often adjust their basic prices to allow for differences in customers, products, location, time/season, etc. Essentially, the company sells its products at two or more prices, even though the difference in price is not always based on differences in costs. Examples may be where different prices are charged to different age groups, e.g. special prices for old age pensioners. Similarly prices may be charged during different times of the day, e.g. telephone calls. Often known as price discrimination, this approach to price adjustments can be very effective in maximizing demand and company revenue. Care needs to be taken, however, not to alienate the customer groups being charged higher prices.

- *Promotional pricing* Our earlier discussed example of promotional pricing is also an example of price adjustment procedures, and as we have seen, is where companies use price as a tactical rather than a strategic approach using temporary changes in prices to generate demand. Obviously, usually prices in promotional pricing are set below list price and sometimes below cost prices. The example shown earlier under promotional pricing, can also be described as a price adjustment policy.

Overall policies for pricing

It is important that pricing decisions are taken within and guided by a policy for pricing. As with all policies in organizations, such a policy should serve to provide an indication of what is acceptable and unacceptable in decision-making and action. A pricing policy should encompass the following:

- Responsibilities and authority for pricing decisions.
- Discretion with regard to price discounts, special deals, etc.
- Procedures for responding to competitor price changes.

- Procedures for changing prices in the company.
- Credit policy.

Activity 5.16

If you are working for a company at the moment, try to establish what your company's policies (if any) are with respect to our list of pricing policy areas.

Pricing and the Internet

There is no doubt that one of the major areas of marketing affected by the growth of Internet marketing is that of price and pricing decisions. At its simplest, the effect of the Internet has been to provide the opportunities for customers to compare and contrast competitors' prices much more widely and easily than they have ever been able to do so in the past. This has put extra pressure, particularly on non-Internet conventional suppliers of products and services to be cost and hence price effective. Customers can and do shop around for the cheapest prices. Moreover of course, many of the Internet suppliers of consumer products, because they do not have expensive retail premises and properties to support, can often undercut many of their more conventional competitors' prices. Because of this, as use of the Internet grows for things like home shopping, we can expect price competition to become even more important in the future. Companies, who because of their costs etc., cannot compete on price will have no alternative but to withdraw from markets or more positively to develop strong brand loyalty and customer franchises again to desensitize customers to the price element of the mix.

Summary

- In this unit we have seen that price plays a central and unique role in the marketing mix.
- The economist, the accountant and the marketer each have different perspectives on pricing, but each has something to contribute to the pricing decision. The major inputs to pricing decisions are the 4Cs of cost, customers, competition, and company.
- The pricing decision should be systematically structured as a series of steps or stages.
- Pricing methods include cost-based methods, competitor-based methods and demand/market-based methods.
- Pricing decisions should reflect company objectives and strategies.
- Pricing strategies may vary over the life cycle of a product.
- Two alternative pricing strategies for new products are price skimming and price penetration. A company needs to establish pricing policies, including responsibilities for pricing, credit policies and price adjustment policies.
- The growth of Internet marketing is increasing price competition and shopping around on the part of customers for low prices in many markets.

Further study and examination preparation

Now do these questions:

Question 5.2

What are the strengths and weaknesses of cost-plus pricing?

Question 5.3

Identify the type of information required by the marketing department before a pricing strategy can be agreed.

Question 5.4

What are the advantages and limitations of a market penetration pricing policy?

Question 5.5

How could the pricing policy alter for maximum returns at each stage of the product life cycle?

Question 5.6

Explain three types of price-adjustment policies which a marketer could adopt.

Previous examination question

Study tip

This question is taken from Fundamentals of Marketing paper June 2000 question 5. Remember, you can access the full specimen answer for this question on the following website addresses: www.marketingonline.co.uk or www.bh.com/marketing.

Question E5

a. Identify and explain the key factors, based on financial and economic issues which may affect the marketer's pricing decisions for a consumer product of your own choice.

(12 marks)

b. Using specific examples, explain ways in which other marketing mix variables affect pricing decisions.

(8 marks)
(20 marks in total)

Bibliography

F. Brassington, S. Pettitt, *Principles of Marketing: 2nd Edn. Chaps 10 and 11*, 2000

Further reading

S. Dibb, L. Simpkin, W. Pride, O. C. Ferrell, *Marketing Concepts and Strategies: 4th European Edn. Chaps 18 and 19*, Houghton, Mifflin, 2000.

G. Lancaster, L. Massingham, R. Ashford, *Essentials of Marketing: 4th Edn, 2002 Chap 7*, McGraw-Hill, 2001.

Objectives

By the end of this unit you will:

- Understand the importance of distribution and logistics in marketing (3.10).

- Appreciate the process of designing channels of distribution including the factors that affect decisions in this area (3.11).

- Be aware of some of the key trends and developments in distribution including the effects of new information and communications technology (3.11).

Study guide

This unit covers our third key element of the marketing mix and encompasses the means and mechanisms whereby products and services are made available to customers.

Variously referred to as either distribution or (in the context of our 4Ps) 'place', this element for a variety of reasons has been perhaps a neglected area of marketing. However, as we shall see, and as no doubt you can appreciate, the place element is just as important as each of the other three elements of the mix, and is very much the responsibility of the marketer – though increasingly the management and planning of channels of distribution and logistics is a task for a specialist in this area. In fact many organizations now employ such experts. While acknowledging that this is an increasingly specialized field and therefore it is not necessary, appropriate, or possible for you to become an expert in this area, we must add that the focus for the design and planning of distribution and logistics must be the customer and his or her needs. Because of this and because of its central importance to effective marketing plans, it is vital that you at least appreciate the role of the marketing function in the design, operation and control of place.

We would expect it to take you about 3 hours to work through this unit and suggest you allow a further 3 to 4 hours to undertake the various activities suggested. Other than your notebook and writing equipment you will not need anything further to complete this unit.

The role and importance of place in marketing

Put simply, the role of this element of the marketing mix is to ensure that products and services are available to target customers in the 'right place' and at the 'right time'. However, there are other important aspects to the place element. For example the marketer's product and services also need to be available:

- In the 'right quantities'.
- In the 'right condition'.
- With the 'right degree' of advice, installation, and after-sales service.

If place is badly planned, these requirements to be 'right' will not be fulfilled, and as a consequence all the other possibly perfectly planned efforts of the marketer, such as an excellent product, a competitive price and an exciting advertising campaign, will be to no avail. Indeed companies have often gone out of business and new products failed because of problems with distribution and logistics.

Another way of illustrating the role and importance of place in marketing is to consider some of the things that can go wrong and the implications for the marketer and the company. Here are just some examples:

- 'Nobody could be persuaded to stock the product.' Perhaps the marketing implications of this are obvious.
- 'Most of the retailers who carry the product are out of stock.' Customers go elsewhere, become angry, and brand disloyal.
- 'At the moment our retailers are carrying too much stock, owing to our unwillingness to deliver in smaller quantities.' Retailers go elsewhere, become angry, and supplier disloyal.
- 'Ten per cent of our products are being damaged in transit.' Customers, distributors, and our own board of directors become angry.
- 'Our competitors will now deliver direct to the customer's home.' We have lost 10 per cent market share.
- 'The costs of our distribution are much too high, owing to ineffective warehousing and delivery.' We have lost 10 per cent of our profits.

We could go on citing examples of the types of problem companies can have with a badly planned place element, but it should now be obvious to you that ineffective management in this area has a major impact on levels of customer satisfaction and levels of company sales and profits. Put another way, effective management of place is now recognized as being a major factor in competitive marketing strategy and company success.

A heightened and changed role for place

Everything we have said so far about place underlines its importance in marketing. In recent times, though, this importance has increased, bringing with it a changing role for place in marketing and the development of new techniques and approaches to its management. We can briefly explore the reasons for these changes.

The high costs of distribution/potential for savings

Until relatively recently distribution and logistics have been neglected areas for potential cost savings. This is perhaps surprising, given that costs associated with distribution and logistics account for 30 per cent or more of a product's total cost. Somewhat belatedly but now increasingly rapidly, companies are recognizing that these potential cost savings represent significant opportunities for improving profits.

The potential for competitive advantage

We have already noted the impact (both good and bad) of place and its management on customers. Effective distribution and logistics designed to increase customer satisfaction can have a tremendous effect on sales and market share. Customers, in fact, now demand levels of service from distribution unheard of even 5 years ago. In addition, as we shall see later, some of the trends in industrial manufacturing and production, such as 'just in time' management, have resulted in a premium for those marketers who can plan their distribution logistics to meet the increased demands placed on them by such developments.

Improved techniques for planning and managing place

Partly as a result of the recognition of the potential for cost-saving and competitive advantage, significant strides have been made in recent years in the tools and techniques for managing place more effectively. In addition, as mentioned earlier, we now have specialists in this area of marketing. The concept of place has moved from looking at individual elements of the distribution network such as channels, to viewing and planning distribution as a complete interrelated system in which the whole process of moving products and services into, through and out of the organization is planned.

With these points in mind we can now turn our attention to planning the place element of the marketing mix.

Broadly there are two key and interrelated areas in planning the place part of the mix. In fact because they are interrelated, they should ideally be planned together. However, we shall discuss each area of planning separately before looking at them as two sub-elements in a total system. The two areas are:

- Planning marketing channels.
- Planning physical distribution/logistics.

We shall start with channels.

Marketing channels

The use of the word channel is appropriate in that in itself it indicates a pipeline and flows through it. In fact perhaps the easiest way to understand the notion of a marketing channel is to use a simple diagram. See Figure 6.1.

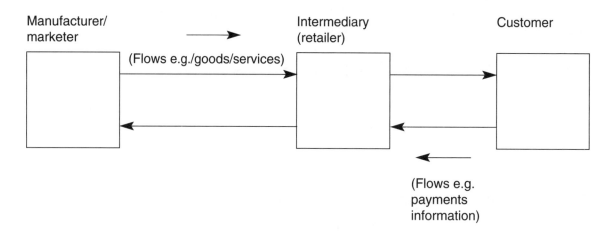

Figure 6.1 *A simple channel of distribution*

As an example, Kelloggs manufactures its range of breakfast cereals, packaging its various products in sizes suitable for the target market. From its production plants the company's different products are delivered directly to retail outlets throughout the world based on pre-negotiated contracts and according to customer demand. Through these retail intermediaries, Kelloggs products are then made available to final customers, with these customers being required to make payment there and then. Information on demand including, for example, responses to new products or special promotional deals can be fed back via the retailer direct to Kelloggs marketing and production teams. Payment to Kelloggs is made by the intermediaries on pre-negotiated terms. The retailer provides stocking and assortment functions for Kelloggs with promotional and other marketing tools often being shared between both parties. Information about the customer and demand is fed back by the retailer to Kelloggs and can be used to adjust marketing tactics and to help develop new products.

Activity 6.2

Using Figure 6.1, list what you think are the key elements of a channel of distribution.

Not all channels look like the one shown in Figure 6.1. Some are longer, with more intermediaries; some have different types of intermediary; some are shorter. Often different flows, outward and inward, occur. In fact these elements of the channel are decision areas. The marketer must plan the configuration of the channel, using these elements as variables. The key decision areas, therefore, in planning a channel of distribution are as follows:

1. Channel length, i.e. the number of intermediaries or 'levels' in the channel.

2. Types of intermediary (if any) in the channel.

3. Channel/market coverage, i.e. the number of intermediaries at any one level.

4. Respective tasks, responsibilities and terms for various channel members.

Channel length

In Figure 6.1 there is only one intermediary level between the producer/marketer and the final customer. The channel, therefore, is relatively short and is in fact a 'one-level channel'. A 'two-level channel' has two sets of intermediaries, a 'three-level channel' three sets, and so on.

Activity 6.3

What do you think a 'zero-level channel' is?

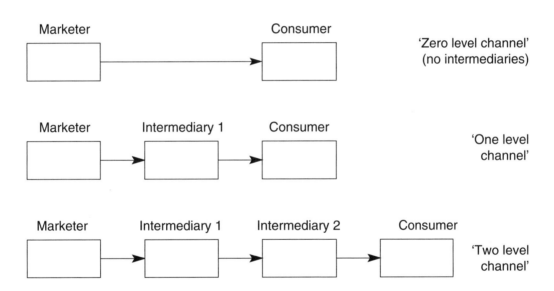

Figure 6.2 *Channel length/levels*

Examples of markets where the various channel lengths tend to predominate include:

*   Zero level (direct): e.g. mail order books/records, direct flight bookings, Internet sales and bookings of various kinds.

*   One-level channel: Many fast moving consumer goods fall into this category, e.g. branded foodstuffs, clothing, DIY products, cars.

*   Two or more level channels: Many smaller companies tend to use two or more level channels, as their size means that they have to deal through, e.g., wholesalers.

Generally speaking the longer the channel, i.e. the more levels, the further the marketer is from the final customer, and therefore the less control the marketer can exert. In addition, each level of the channel will normally wish to make a profit; hence either final prices to the customer are increased and/or profit margins at each level are decreased. This would seem to imply that the shorter the channel, the better. In fact it raises the question as to why a marketer should use intermediaries at all instead of marketing direct.

Activity 6.4

On the basis of your own experience/knowledge try to list any reasons why the marketer might use intermediaries in distributing products and services.

Ultimately, a decision to use intermediaries at one or more levels in a channel is based upon their superior effectiveness in performing the required channel functions and flows. We have already seen a little of the flows involved in channels in Figure 6.1, but examples of other functions and flows required to be performed in channels include:

- Storage and movement of products.
- Transfer of ownership/title.
- Promotion.
- Negotiation.
- Risk-taking.

If the marketer cannot perform these functions and flows more effectively than intermediaries then they should be assigned to such intermediaries. If one level of intermediaries is not sufficient, then a two-level channel should be used, and so on.

The growth of direct marketing

In recent years there has been a trend towards shorter channels. In fact direct marketing, i.e. a zero-level channel, is increasingly being used. As the term implies in direct marketing, the marketer sells direct to the final customer.

Activity 6.5

List four examples of types of direct marketing. Then compare your list with the one shown in the debriefing.

As we saw earlier, direct marketing can only be justified where it is more efficient and effective than using intermediaries. A number of reasons explain the growth of direct marketing in most countries of the world.

Activity 6.6

Try to list four possible reasons for the growth of direct marketing. Then compare your list with that shown in the debriefing.

The reasons for the growth in direct marketing shown in the debrief above explain the reasons why marketers have been interested in using this form of distribution more and more in recent years. However, this desire and willingness to use direct marketing on the part of marketers, important though this is, is not on its own sufficient to explain the significant growth in this area in recent years. Equally important to the growth in direct marketing, therefore, have been two other factors which have been equally significant in helping the growth of direct marketing. These two factors are first, the advances in information technology and particularly databases, and second, developments and advances in direct response media. We shall now consider each of these a little more.

Information Technology and direct marketing: use of databases

The advances in information technology have enabled organizations to develop and use sophisticated databases to identify their customers, their behaviour and characteristics, and as a result, to market to them directly without the need for intermediaries. There is no doubt that the database is central to successful direct marketing activities. Increasingly powerful and low-cost computer power has enabled companies to collect and store data on customers which can be used to, for example, determine appropriate segments and target markets, produce mailing lists, store information on customer responses to direct communications, and so on. Information may be stored regarding transactions with customers in the past, but can also be bought in from, say, list agencies for targeting direct mail and other forms of direct marketing contact. The databases can be used to track, analyse and develop relationships with customers. Many companies are now using their databases to develop these relationships as a key part of their overall marketing and promotional strategy. We shall examine the use of databases and information on customers in the development of relationship marketing, together with the meaning and implications of relationship marketing itself in more detail in later units and in particular in Unit 9 when we consider customer care. Databases now include information on customers from very many sources which can be layered and amalgamated together to give a comprehensive profile of customers. Examples of sources of information for databases which facilitate direct marketing include, for example: census data, postcode data, electoral role data, credit data, transactional data, vehicle ownership data and lifestyle databases.

Often database information is available from commercial databases and indeed there are some companies whose whole business is the provision of data including for example, list companies which specialize in supplying information for direct marketing.

A good example of a company developing business opportunities through the provision of databases and database information is the Royal Mail in the United Kingdom. As you would expect, the Royal Mail's database centres around address and post code information. But this information is also linked to huge amounts of other consumer information in their database. In this way, for example, post code addresses can be linked to, for example, purchasing behaviour variables and/or lifestyle information to provide insightful information for marketing decisions. Direct marketers in particular have found this and other similar databases useful.

Extending Knowledge

You might want to look further at some of these database providers to see what sort of services they can offer. Needless to say, many of them can be accessed through their company websites. So, for example, information about the Royal Mail database services can be accessed through www.royalmail.com/my solution.

In addition to these commercially available databases, many companies of course develop their own databases on customers. So, for example, many of the leading UK retailers have developed in-house databases. The use of loyalty card systems, mentioned earlier in our discussion of relationship marketing have proved invaluable here. A good example of a company using loyalty cards and schemes in this way is the Boots Company who use their Advantage loyalty card system to build a database which in turn helps them to develop effective promotional and other marketing campaigns based on a detailed knowledge of its cardholders and users.

As you would expect, the internally developed database has several potential advantages compared to its bought-in counterpart. In particular, there is greater potential for control, greater potential accuracy, and a tendency for the information in the database, perhaps for understandable reasons, to be more relevant to the marketer's activities.

Against these potential advantages of developing an internal powered database are the costs and complexity, not to mention the skills required for a company to build and use its own database systems. Database providers are now very professional and bring high degrees of expertise and experience to the marketer. Further examples of information database services include, for example, the British Market Research Bureau, CACI, and Nielson Audits. Again, remember many of these marketing databases can be accessed via the Internet. In their text *Principles of Marketing*, Brassington and Pettitt suggest that there are currently over 4,000 companies offering database services in the United Kingdom with a further 20,000 throughout the rest of Europe.

To some extent, if anything, marketers' problem today is not lack of information and data, but rather a surfeit of it, leading to the potential for information overload. It is important to remember that information costs money and a substantial amount of money can be wasted building, accessing and using databases if great care is not taken in their design and operation. Examples of the sorts of potential problems which marketers must seek to avoid in their database systems include data which is out of date and/or inaccurate, data which cannot easily be accessed and analysed, and above all, data which is not useful in helping to improve marketing decisions. Effective database design and operation therefore is extremely important and must be suitable for the purpose the marketer intends. In the case of direct marketing programmes, the following represents the types of information which might be required for developing and executing a consumer goods direct marketing campaign.

- Customer name.
- Customer address – and in particular, post code.
- Customer status, e.g. user, non-user, lapsed user, etc.
- Age.
- Income.
- Socio-economic group.
- Purchase history (where appropriate).
- Geodemographic profile.
- Previous response profile (where appropriate).

Remember, these are just examples of the sort of information that might be contained in a typical database for a direct marketing campaign. Obviously the more information, the more accurate this information, and the more relevant to the marketing campaign in question, the better. Though again we need to remember that information costs money. The database should help to ensure that the direct mail campaign is aimed at the right target customers and that the content of the direct mail programme is designed with these target customers in mind. In doing so, there is likely to be a much higher response rate and of course a reduction in the number of customers feeling that they have been sent junk mail.

Not surprisingly, the difference between an effective and an ineffective database with regard to the impact of direct mail and marketing campaigns can be significant. The marketer needs to ensure, therefore, that the database is kept up to date and clean. This helps to not only improve response rates but also helps to mitigate against some of the worst of the horror stories which have in the past been associated with some direct marketing campaigns. For example, some companies unfortunately send out direct mail shots to customers who are deceased. Or, for example, offering pregnancy testing services to pensioners.

Developments in direct distribution technology: electronic methods

Although direct marketing represents a zero level channel, and therefore is legitimately a consideration in developing the place element of the mix, direct marketing campaigns also make use of promotional tools and media, indeed they are essential in the development and implementation of a direct marketing approach. Because of this, therefore, we shall also return to direct marketing, and in particular to some of the main tools used in direct marketing in the Unit 'Tools of marketing: promotion' covering the promotional tools of marketing.

However, there have been several major developments in the last few years with regard to the technology available for distribution which have in turn facilitated further growth and potential for more direct channels of distribution which you need to be familiar with. In particular, the growth in direct marketing in recent years has been underpinned by the development of direct distribution via electronic methods which in turn have given rise to a move towards convenience driven access such as, for example, home shopping. Of particular significance here of course is the Internet and the World Wide Web.

The Internet and the World Wide Web

The growth of the Internet and the World Wide Web represents probably the most significant development in direct marketing. The customer can now shop from home surfing the World Wide Web for products and services to buy on-line.

At first restricted in many countries by the incidence of PC ownership and by concerns about security, the Internet and the direct marketing which goes with it has finally taken off and there is no doubt that it will continue to grow in importance. In some ways the Internet probably represents the most direct marketing channel possible; other than a service provider and perhaps an Internet search engine no intermediaries are involved at all in the channel. Hence, as we have seen in the previous unit, prices can therefore, potentially at least, be much lower than through conventional channels. Perhaps above all, however, the Internet represents one of the most convenient ways of purchasing for the customer. No longer does the customer have to turn out in inclement weather and struggle to find a parking space at the shopping centre; the customer can now not only shop, but shop around from the comfort of their homes. Although the Internet is growing rapidly as a marketing channel throughout Europe and particularly in the United Kingdom, many marketers have still not woken up to the potential and impact from a channel and marketing perspective. Even those companies that have developed websites, have often not got to grips with the fact that in order to be effective great care must be taken in the design of the website and, for example, its links with search engines etc. Put bluntly, website and Internet marketing skills in general are poorly developed in many companies. Many companies make the mistake of thinking that a website is just another way of advertising or presenting information about the company and its products. Many companies and certainly many marketers who would never dream, for example, of designing their own advertising and copy content, are quite happy to design their own websites. As a result, and again to be blunt, many websites are unprofessional, under-utilized and unimpressive. Marketers must realize that website design in all its facets requires specialized skills and knowledge and is far better left to experts in this area. Having said this, of course, this is not a reason for the marketer not understanding at least the basics of website design and Internet usage in marketing. Marketers are now increasingly appreciating how web techniques such as 'chat rooms' and 'bulletin boards' for example can be used in marketing.

Although the growth of the Internet and the World Wide Web is, as previously mentioned, linked to developments in technology and, for example, the incidence of PC ownership, as you would expect this growth is driven by the fact that as a marketing channel the Internet offers several advantages compared to other channels, including other direct channels such as mail order, telemarketing and so on. Some of these advantages accrue to the marketer and some to the customer, but the real driving forces in the growth of this channel are those where the advantages accrue to both. Some of the advantages which serve to explain the growth of the Internet as a marketing channel include:

- Convenience.
- Potential for lower prices to customers.
- Potential for customers to shop around.
- Potential for marketer to build databases based on customer visits, information provision etc.
- Flexibility and speed, e.g. customer orders can be dealt with immediately, quick delivery, etc.
- Customers using/visiting websites already predisposed towards product, i.e. have already indicated interest.
- Websites potentially much more interesting than other direct promotional material, i.e. can include movement and sound.

In addition to PC ownership and the cost of access to the Internet, probably the major factor determining future growth of this area of marketing will be consumer attitudes towards security factors. A recent government survey in the United Kingdom, for example, indicated that worries about security amongst Internet users represents the major barrier to an increased growth in shopping via this channel. Some 70% of regular Internet users expressed concern and said that it was the main reason for their not having bought anything through this channel. Certainly there have been problems in some instances with, for example, protecting customers' information and interests, but perhaps as much as anything this is really a marketing problem, i.e. potential shoppers need to be convinced and persuaded about the levels of security in Internet shopping systems.

Despite these concerns, however, the advantages of the Internet as a channel of distribution mean that it will certainly continue to grow in importance.

Other technology driven advances

Although the Internet probably represents the most important technological development affecting channels, it is by no means the only one. Again, we shall consider some of these developments in other units in the context of, for example, the promotional mix (in the Unit 'Tools of marketing : promotion') and again our unit on technological advances in marketing fundamentals (Unit 'Technological advances in marketing fundamentals'). Specifically in the context of channels, however, and even more specifically in the context of direct marketing channels, other technological developments have had or are beginning to have a major effect. Two of the more important are introduced below.

Telemarketing

Although obviously the telephone is not a new technology, ownership is now so widespread in many countries that marketers have turned more and more to using the telephone as a way of directly selling, or at least communicating, to their customers. Both outbound, where the organization contacts a potential customer and inbound, where the potential customer is encouraged to contact the organization, are used as in, for example, direct response advertising. As with direct mail and the Internet, telemarketing is both a promotional tool and a marketing channel. With telemarketing customers are contacted in their own homes or businesses with a view to creating some sort of response. Sometimes the response sought will be a direct sale, but more often the response sought will be to encourage interest and to generate sales leads and opportunities including the establishment of appointments for a salesperson to visit for example. Because customers are being contacted in their own homes or premises and because calls are usually unsolicited there are some who feel that this type of marketing is intrusive and even unethical. Certainly, telemarketing can be annoying to some customers and great care needs to be used in its application. In addition, there are industry codes of practice and regulations which govern the use of this tool. For telemarketing to be successful like direct mail, good lists are important. It is also important to ensure that company personnel making the calls are well trained and polite. Success rates in terms of, for example, generating appointments and certainly for generating sales are relatively low with often as many as 100 calls being required to generate only one or two successes. However, compared to other forms of promotion and channel arrangements, costs are also relatively low. It is likely that, despite some customer resistance to this method of direct marketing, usage of this channel will continue to grow.

Teleshopping

The growth of this type of channel and promotional method is underpinned by developments in communications technology. For example, cable and satellite television allied to digital technologies are giving rise to significant growth in home-based shopping via the television. Many of the cable and satellite companies offer channels specifically devoted to shopping but in addition, of course, conventional programming often now includes opportunities for teleshopping during the normal commercial breaks between programmes. Current developments such as, for example, 3D television and television linked directly through a modem to the Internet will only increase the use of this type of channel. Again, the underpinning reason for the growth of this channel is its convenience allied to an increase in satellite and cable systems and companies. There are those who believe that it is teleshopping via the Internet which represents the channel of the future as opposed to PC-based Internet usage. Certainly the familiarity of the television as opposed to PCs for many people gives it a great advantage, but there is still a reluctance on the part of consumers to participate in television shopping.

Types of intermediary

To a certain extent this facet of channel design and planning is closely related to the previous decision about levels. For example, a company may decide that the most effective channel would include distributing through wholesalers and retailers. However, although the decision has been made to use these groups of intermediaries, there are often different types of intermediary within each group that the marketer can use, e.g. in wholesaling there are merchant wholesalers, full service wholesalers, cash and carry wholesalers and so on. Similarly, examples of types of retailer might include independent single retailers, chain stores, variety stores, multiples, etc. The marketer therefore must decide which of this possible variety of intermediaries is most effective and efficient.

Activity 6.7

If you are currently working for an organization or company, try to find out what sorts of intermediary (possibly at various levels in the channel) are available/used to distribute the types of products or services that your company markets.

Channel/market coverage (number of intermediaries)

The third key element of channel design is the decision as to the number of intermediaries to be used at each level. There are three broad choices:

- Large numbers of intermediaries are used. This is known as 'intensive distribution'.
- Only one or two specially selected intermediaries are used. This is known as 'exclusive distribution'.
- In between these two extremes comes 'selective distribution', where a relatively small number of intermediaries are used at each level.

Question 6.1

Which of the following products would probably be best distributed on an intensive, exclusive or selective basis.

Compare your answers with those shown in the debriefing.

- Rolex watches.
- Cigarettes.
- Mid-priced hi-fi systems.
- Toilet rolls.
- Haute couture fashion.

Tasks, responsibilities and terms

Our final key elements of channel design are decisions regarding what is required to be performed in the channel of distribution and who is to perform these tasks. These tasks and responsibilities should ideally be agreed between channel members. For example, we have seen that one of the functions in the channel is flows of information. Similarly, another channel function is promotion. It is important to ensure that these tasks are allocated and agreed between channel members. In the same way facets such as 'territorial' rights of channel members and other terms on which channel agreements are entered into should be established and agreed.

Factors affecting channel choice and design

It has been stressed that ultimately the rationale underpinning channel design is the need to achieve the most effective and efficient channel possible for the marketer. With this in mind a number of factors will influence channel choice.

Only the major factors have been listed in the debrief but you should be able to assess many of these in the context of your own organization's products and channels of distribution.

Trends and developments in channels of distribution

Although it is impossible in what is one of the most dynamic areas of marketing to cover all the recent trends and developments in channels of distribution, the examiners will look for at least some appreciation of contemporary events. In addition to the problem of scope regarding trends and developments, at least some of these are country-specific. For example, certain important trends in, say, retailing in the United Kingdom are not relevant to other parts of the world. However, with these caveats in mind it is possible to identify some broad general trends and developments in distribution which are affecting marketers on a broad scale.

Among some of the most significant trends and developments affecting channels of distribution are the following:

- *The increased power of the retailers.* In many developed economies, and particularly in the United Kingdom, retailing has become very concentrated. The multiples are now very powerful and can often dictate terms to suppliers.

- *The growth of own branding.* Related to the above, the power of the retailers has enabled them to market their own brands in direct competition with the suppliers' brands.

- *The growth of 'vertical' marketing channels.* Vertical marketing channels are channels where the different levels and members in a channel are co-ordinated or managed by a single channel member so as to achieve efficient and effective distribution to target market customers. Vertical marketing channels also potentially reduce the inherent conflict between different levels and members in a channel. There are a number of ways in which vertical channel integration can be achieved. For example, one member of the marketing channel may simply purchase the operations of other members/levels of the channel. This is sometimes referred to as a *corporate* vertical marketing system. A retailer that purchases for example wholesaling and production facilities would be an example of a corporate VMS. Similarly, but this time working from the other end of the distribution channel, a manufacturer may purchase wholesaling and retailing facilities in order to consolidate and co-ordinate this channel. A second approach to achieving vertical channel integration is known as an *administered* VMS. Here the different channel members remain independent with vertical integration and coordination being achieved on the basis of informal agreements between the members of the channel. Although channel members remain independent, normally one channel member will effectively control and administer the channel so as to optimize the operation of the channel as a whole. Often such control will fall to the largest and most powerful member of the channel. For example, in the United Kingdom the power and size of Marks & Spencer, the retailer, enables them to operate an administered vertical marketing system over which they have control. The third type of vertical marketing system for achieving vertical integration is the *contractual* VMS. Under this sort of system, the channel relationships and coordination are achieved through formalized agreements and contracts. A good example of this, and an area of rapid growth in distribution in recent years, is the franchise organization such as MacDonalds, Dynarod and Kentucky Fried Chicken. Members of the channel enter into legal agreements that set out duties and rights.

- *The growth of 'horizontal' marketing channels.* This is where institutions at the same level of the marketing channel are combined under one management. For example, an organization may integrate horizontally by merging with another organization at the same level in a marketing channel such as the merger of a college with a university. Horizontal integration is done to achieve efficiencies and economies of scale in areas such as purchasing, promotion and so on. However, horizontal integration can lead to a decrease in flexibility and difficulties in coordination.

- *The growth of direct channels and the use of electronic methods*: these have been outlined earlier.

Activity 6.9

See if you can find examples of franchising arrangements in your own country and, where appropriate, preferably in your own area of marketing.

NB You are not allowed to use McDonalds, Burger King, or Kentucky Fried Chicken. (These are too easy!)

Physical distribution/logistics

Our second major element in planning the place decisions of a marketing mix is the planning of the systems and procedures for physically moving products and services from a marketer to the customer. This element is known therefore as physical distribution. In line with the increase in sophistication of planning place recently, the scope of planning physical distribution has widened to include all the physical flows of products and services into, through and out of the marketer's organization. This wider, and what was referred to earlier as a systems, approach to physical distribution is termed 'logistics'.

In examining physical distribution and logistics we shall cover the following areas:

1. The importance of physical distribution/logistics.
2. Key planning areas/decisions.
3. Inputs to planning physical distribution and logistics.

The importance of physical distribution/logistics

Earlier we referred to the high cost of distribution and the potential for savings in this area. In most companies a large proportion of this cost and therefore potential for saving is associated with the physical distribution element of place. Perhaps this is easier to appreciate if we think of some of the functions and activities encompassed by physical distribution.

Activity 6.10

Before proceeding, see if you can write down what you think might be types of activity in physical distribution.

Much more important, however, for the marketer is again something we raised earlier in the unit that serves to underline the importance of physical distribution. This is the fact that physical distribution decisions have a major impact on levels of customer satisfaction (or dissatisfaction) and hence are a major source of potential competitive advantage.

This impact centres on levels of customer service, which are directly affected by the design and activities of the physical distribution system.

Activity 6.11

Before we proceed, see if you can write down any examples of elements of customer service that might be affected by physical distribution.

We can see that if a company can improve its level of service in areas such as this, it might increase sales and market share. This is especially true in markets where it is difficult to differentiate one's products and services in any other way.

In addition, particularly in industrial markets, many customers are operating just-in-time systems of production. In this situation service delivery is crucial. In many industries it is impossible to become a supplier unless one has a physical distribution system geared to supplying on a just-in-time basis.

Key planning areas and decisions

Our outline of the major activities in physical distribution, together with our discussion of the various areas of customer service affected by the physical distribution system, already points us to what are the key decision areas in planning physical distribution and logistics.

First of all we must decide the objectives for our physical distribution system. These objectives should be couched in terms of objectives with regard to desired levels and areas of customer service. These should be specified in advance, preferably in quantitative terms, e.g. 'All customer orders must be fulfilled within a maximum of 36 hours from receipt of order'.

Once objectives for the output of the physical distribution system are set, then the system itself and its component activities can be planned to achieve the specified objectives. Key decisions would include, for example:

- Inventory levels.
- Order-processing systems.
- Methods of transport.
- Warehousing: numbers and locations.

Inputs to planning physical distribution and logistics

We have seen that the design of a physical distribution system and its component activities should centre around meeting predetermined objectives with regard to the elements of customer service. Because of this, the first and most important input to planning physical distribution and logistics is 'information on customer requirements with regard to areas and levels of service'. Remember what we are looking for is at the very least to provide the minimum levels of service required, and preferably to use improved service levels as a basis for competitive advantage.

We should find out, therefore, what the customers' requirements are and what constitutes value in terms of service levels to the customer. For example, would the customer value speedier delivery? Would the customer value the ability to deal with special orders?

If customer requirements are the first and most important input to planning physical distribution and logistics, we should also remind ourselves that costs and profit to the company are also important. For example, most customers, if asked, would probably say they would value the ability to deal with special orders. However, improved levels of customer service usually cost the provider more. The real issue, therefore, is the extent to which this 'value' to the customer is sufficient to offset the potentially higher costs of providing it. Put simply, in designing the physical distribution system the second key input is 'cost'. We must carefully balance competitive advantage against cost. Most physical distribution systems are designed to provide pre-specified levels of customer service at minimum cost.

The third key consideration with regard to the design of the system is that it should be considered *as that,* i.e. 'a system'. It is no use minimizing costs in one area of the system, e.g. inventory costs, only to find that this is more than offset by a corresponding increase in costs elsewhere in the system, e.g. delivery. This is why in recent years much more emphasis has been placed on planning the whole of physical distribution and the channel element as a complete logistical system.

Our fourth input to the design of the physical distribution system is a consideration of 'competitors'. After all, every marketing decision should reflect the competitive situation. It is important to assess the levels and types of service being offered by competitors in the market.

The fifth and final consideration in the design of physical distribution is to remind ourselves that this is a very dynamic area of management and marketing. Changes in technology, techniques of production, and customer needs mean that physical distribution systems need to be constantly evaluated and, if necessary, updated and changed to reflect these changes and to remain competitive.

146

As we have seen so many times already in our discussion throughout the units, physical distribution and logistics planning has been enhanced and facilitated in recent years by developments in information technology. There is no doubt that this area of distribution is complex due to the number of elements comprising the physical distribution and logistics system and the interrelationships between them. Cheap computing power has enabled the marketer to take account of these complexities and interrelationships, and design the total logistic system so as to provide optimum service at minimum cost.

Activity 6.13

Try to think of any changes in physical distribution over the last few years either in the industry in which you work or in an industry with which you are familiar. How have these affected marketing in the industry?

Summary

In this unit we have seen that:

- Place decisions have a major impact on levels of customer satisfaction.

- Place costs a company a great deal.

- Place should be designed to provide pre-planned levels of customer service at the minimum cost for each level of service.

- The two broad and interrelated areas of planning place are planning marketing channels and planning physical distribution/logistics.

- In planning both these areas the key considerations are customer needs, company objectives and costs, and competitors.

- Channels are one of the most dynamic areas of marketing these days with many changes taking place, often underpinned by developments and changes in technology, in particular the growth of more direct channels based on electronic and communication technologies.

Further study and examination preparation

Now do these questions:

Question 6.2

What are the key benefits of an effective management programme for the physical distribution of products?

Question 6.3

Define what is meant by:

1. Exclusive distribution.
2. Intensive distribution.
3. Selective distribution.

Question 6.4

What are the key issues which a marketing manager will need to take into account when considering alternative or new distribution channels?

Question 6.5

Explain what is meant by the two terms:

1. Vertical channel integration.
2. Horizontal channel integration.

Question 6.6

Explain the reasons for the recent growth in direct marketing, giving examples to justify your thoughts.

Previous examination question

Study tip

This question is taken from Fundamentals of Marketing paper June 2000 question 7. Remember, you can access the full specimen answer for this question on the following website addresses: www.marketingonline.co.uk or www.bh.com/marketing.

Question E6

a. What are the key issues which a Marketing Manager will need to take into account when considering alternative distribution channels?

(10 marks)

b. Explain with examples the reasons for the recent growth in the use of direct marketing channels.

(10 marks)
(20 marks in total)

Bibliography

F. Brassington, S. Pettitt, *Principles of Marketing: 2nd Edn. Chap 12*, 2000.

Further reading

P. Bickerton, M. Bickerton, U. Pardesi, *Cybermarketing 2nd Edn*, Butterworth-Heinemann, 2000

D. Chaffey, Maher, Johnston, Ellis-Chadwick, *Internet Marketing*, FT/Prentice-Hall, 2000

S. Dibb, L. Simpkin, W. Pride, O. C. Ferrell, *Marketing Concepts and Strategies: 4th European Edn.* Chaps 12 and 13, Houghton, Mifflin, 2000.

G. Lancaster, L. Massingham, R. Ashford, *Essentials of Marketing: 4th Edn, Chap 8*, McGraw-Hill, 2002.

Unit 7
The marketing mix: promotion

Objectives

By the end of this unit you will:

- Understand the role and importance of communications and promotion in marketing (3.12).
- Understand the process of communication (3.12).
- Understand the range of tools that comprise the marketing communications mix (3.12).
- Understand the factors that contribute to the development and implementation of the marketing communications mix (3.12).
- Be aware of key trends and developments in promotion (3.12).

Study guide

This unit covers our fourth so-called 'P' element of the marketing mix, and encompasses the tools available to the marketer to communicate with customers and others about products and services.

Although essentially about communication, then, this particular tool of the marketing mix is normally referred to as promotion. This is a very wide area of marketing encompassing, as it does, decisions about advertising, sales promotion, personal selling, publicity/public relations and direct mail. Because this is such a wide-ranging area of marketing, including factors as diverse as media selection for advertising through to recruitment and selection of the sales force, etc., we cannot hope to cover all the areas in promotion. Instead, a more realistic objective is to make sure that you understand the process of communication, the key elements of the promotional mix and how to plan these, and how to manage the individual tools of promotion.

We would expect it to take you about 3 hours to work through this Unit and suggest you allow a further 3 to 4 hours to undertake the various activities suggested. Other than your notebook and writing equipment, you will not need anything further to complete this unit.

The role and importance of promotion in marketing

Marketing promotions or, as we shall alternatively call this area, marketing communications, are an important tool of marketing for a variety of reasons. However, it is useful to highlight two major reasons that serve to underpin the vital role this element of the marketing mix plays.

The first reason why promotion is vital is quite simple. It is impossible to sell your products and services if nobody knows of their existence. Similarly, it can be difficult to market a product if customers have little information about your company. As we all know, even if the customers are familiar with both product and company, they may still require 'a little persuading' in order to be convinced that they actually need the product. All these are situations where, without effective marketing communication, making a sale is difficult. What we are talking about here are processes such as creating awareness, generating interest, heightening desire, and ultimately creating action in the form of a sale. Each in their own way, the various tools of promotion are aimed at fulfilling one or more of these functions.

This important communication role of marketing promotions is not just applicable to products and services but also to any other area where marketing tools and concepts are applied.

For example:

- Marketing 'ideas and causes' needs effective communications.
- Marketing 'people and celebrities' needs effective communications.

In short, everything that can be marketed needs to be communicated to customers. A company can have the best possible product for the target market, the most effective channels and systems of distribution, and a very competitive price, but if marketing communications are ineffective, all this can amount to nothing. In addition, ineffective marketing communications may result in substantial sums of money being wasted.

This brings us to our second reason for the importance of this area of the marketing mix. The second reason is that spending on promotional activities by companies and organizations is costly.

Last year in the United Kingdom organizational spending on promotion amounted to several billion pounds. In some cases a single promotional programme for, say, a new product launch can cost a company several millions. Clearly it is not being suggested that all promotion necessarily costs a company so much, but there is no doubt that in contemporary marketing, where competition is intense, high levels of promotional spend are common and sometimes obligatory. Because of this, it is essential that the marketer understands the process of marketing communications, the range of promotional tools available and their characteristics, and how to plan promotion so as to have the greatest impact for any given level of spend.

As we did with place, perhaps another way of illustrating the role and importance of promotion in marketing is to consider some of the things that can go wrong if promotion is badly planned and executed, together with the possible implications for the marketer and the company. Here are just some examples:

- 'We have just launched our new product and dealers did not have any brochures to give to customers who expressed an interest.'

- 'Because we chose the wrong media for our advertising campaign, the target market is still unaware of the merits of our product.'

- 'We have still not managed to overcome the damage to our company image from the pollution scare last year.'

- 'Half our advertising spend is wasted. The problem is we are not sure which half.'

- 'I don't know you, I've never heard of your product, I've never heard of your company, now what was it you wanted to sell me.'

We could go on citing examples of the types of problem stemming from badly planned and implemented marketing communications, but it should now be obvious to you that this area has a major impact on marketing effectiveness.

Activity 7.1

Try to recall any 'bad experiences' you have had as a customer or a potential customer for a product/service in the past that perhaps on reflection have been due to badly planned and managed marketing communications.

Reflect on the effect of this experience at the time with regard to your attitudes towards the product or brand and its supplier.

The process of communication

If the marketer is to manage the promotional element of the mix effectively, it is essential for him to understand the basic process and concepts of what is after all a communication process. For this reason virtually every basic marketing textbook in this area starts by examining this process and the key concepts which underpin it.

Exam hint

Because this part of marketing communications appears to be a little 'theoretical', there is perhaps an understandable temptation to skip over this process and concepts. However, not only is a basic understanding of the process and concepts of communication useful in very practical terms to the marketer, but, perhaps reflecting this usefulness, there have in fact been questions in the past in the Fundamentals paper on these aspects.

Communication is a vital part of all of our lives. We attempt to communicate with our husbands or wives, with our neighbours next door, or with our employees or managers. Nations attempt to communicate with other nations, often unsuccessfully. We are entertained, informed, often annoyed by communications. Whole industries are based on communicating. In short, communication and the need to manage it effectively is not something that is only relevant to marketers.

Definition

Communicate

To impart; to transmit; to receive; to administer. Hold intercourse; have common door or opening with.

Definition

Communication

Imparting; access or means of access; connection between places.

With such an extensive and varied scope for communication activities and meanings perhaps surprisingly we can distinguish a number of basic elements which, irrespective of the precise type of communication, make up the process. In virtually all types of communication, and certainly marketing communications, the elements are shown in figure 7.1:

Figure 7.1 Key elements of the communications process

The sender (source, transmitter)

All communication requires that there be a sender from which the communication stems. This could be, for example, a broadcasting authority, the editor of a newspaper, an employer or in our case the marketer.

The receiver (audience)

Our second key element in the communication process is the party or person with which we wish to communicate. As we shall see, unless and until the intended audience receives the message, there is no possibility of effective communication. In many cases the target audience for marketing communications is the customer or at least the potential customer. However, much marketing communication is also aimed at persons or parties other than the customer. For example, communications may be aimed at others who influence the purchasing process. Similarly, communications may be aimed at 'publics' important to the company, such as shareholders, local communities, and even politicians and governments.

The channel (media or medium)

If we have a sender and a receiver at either end of the communication process, then we also need a channel through which they can communicate. There are many types of channel of communication and these various types are very important to the marketer in planning marketing communications. A broad distinction can be made between 'personal' and 'impersonal' channels of communication. One of the most important areas in marketing communications is media selection and planning.

These are the first three basic elements of a communication process: a sender, a receiver and a channel. In addition to these three basic building blocks, we have a number of other elements that might be called 'technical aspects' in a communication process. These are aspects a communications engineer would perhaps be more familiar with, but, because they are endemic to the communication process, they are relevant to marketing communications.

Encoding

In order to transmit and share messages and information the sender must translate the message or information by means of a variety of signs and symbols appropriate for both the channel and the receiver. This process is known as encoding. It is important that the sender should use signs and symbols the receiver can interpret and understand. For example, the marketing communicator must not use words or symbols that make no sense or perhaps, even worse, can be misinterpreted by the receiver. So, for example, if we were promoting a new product such as a waterproofing agent to householders, it might not be a good idea to use the technical terms for the chemicals in the product, as most consumers would probably not understand them. Similarly, the marketer should use signs and symbols the customer can relate to: advertising messages for teenagers, for instance, might be very different to those we would use for the more mature end of the market. Encoding and its principles is particularly important when marketing crosses national frontiers, i.e. in international marketing. There are many examples of marketers making classic faux pas in their use of language and symbols in such markets.

Activity 7.2

Try to look out for and make note of any advertising and promotion for products you feel are inappropriate for the target market. This might be, for example, promotion for an imported product or service you feel the marketer has not got quite right for the intended market.

Decoding

Obviously if there is an encoding process in communication, there must be a decoding process at the receiver's end of the process. Many of the comments with regard to the appropriate signs and language we made about encoding apply here. In the decoding process the target audience tries to interpret and make sense of the messages that are being conveyed. We know that very often in the decoding process the intended message can become changed or distorted. The receivers will have their own perceptions and beliefs, which can cause changes and distortions.

Noise

Where the message received after transmission and decoding is not the same as that intended, or where the receiver has difficulty even receiving the message, we say there is 'noise' in the communication system. In fact one source of such noise is the different perceptions and beliefs that can influence the decoding process referred to above. There are many sources of noise, however, in communication systems. For example, each and every day most of us are bombarded with dozens of selling and promotional messages. In this clamour for our attention by the marketer much of the information intended for us is simply lost. We suffer from what the communication specialists call 'information overload'. Two further sources of noise in the communications process are the encoding and decoding elements and in particular the use of signs and symbols used to encode and decode including, of course, the major one of language. Many marketers, particularly in international markets have found to their cost that the words and symbols they have used to encode their messages to reach and influence the receiver of the marketing communications are decoded in an entirely different and often wholly inappropriate and unintended way so far as the marketer is concerned. So for example the Swedish marketer who used the brand name 'Krap' for his toilet paper products to be sold in the United Kingdom obviously was unfamiliar with the way this would be decoded by the target market. In fact, although at first sight amusing, mistakes such as this in the encoding and decoding process, and often much subtler ones, can be disastrous for the marketer and are much more frequently encountered than one might imagine and certainly hope for. Clearly the marketer must understand the sources of noise in a communication system and how best to minimize this through careful planning.

Feedback

Our final basic element of a communication system is what is known as feedback – information from the receiver this time, as a result of the communication sent. Such feedback may be intended or unintended, voluntary or involuntary, personal/direct or impersonal/indirect. Such feedback serves a number of useful purposes in a communication system. But in particular feedback enables the sender, e.g. the marketer, to ascertain the extent to which the intended message has been received and interpreted correctly. As importantly, it will also help to indicate the extent to which it has achieved the desired result. Perhaps the most obvious form of feedback in marketing communications is where the message is intended to create a sale, whether or not the customer has actually purchased. As we shall see, however, there are many possible objectives for marketing communications, of which creating a sale is only one. The marketing communicator must ensure that feedback is planned for and obtained as a way of evaluating the effectiveness or not of marketing communications.

Activity 7.3

Try to think of ways in which the marketer can obtain feedback from customers regarding the effectiveness of marketing communications. Compare your list with that shown in the debriefing.

The tools of promotion: the promotion mix

Later in this unit we are going to be looking at the planning of marketing communications. Before we do this, we need to ensure that we are familiar with the major tools of promotion that are available to the marketer. The selection and combination of these tools in a communications campaign is referred to as the 'promotional mix'.

> **Definition**
>
> **Promotional mix**
>
> The promotional mix is that combination of individual promotional tools selected by the marketer in order to promote a particular product to a particular target audience.

In fact there are dozens of individual promotional tools from which the marketer may select. We may, however, group these tools into one of five major sub-categories to represent the main constituents of the promotional mix. They are listed below and we shall discuss each in turn.

- Advertising.
- Personal selling.
- Sales promotion.
- Publicity and public relations.
- Direct mail.

Advertising

Perhaps the first promotional tool we tend to think of in marketing communications is advertising.

> **Definition**
>
> **Advertising**
>
> Any paid-for type of marketing communication that is non-personal, aimed at a specific target audience through a mass media channel.

This definition encompasses a wide variety of different types and reasons for advertising. For example, advertising may be used in:

- Advertising products and services: Ford cars, McDonalds restaurants.
- Advertising ideas and issues: Greenpeace, Oxfam.
- Advertising people: Jennifer Lopez, President Bush.

Types of advertising may include:

- Trade advertising: 'C&Q warehouses for professional decorators'
- Consumer advertising: 'Robinsons Barley water – refresh your ideas'
- Corporate advertising: 'Shell: the caring company'

In many markets advertising constitutes the largest spend area for marketing communications, especially in consumer goods markets. Advertising has several advantages as a tool of marketing communications.

> **Activity 7.4**
>
> Make a list of what you feel might be the advantages of advertising as a promotional tool. When you have completed this list, compare it with that shown in the debriefing.

We can see some of the reasons why advertising is used so extensively by some marketers. There are, however, potential disadvantages associated with advertising, the main ones being the following:

- Potentially high absolute costs.
- Often difficult to evaluate effectiveness.
- Persuasive value may be less than more personal promotional tools.

Personal selling

Anyone new to marketing might not have first thought of personal selling as a tool of marketing communications. However, to the extent that personal selling and other tools in the promotional mix are substitutable one for another, this is a major promotional tool. In many industrial markets spending on personal selling is the major promotional spend.

Definition

Promotional spend

A paid-for type of marketing communication that normally calls for personal and often one-to-one contact between marketer and customer.

This definition encompasses a wide variety of different types of selling. For example:

- Telephone selling.
- Technical selling.
- Missionary (or pioneer) selling.
- Retail selling.

Each of these types of selling can be found across a wide variety of markets and marketing situations, but below are some examples of situations and markets where each type tends to predominate.

Telephone selling: is used widely for home improvement products such as double-glazing.

Technical selling: as one would expect is particularly prevalent in business-to-business markets involving products such as computers, machinery, and even consultancy.

Missionary selling: used widely for selling new products and/or in new markets. So this type of selling is often found in international markets where a marketer is selling for the first time.

Retail selling: perhaps self-explanatory, but many retail situations do not actually involve any selling as such, so retail selling tends to be associated with, for example, household appliances, cameras and electrical equipment, holidays and cars.

Activity 7.5

Make a list of what you feel might be the advantages of personal selling as a promotional tool. When you have completed this, compare your list with that shown in the debriefing.

Personal selling has many advantages. However, the potential disadvantages associated with personal selling are as follows:

- More difficult to vary spend in short term compared to other promotional tools.
- Cost per customer contact high.
- Depends on people and therefore potentially suffers from 'people problems'.

Sales promotion

Our third major category of promotional tools represents what is probably one of the fastest growing areas of spend in marketing communications. In some markets spending on sales promotion is equivalent to or greater than spending on either advertising or personal selling.

Definition

Sales promotion

Any intermittent and/or short-term incentive designed to encourage purchase or sale of a product or service. Usually but not always impersonal in nature and usually non-media-based.

This definition encompasses a wide variety of different types and reasons for sales promotion. For example, sales promotion may be aimed at:

- Trade and intermediaries.
- The sales force.
- Consumers.

Types of sales promotion activity and tools include:

1. Premiums.
2. Coupons.
3. Self-liquidating offers.
4. Buy-back allowances.
5. Bargain packages.
6. Giveaways.
7. Dealer loaders.
8. Discounts and cash allowances.
9. Merchandising allowances.
10. Exhibitions.
11. Sales contests.

Question 7.1

What are:

1. Self-liquidating offers?
2. Giveaways?
3. Coupons?
4. Premiums?
5. Dealer loaders?
6. Buy-back allowances?

When you have completed this, compare your answers with those shown in the answer.

Publicity and public relations

Perhaps at one time the most neglected promotional tool, recent years have witnessed an increasingly professional approach to managing this area of marketing communications.

Definition

Publicity

Publicity is any type of news story and information about an organization and/or its products transmitted at no charge through a mass medium. Public relations are activities designed to create understanding and goodwill between an organization and its publics.

Publicity and public relations are often planned together, frequently using the services of a specialist publicity and PR agency. There are a wide variety of different types of activity in publicity and PR. For example:

- Press releases.
- Company open days.
- Press conferences.
- Third-party endorsements.

Some of the potential disadvantages associated with publicity and PR:

- Difficult to control media comments/reactions to publicity and PR.
- Difficult to assess impact, if any, on sales/profits.
- More difficult to control content and timing of communication.

Direct mail

Direct mail is, of course, part of direct marketing which was discussed in the Unit 'Tools of marketing: place' as part of the place element of the marketing mix and is one of the main communicational tools used in direct marketing. We have stressed several times that this area of marketing has grown substantially in recent years and you are now familiar with some of the reasons for this. As a result, many marketers and marketing academics, including for example, Kotler, now consider direct mail to be the fifth element of the traditional promotions mix. Certainly direct mail can be considered as one of the most effective methods of communication especially when linked to a company database and loyalty scheme. This method is particularly useful in building consumer relationships and is very easy to control and evaluate. We shall be looking at these uses of database and loyalty schemes in building effective consumer relationships in more detail in the Units 'Customer care' and 'Marketing fundamentals: the examination'.

Direct mail is usually a personally addressed marketing communication that is delivered direct to targeted respondents through the postal system. As already mentioned, its effectiveness depends on the accuracy and completeness of the list of addresses, together with the comprehensiveness of the information on the individuals or households to which the direct mail is being sent. Provided this database and the resulting mailing lists are effective, direct mail can be personalized and targeted very accurately. Most direct mail is aimed at generating enquiries and leads, and as already mentioned can be used to build relationships with customers. In part, the growth of direct mail has been a response to the increasing frustration and concern of marketers with regard to mass-media channels such as television, newspapers, etc. with respect to their cost-effectiveness in reaching target customers.

Although, at first sight, direct mail can appear relatively inexpensive compared to other forms and methods of communication such as TV advertising, in fact the return rates from direct mail, which can vary enormously but are often as low as 0.5%, can make this an expensive way of targeting promotional activities. Nevertheless, its advantages mean that direct mail will continue to grow, especially in consumer markets.

Study tip

It is important to remember that, although the syllabus is divided up into distinct sections with sub-sections, the different parts of the syllabus are interrelated and in some areas often overlap substantially. So, for example, we have seen that direct mail, as well as being a promotional tool, is also a channel. You will recall in this respect that for this reason we discussed the growth of direct marketing, of which of course direct mail is a major tool, in our previous unit. We also discussed some of the developments in direct marketing, and in particular the impact of databases and new technologies such as the Internet. It would be useful therefore to now re-read our previous discussion of the growth of direct marketing, but this time considering it from the perspective of the promotional elements of the mix. We shall also be considering these elements further shortly in this unit, but again from the perspective of promotion this time.

These then are the four major conventional promotional tools available to marketers. It is important to stress, though, that virtually everything a company does, says, or stands for potentially communicates something to the outside world. For example, the appearance of the employees of an organization can send signals to customers. Similarly, the state of, say, a company's vehicles can also communicate images. Even the other elements of the marketing mix contain signs and signals (planned or not) for customers and publics. Because of this, companies increasingly need to plan all the elements of communication so as to ensure consistency and co-ordination. Planning promotion should be looked on as planning a total package.

In addition, as we shall see we have recently seen the growth of new promotion tools, and in particular the Internet which we shall consider later.

Managing/planning promotional strategies

In this part of the unit we turn our attention to the issues, steps, and procedures in planning marketing communications. As mentioned earlier, it is impossible to look at detailed issues in planning each of the elements of the promotional mix. For example, management of personal selling includes recruitment and selection, motivation and compensation, territory design, sales planning, sales training, the sales process itself, and so on. We shall be looking briefly at the management and planning associated with each of our four major tools of promotion but the emphasis is on the management of the total promotional package. In doing so, many of the issues that will be considered at this level, such as setting promotional budgets, can also be applied at the level of planning each individual element of the mix.

In planning promotion we can identify a number of sequential but interrelated steps. The examiners will at the very least expect you to be familiar with and understand each of these steps. We shall consider each in turn.

Identifying the target audience

We saw earlier that the process of communication is about passing messages/information from a sender to a receiver. The starting point, however, in planning marketing communications is to identify who this receiver is to be; or, in marketing terms, who is the target audience.

In many cases, of course, the target audience will be the target market, i.e. customers. In other cases the target audience may be intermediaries, the general public, shareholders and so on. Even this identification of broad target audiences is not sufficient to plan marketing communications effectively. For example, if the target audience for marketing communications is customers, we need to define these customers precisely. Parameters that might be useful if the target audience is customers might include customer characteristics (age, sex, etc.); customer attitudes (interested customers, disenchanted customers, etc.); customer behaviour (regular customers, infrequent customers, etc.).

Espccially where the target audience is customers, details on the profile of the target audience are very closely related to something we shall be looking at in a later Unit and which you are already probably familiar with, namely market segmentation and targeting. At this stage it is sufficient to note that the identification and profiling of the intended target audience for marketing communications are essential.

Setting promotional objectives

Having identified the target audience for our marketing communications, we must next determine what we wish to achieve with our promotional activities. There is a temptation here to think of promotional objectives exclusively in terms of sales and profits, i.e. that all promotion is ultimately aimed at maintaining or increasing these sales and profits. Certainly it is true that in many cases this is the ultimate objective of all marketing activities, including promotional activities. However, it is much more useful to think of promotional objectives in terms of the communication tasks that our promotion is designed to fulfil. After all, communication is what marketing promotion is about. In addition, not all promotional efforts are in fact aimed at increasing sales and profits. Finally, in terms of setting promotional objectives in terms other than sales and profits, it is important to remember that promotion is only one factor affecting sales and profits. Certainly in some cases, such as direct response advertising, it is possible to relate sales to promotion. More often than not, though, promotion works in tandem with other elements of the marketing mix with regard to its effect on sales and profits. It is preferable therefore to think of promotion in terms of its desired communication effects. In other words, we should set promotional objectives in terms of what we wish to achieve with the target audience identified in the first stage of planning.

A number of models have been developed to help the marketer consider what audience response is being sought as a result of promotional efforts. We shall describe some of the best known of these models in order to help you understand how they relate to the setting of promotional objectives.

Response hierarchy models

As the term implies, these models are based on the notion that there are a number of possible responses to marketing communications on the part of the target market. Furthermore, the word 'hierarchy' suggests that there is an ordering or sequencing of responses, each one representing a 'higher level' of response on the part of the customer in the buying process. These notions will become clearer if we discuss some of the best known of these response hierarchy models.

The 'AIDA' model.

One of the earliest but still widely used and discussed models that can be used to consider promotional objectives suggests that the buyer, or potential buyer, passes through four key stages in the buying process. Each of these stages corresponds to one of the initial letters of the AIDA mnemonic.

Question 7.2

What do the initial letters of the AIDA model stand for?

If you have not heard of this model before, turn immediately to the answer before proceeding. If you think you already know what the letters stand for, write down your answer and then compare it with the answer shown in the debriefing.

The initial letters of the AIDA model are meant to represent the various stages a customer passes through in the purchasing process. It suggests that the marketer must first gain the 'Attention' of the customer, and then create 'Interest', which can be translated into 'Desire', and the final stage of course is where the customer translates desire into 'Action' by actually purchasing the product or service.

These four key stages in the AIDA model are shown in Figure 7.2.

Attention → Interest → Desire → Action

Figure 7.2 The AIDA model

Although a simple, and still useful model, there is now general agreement that this particular response hierarchy model is probably too simplistic in as much as it does not consider a range of very important issues which are important to the marketer because they affect the purchasing process and the role of communication on this.

Some of these issues which are not considered are related to the influences on the consumer such as perceived risk, level of involvement, environmental issues such as the economy related to disposable income, the buyer's experience of the product recently, competitor strategies, etc. Because of this, many suggest that AIDA is in fact now very limited in helping us to understand the issues involved in planning effective promotion.

The 'innovation-adoption' model

This too is a well known alternative model of the steps and stages *en route* to purchasing a new product, which, you may recall, we first introduced in the Unit 'Tools of marketing: product'. The model simply proposes a slightly different view of the steps in the purchase process compared to the AIDA Model.

Question 7.3

What are the stages the customer is said to pass through in the innovation-adoption model?

If you cannot recall the steps in this model turn immediately to the debriefing. If you possibly can, however, try to recall the steps in this model, write down your answer and compare it to the one in the debriefing.

This model was specifically developed for the process of purchasing new products. The first two stages are very similar to the AIDA Model, in that it is suggested that the customer needs to be made 'Aware' of the new product or service followed by the development of an 'Interest' in the product. If the customer is sufficiently interested, then he or she will be prepared to 'Evaluate' the product in more detail, followed by 'Trial'. If the trial is satisfactory, the customer 'Adopts' the product or service and – provided the customer continues to be satisfied with the product or service – enters post-adoption confirmation and becomes a regular/loyal customer.

The innovation-adoption model is shown in Figure 7.3.

Awareness → Interest → Evaluation → Trial → Adoption → Post adoption confirmation

Figure 7.3 *The innovation-adoption model*

Activity 7.8

Try to think of a product or service where customers might have conceivably passed through the steps described in the innovation-adoption model. Preferably try to think of an example where you yourself might have passed through these stages.

Hierarchy of effects model

Developed by Lavidge and Steiner in 1961 this model actually uses the term 'hierarchy'. Again, as is common to all of these models, the Lavidge and Steiner model (Lavidge, R. J. and Steiner, G. A. (1961) 'A model for predictive measurements of advertising effectiveness.' *Journal of Marketing*, 61), is based on the notion that the customer passes through a series of hierarchical steps *en route* to making a purchase. This model posits six steps in the process as shown in Figure 7.4.

Awareness → Knowledge → Liking → Preference → Conviction → Purchase

Figure 7.4 Hierarchy of effects model

Perhaps more than the first two models described here, this model clearly links the sequence in the hierarchy to the major functions of the promotional tools and in particular to advertising. The first two, awareness and knowledge, relate to information or ideas; the second pair, to attitudes or feelings towards the product; and the final two steps, conviction and purchase, produce action – the acquisition of the product. Lavidge and Steiner suggest that this model can help to develop advertising objectives and campaigns. It is also a useful model for helping to measure the effectiveness of advertising.

The DAGMAR model

First proposed by Russell Colley, DAGMAR stands for the title of Colley's book, *Defining Advertising Goals for Measuring Advertising Results*, Colley, R. (1961) Association of National Advertisers, New York. Again, this model is based on the notion that promotion, or in the case of Colley, specifically advertising, must move the customer through a number of stages towards purchase. The model is shown in Figure 7.5.

Unawareness → Awareness → Comprehension → Conviction → Action

Figure 7.5 The DAGMAR model

Colley refers to these stages as a *marketing communications spectrum*. The successive levels of the spectrum are as follows:

- *Unawareness/awareness* At this first stage of the spectrum we must move those customers who are unaware of the product through to a stage of awareness. Without this of course, there is no possibility of moving to the next stages of the spectrum. Advertising, therefore, is specifically aimed at creating awareness.

- *Comprehension* This next level in the spectrum is where the customer moves from simply being aware to understanding and appreciating what the product or brand is about. Clearly, marketing communications can play a key role in this process either through advertising or perhaps through the sales person and in-store information.

- *Conviction* At this stage the customer is moving towards preferring the brand. Again, this may be based on a number of factors including important word of mouth communication.

- *Action* As the term implies, it is here that the customer actually acts to purchase the product. It may be felt that advertising and other forms of marketing communication are irrelevant at this stage, but remember the customer can always change their mind and may need that final impetus or persuasion to purchase.

Colley's DAGMAR model, like the other response hierarchy models, illustrates that marketing promotions move the customer through a series of steps or stages towards purchase.

In terms of setting promotional objectives the value of such models is that they force the planner to consider what type of response is being sought from the target audience. Rarely can a single promotional campaign take a customer through all the stages in the buying process. More realistically, the promotional campaign will nudge a potential customer from one stage to the next or possibly through a couple of the stages. So, for example, an objective for a promotional campaign might be to make customers who are already aware of our products and services more interested in them. The promotional objectives for such a campaign therefore need to be expressed in terms that reflect this intended outcome for the promotional spend. An example of promotional objectives set in the context of the notion of response hierarchy models is shown below. For example:

'The objective of the promotional campaign is to increase customer awareness in the target market from its current level of 10 per cent to 15 per cent over the 12 months of the promotional campaign'.

We can see that setting objectives in this way helps in planning the next stages of the promotional campaign, e.g. message, channels, etc. In addition, setting objectives in this way facilitates the measurement and control of the effectiveness of our promotion.

Activity 7.9

Using the examples of the audience response hierarchy models shown earlier in the unit, practise setting illustrative but realistic possible objectives for promotional campaigns.

Extending knowledge

Find out about these models if you can. You will find further examples in G. A. Lancaster and L. Massingham, *Essentials of Marketing*, 4th Edition, Chapter 9.

Determining the message(s)

Having identified the target audience and the response sought from the promotional campaign, the marketer can then begin to think about the message(s) that will be needed to achieve this. Very often the marketer will make use of specialist outside help in formulating messages, in particular an advertising agency. Of special importance is the message content, where the marketer must determine what appeals or themes are going to be used. In promotional terms we often refer to the identification of the 'unique selling proposition' (USP) as the basis for the message content.

In addition to USPs as the basis for designing message content in promotion, the following are also used as the focus for message design:

- Fear.
- Guilt.
- Joy.
- Pride.
- Morality.
- Humour.

Selection of channels

We saw earlier in the unit that messages and information are communicated through channels. There is a wide range of possible channels for marketing promotion, each with its own characteristics, advantages and disadvantages, etc. We often refer to these as 'media'. No doubt you can think of plenty of examples, including television, newspapers, magazines, posters, exhibitions, etc. Selection of channels should stem from the preceding stages of promotional planning, e.g. target-audience selection.

Although there are dozens of types of specific media available in broad terms the marketer must choose between one or a combination of personal channels, e.g. personal selling, and/or impersonal channels, e.g. advertising.

Setting the promotional budget

Perhaps one of the most vexed questions in planning promotion is how much to spend, i.e. the total promotional budget.

Of the four methods shown in the debriefing, the first three are probably self-explanatory. Each method has its advantages and disadvantages but by far the most analytical of the methods is the one that perhaps needs a little explanation, namely the 'objective-and-task' method.

In this method the promotional budget is set up by means of the following steps:

- Establishing specific communication objectives.
- Establishing tasks required to achieve objectives.
- Estimating costs of these tasks.
- Calculating required budget on basis of first three steps.

Determining the promotional mix

Having determined the broad division between personal and non-personal channels, together with the promotional budget, we must determine the allocation of this budget between the different elements of the promotional mix, i.e. personal selling, advertising, sales promotion, publicity and public relations and direct mail. Many factors affect what is the most appropriate mix.

You will see from the debriefing, and you probably already knew, that many factors affect what is an appropriate promotional mix in any given situation.

Factors affecting the choice of the promotional mix

Many factors will affect the choice of an appropriate promotional mix. Some of the most important of these factors are as follows.

Target market/customer type

Target markets or more broadly the type of customer being targeted will affect the choice of the promotions mix. This is most easily demonstrated if we consider the promotions mix for an industrial versus a consumer target market. For the industrial customer it is more likely that personal selling will predominate in the promotional mix. This is because personal selling techniques are usually much more effective for industrial buyers as the products are often technical and the message can be tailored to the needs of the buyer. In addition, because there are likely to be fewer numbers of buyers in the market, mass advertising is rarely appropriate. What advertising is done will probably be only a small amount conducted in the trade press. Also useful in the promotional mix to industrial buyers will be sales promotions, and particularly techniques such as discounts for bulk purchase, free trials, etc. Personal selling also helps in this type of market because there are different members of the decision making unit (DMU). Finally, often the industrial marketer has a smaller promotional budget which restricts the use of some of the more expensive promotional tools.

In the consumer market, on the other hand, advertising is likely to predominate in the promotional mix. Personal selling will normally be confined only to more expensive consumer products. Sales promotion and direct mail, however, will also be useful in this market, especially for encouraging brand switching, initial purchasing and in the case of direct mail, enquiries.

Characteristics and cost effectiveness of the promotional tools

As implied in our discussion of the promotional mix in industrial versus consumer markets above, each of the promotional tools has its own characteristics and relative advantages and disadvantages compared to the other promotional tools. This means that some tools are much more appropriate and hence cost-effective in achieving certain objectives or reaching certain target customers. So, for example, advertising is much more appropriate where there are large numbers of geographically dispersed customers. It is, however, an impersonal form of promotion and therefore is inappropriate where customers require a high degree of personal contact and/or source credibility. Personal selling, on the other hand, although expensive from the point of view of the cost of each sales person, can be a very cost-effective way of communicating with customers, especially where products are technical or complex, and where therefore the customer requires clarification. Sales promotion is particularly useful for encouraging one-off purchasing and short-term interest in a product or service. If used excessively however, sales promotion can cheapen the image of a product or company.

Company resources, objectives and policies

As already indicated, mass advertising at a regional, national and certainly international level, will often require substantial promotional resources. Some companies simply cannot afford to spend on advertising. Also, the objectives of the organization will affect the promotional mix and certainly the extent to which the different promotional tools will be used. For example, if a company aims to develop and launch new products and therefore is required to create extensive awareness, it is likely to use more advertising in its promotional mix. Companies whose objective is to steal market share will often concentrate more on sales promotion efforts. Finally, a company may have policies which restrict the use of certain promotional tools. So, for example, some companies will not use direct marketing because they feel that this does not fit with the overall image which they wish to project.

Availability of promotional tools

We sometimes forget that not all the promotional tools are as easily or widely available to all marketers throughout the world. So, for example, in some countries, direct marketing, and in particular, direct mail, would be very difficult to use because mailing lists are simply not available. Similarly, mass advertising and in particular the media channels on which it depends are very poorly developed in some countries.

Product life cycle

We have already seen in an earlier unit the stage in its life cycle at which a product is has implications in the selection of marketing strategies. An important area of strategy affected by the product life cycle is, of course, the promotional strategy and, in particular, the promotional mix. So, for example, at the introductory stage of the product life cycle, advertising may predominate in the promotional mix in order to develop awareness. In the maturity and decline stages in contrast, emphasis on the promotional mix may switch to the use of sales promotion in order to try and extend the life and sales of a product.

Push versus pull policies

The overall communications strategy will of course affect every element of planning a promotional campaign including the choice of the promotional tools. Of particular importance, though, is the extent to which a company chooses to use a push versus a pull strategy.

- A *push strategy* is where the communication messages are targeted at the channel intermediaries (trade channels) such as dealers, wholesalers, agents, distributors and retailers. Often with a push policy the producer promotes a product to the next member in the marketing channel, with this member in turn promoting to the next level in the channel, and so on. This strategy should allow the trade channel members to facilitate the distribution of the products to consumers or end users, thus 'pushing' the products to the consumers. A push policy often uses predominantly personal selling, but also may involve advertisements in the trade press and sales promotion techniques such as discount for bulk orders, dealer competitions for the best sales figures, etc. The idea of a push strategy is shown in Figure 7.6.
- A *pull strategy* is where the promotion is directed at the end consumer or buyer in an attempt to get the customer to demand the product or service and hence 'pull' the product through the channel. The promotional objective is usually to generate increased

awareness, build attitudes and provoke motivation within this group of buyers. With this type of communications strategy examples of promotional tools in the promotional mix would be, e.g. television advertisements, direct mail, and sales promotions such as 50% extra free, etc. The idea of a pull strategy is shown in Figure 7.7.

Manufacturer → Trade channel → Reseller ← Consumer
e.g. distributor or buyer

Message Message Buy

Figure 7.6   *A push promotional strategy*

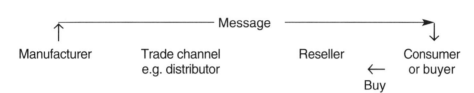

Message

Manufacturer   Trade channel   Reseller   Consumer
e.g. distributor ← or buyer
Buy

Figure 7.7   *A pull promotional strategy*

Measurement and control of promotional effectiveness

As with all marketing activities, it is important to measure the impact of promotional programmes and the effectiveness of what we have seen can be a substantial spend. We also know, however, that measuring promotional effectiveness in terms of its effect on sales and profits is complicated by the wide range of factors that impact sales and profits. This is where setting objectives in communication terms comes into play. It is much easier to measure the impact of the promotional programme in terms of pre-specified audience response objectives, such as impact on, say, awareness. Measurement of the impact of the promotional programme is never easy but every effort must be made to ensure that the programme is cost-effective.

Managing/planning individual elements of the promotional mix

In addition to planning promotional strategies, the marketer must also plan, implement and control each of the individual elements of the promotional mix being used. In other words, if all four elements are being used, the marketer must plan advertising, sales promotion, publicity and public relations, and personal selling. As already emphasized, we cannot look at each of these individual elements separately. However, as you will appreciate, in the Fundamentals paper it is unlikely that the examiners will look for detailed knowledge of, say, sales planning. They may, however, realistically expect you to know a little about managing each of the promotional tools. Perhaps with the exception of the personal selling element of promotion, which raises special issues in terms of its management, at least some of the steps in the framework used here for planning promotion can be used to structure the planning process for each of publicity/PR, sales promotion, and advertising.

In planning each of these elements we can use the following steps from our framework:

- Identifying the target audience.
- Setting promotion objectives for each tool.
- Determining the message/theme.
- Selecting the media.

- Determining the budget.
- Implementing, evaluating and controlling.

Trends and developments in promotion

Just as in other areas of marketing, promotion has witnessed some interesting changes in recent years. Although the major promotional tools outlined so far in this unit still dominate, we have seen the increased use of the following promotional tools.

- Corporate advertising.
- Sponsorship.
- Packaging.

We shall discuss the important promotional aspects of packaging in a little more detail.

Packaging and promotion

In the Unit 'Tools of marketing: product' we considered packaging as part of the product element of the marketing mix – in particular, in this context, its roles as protection and containment of the product itself. We also suggested, however, that packaging also plays an important promotional role and is sometimes said to act as the 'silent salesman'. If anything, this promotional role for packaging has become even more important in recent years. Many factors underpin this growth in importance including:

- The growth of self-service.
- The proliferation of brands and branded products.
- Increased consumer affluence.
- Problems associated with differentiating the core product.

These and other factors have placed packaging and packaging decisions at the centre of many promotional programmes. Innovatory packaging can often lead to increased sales and market share, giving the marketer a competitive edge at least for a period of time until competitors catch up.

Activity 7.13

Try to list examples of innovation in packaging that, at the time of their introduction, led to a competitive advantage for the marketer first using the packaging. Compare your list with that shown in the debriefing.

Whatever the examples on your list you will probably appreciate the powerful competitive edge that can be gained through packaging and some of the significant developments that have taken place in this area.

Decisions about packaging need to be taken by senior management and at an early stage in product development. Any proposed changes in packaging, however minor they may seem, should be carefully evaluated against customer perceptions and competitive activities. In the case of a new product a 'packaging concept' should be developed and researched with both customers and distributors. Care should be taken to ensure that the packaging fulfils both its protective and promotional roles.

It is difficult and dangerous to be definitive about what constitutes 'good packaging'; after all, many factors from target market to the type of product affect this decision. With this in mind, though, effective packaging usually meets the following criteria from a promotional point of view:

- It is distinctive.
- Related to the above, it is recognizable by customers.
- It fits with both product and corporate image.
- It is appropriate to the needs and perceptions of the target market.

Packaging must appeal, not only to consumers, but also to resellers. Rising consumer affluence can mean that consumers are willing to pay a little more for the appearance and prestige of better packages.

If there is no real product difference between rival brands, it is essential that the packaging is used with the branding strategy to differentiate the product, for example, the cat food, Felix, has a distinctive ring-pull opening top showing a cat's paw mark which reinforces the 'Felix' character used on the label and in the commercial television advertisement.

Decisions about packaging that must directly influence the promotional effect of the packaging include the following:

1. The pack should be *attractive and attract attention* in helping to promote the advertising and brand image – the logo should be clearly identifiable on the packaging. It should facilitate self-selection. Ferrero Rocher recently offered their individual chocolate products in a clear box shaped like a distinctive pyramid - the objective was to appeal to the mainstream audience while managing to break out of the sea of 'sameness'. The result was that this product was one of the fastest selling chocolate packs on the UK market during the Christmas period when it was launched.

2. *The shape and colour* should relate to the customer motivation and positioning of the product – such as the distinctively coloured tube packaging with re-sealable top and foil peel-back seal for Pringles crisps (a premium potato crisp product aimed at the trendy and affluent market).

3. *Social and ethical issues.* As with all areas of marketing, it is important to conform, not only to legal and regulatory requirements, but also to social and ethical issues. There is much criticism among some consumer groups regarding the 'wastefulness' of some types of packaging. Increasingly 'green' consumers are looking for recyclable packaging and will make brand choices on this basis. In addition, packaging should not be misleading to consumers by, for example, making them think there is more of the product in the container than there actually is. Finally, several recent controversies over packaging show that care should be taken with regard to, for example, the promotional message used in the packaging. For example, some of the 'alcopop' products (fizzy, drink type products which are alcoholic) were criticized with regard to their labelling and packaging because it was suggested that some of the images and messages used in the packaging made them particularly appealing to under-age drinkers.

4. Packaging may be designed to *promote impulse buying*. For example, many confectionery products and counter line products are effectively marketed through packaging in this way.

5. Packaging should convey or *reinforce the promotional messages* related to sales promotion offers, sponsorship or tie-ups. For example, Walkers crisps used their packaging to support a promotional campaign based on instant Spice Girls prizes.

6. As indicated above, the packaging should be integrated with all of the promotional elements and the marketing mix, e.g. Ferrero Rocher individual chocolates. The packaging echoes the quality statements made in the promotional advertisements, pricing strategy and product ingredient quality.

Information technology and promotion

Perhaps as you would expect marketing promotions have been substantially affected by the advances in communication and information technology within the past ten years. Indeed, this has had a major impact for marketers planning the promotional mix for their products and services. Some of the key issues are as follows:

- The growth of electronic communications such as the Internet, e-mail, fax, etc. has allowed information to become more rapid and global.

- The increasing power of the computer has allowed the marketer to gather and analyse information about their customers more effectively. As we have seen, this is one of the major reasons for the increase in direct mail. As we shall see in some of the later units it has also enabled companies to develop loyalty schemes to build individual relationships with customers.

- Digital technology is growing rapidly, with interactive digital television allowing two-way communications. The growth of satellite television has allowed marketers to target very specific target segments with their television advertisements such as pension plans for the over-50s advertised on the UK Gold channel (Sky). This will also offer marketers the opportunity to evaluate advertisements more effectively.

- The increased use of the Internet as a promotional tool for individuals and companies has offered many marketers a further effective promotional tool, resulting in more control and evaluation of the communications. Remember we have already considered the impact of this on direct marketing and increases in direct sales.

It can be seen that there are a wide range of IT advances which have allowed the marketer to plan more interactive, two-way messages which ultimately convert into an increased knowledge about the consumer. This increase in information allows the marketer to tailor the messages to consumer behaviour, which should ultimately lead to more effective promotional strategies. In this part of the unit, therefore, we shall look at some of the reasons for the growth of the Internet as a promotional tool.

The Internet as a promotional tool

We have already considered the Internet from the perspective of the place element of the marketing mix, but of course the Internet is also a promotional tool in its own right. Moreover, and again as we have seen several times throughout different units, it is a promotional tool which is increasingly being used by marketers throughout the world.

Some of the major reasons for the growth of the Internet for advertising and promotion include the following:

- Internet advertising can be very dynamic compared to, for example, conventional print advertising with the use of powerful graphics and hence movement and sound where appropriate.

- Given that consumers open websites voluntarily, even though sometimes a particular website is reached by accident, then at least some consumers are already predisposed to be interested in the product or service being advertised.

- The marketer can measure the response at least to the website through the number of hits recorded for the site.

- Dependent on the nature of the website and the advertising, the customer may often respond to the advertising immediately by placing an order.

- Carefully designed websites can be used to encourage an element of two-way communication with a target audience with, for example, questions being used to prompt responses from the customer and/or being used to respond to customers' enquiries.

- Compared to print and even television advertising, Internet advertising has a more insistent presence. Conventional advertisers are increasingly worried for example, about customers simply 'turning off' literally or mentally when confronted with advertising. The Internet still has an element of novelty for many users.

- Nominal costs for advertising on the Internet are substantially lower than when using conventional media channels. For many companies the cost of, say television advertising, on a national, never mind an international scale, has become prohibitive.

- Finally, much more information both in extent and detail can be provided through an Internet site, and again, the customer can to some extent pick and choose which elements of the information he or she wishes to receive.

Clearly then the Internet has much to recommend it as a promotional tool, but as with its use as a channel, its use as a promotional tool is still primarily determined by access to and use of the Internet by customers. We have seen that this access is patchy throughout the world with the highest incidence of access to, and use of, being in countries like the United States, Japan, and the United Kingdom. In some other parts of the world Internet access, particularly for home shopping use is still in its infancy. At the moment therefore, the international marketer in particular is restricted to some extent. However, this restriction is to some extent offset by the fact that by definition at least in principle the World Wide Web is global.

Advertising and promoting via the Internet involves the same key considerations as in developing promotional and advertising campaigns through conventional channels. So, for example, the marketer still has to determine campaign objectives, identify the target audience, create the promotional message, develop budgets, implement the campaign and measure and evaluate performance. However, there are some aspects of Internet promotion and advertising which are very different and require different skills and expertise over and above those required for conventional promotional channels and campaigns. So, for example, messages need to be designed with search engines and web access in mind. Similarly, there are several technical and regulatory website design conventions which need to be taken into account. Finally, things like security for customers and protection of data and information are important facets of designing websites and promotional messages on the web. Again we would proffer the same advice with respect to using the Internet as a direct marketing channel, namely that unless the marketer is an expert in website design, including some of the technology aspects which underpin it, then developing websites for use in marketing is best left to the experts, albeit guided by, and in the context of, the marketing manager's objectives and requirements for the promotional and other elements of the marketing programme.

Having said this, more and more marketers are in fact becoming familiar with the intricacies and technicalities of website design and Internet usage for promotional purposes. A familiarity which no doubt will continue to grow as this increasingly important and powerful new advertising and promotional medium develops.

As a guide, some of the key decision areas in using the Internet and websites as a promotional tool are indicated below:

- The website should be designed as an active marketing tool rather than as a sort of trade directory listing of a company on the Internet.
- Communications objectives for the website must be set for each target audience, e.g. increasing awareness, encouraging on-line sales, educating the market, launching a new product, gathering information for a direct mail campaign, etc.
- It should be easy for customers to find the website.
- The website should offer the visitor a rewarding and rich experience.
- The website should be designed to 'fit' with the overall communication strategy, i.e. there should be consistency of message.
- There should be a good design and flow of information.
- Where appropriate, the website should ensure access to secure ordering systems.
- The website should offer added value, perhaps in the form of 'free downloadables' or links to mailed sales promotions.
- The site should be updated on a regular basis as necessary.
- The site should be evaluated and controlled with regard to its efficiency and effectiveness. Several commercially available website-tracking programmes can be purchased for this purpose.

This last point of evaluating and controlling websites is becoming more and more important as marketers and website designers develop more familiarity with the use of websites in marketing and how to evaluate them. Until now, relatively simple measurements such as click-through rates – registered when a person clicks on an advertisement – and impressions – a record of each time a viewer downloads an advertisement onto a browser – have been the standard measures for evaluating the response to Internet campaigns. However it is increasingly recognized that these are extremely unsophisticated and hence potentially misleading measures of effectiveness. In particular, they reveal little or nothing about the nature of activity and consumer behaviour after the Internet site visitor has clicked or downloaded. Because of this there has been much activity in the development of tracking software and measurement services that provide more useful insights into the effectiveness of website campaigns. In the past, the technology under-pinning website campaign tracking systems have been based on cookie-based applications, but it is now recognized that these are imperfect and often inappropriate. The more recent tracking systems are based on providing much more information about people visiting websites by collecting consumer information at the time of the visit. This information is then increasingly linked to subsequent consumer activity, such as, for example, ordering profiles or even product usage information. A large number of companies, such as, for example, WCL, Mailtrack, Broadbase, and Accrue, are now developing much more sophisticated tracking responses to opting e-mail and SMS marketing messages.

Earlier in this unit we asked you to visit some company websites to look at how they were using their websites in marketing. Remember, websites are used in many ways by marketers now and not just as promotional tools. A key issue, perhaps as with all promotional tools, is the extent to which a website is effective, in this case in promoting a company or its products. Needless to say this can be very difficult to assess. Certainly it is easy to measure the number of visitors to a website but does this constitute effectiveness? There is a growing realization that nobody knows much about the way that consumers behave on-line. The most frequent measures for tracking the response to Internet promotional campaigns have been the use of click-through rates, which registers when a person clicks on an advertisement, and impressions, which record each time a viewer downloads an advertisement onto a browser. It is now realized that more sophisticated response tracking on customer behaviour on the Internet is required. Because of this, there has been a rapid increase in companies developing tracking software and bespoke services that can provide more powerful measures of the promotional effectiveness of website campaigns. The evaluation of information technology based communications, including Internet sites, are further explored shortly in the unit.

Websites are often thought of as just another selling device, but the website can be used much more actively, in particular to develop better relationships with a company's customers and publics.

Customer relations

A well designed and operated website allows for very effective communication with customers. If customers can easily find the website and access information on it, and if they find that these visits are rewarding in the sense of offering more than simply information, the customer is likely to be favourably impressed with regard to the company and its offerings.

Media relations

The website can also be dedicated to developing media relations. This can be one of the most potent public relations tools as, for example, reporters can access information which they may need at any time of the day or night, and if prepared carefully, in a format that is ready to use.

Investor relations

As the financial community is increasingly used to using the Internet, a corporate website can also be important for investors accessing information. This would include the annual reports being posted on the site.

Community relations

The website can also be used for developing community relations. This site could include information relating to the promotion of local joint projects, contributions to arts and culture, invitations to open days and educational pages.

We can see, therefore, that the strategic design and use of the website is growing in importance in today's market place and this must be considered as part of an integrated communications strategy.

The evaluation of websites and internet marketing communications

As with all the marketing communications tools, it is vital that the marketer establishes clear objectives and standards for performance for what are often expensive elements of the marketing programme. These objectives and standards can then be used to evaluate the various tools. In the early stages of the application of some of the website and internet marketing communication tools outlined, evaluation and control was not a strong point. However, this is now changing and evaluation is becoming more important and sophisticated. The following indicates just some of the ways in which the internet and websites can be evaluated.

The most frequently used evaluation method for the Internet site is the analysis of what are known as 'hit records' for each file retrieved by the respondent or visitor.

Definition

Hit

A hit is a downloaded file as recorded in a server log.

Although a broad measure of the number of people visiting a site via a server, the hit record gives very little indication of the effectiveness of a website. Accordingly, some much more sophisticated software packages or web tracking programs are now available. Using such web tracking programs, a company can also identify and evaluate, for example, the following:

- Where the website visitor came from – based on their e-mail domain.
- On what page the visitor started.
- What pages were visited and in what order.

- How long the visitor spent on each page.
- What the visitor did on each page, e.g. complete a form, down-load a file, play a game.

Improvements in Internet site evaluation and control are being made all the time now.

Extending knowledge

An excellent source of further information regarding on-line marketing is Bill Eager and Cathy McCall's *The Complete Idiot's Guide to On-line Marketing* – don't be put off by the title!

Other technological developments in promotion

As you will appreciate, the Internet is only one major technological development which is affecting the promotional element of the mix. Some would argue however that it is the most important and potentially the most far-reaching. However, a number of other technological developments are affecting the promotional element of the mix in important ways and indeed the Internet itself also affects other elements of the promotional mix including personal selling and the promotional elements of direct mail. In the context of the syllabus and of course from the point of view of your professional development as a marketer, therefore, it is important that you are familiar with and understand some of these other technological developments and how they are affecting promotion.

Summary

- In this unit we have looked at the role and importance of communication in marketing.
- We have examined the key concepts in and process of communication and their implications for the marketer.
- We have established what are the key ingredients in the promotional mix.
- You should now appreciate the key steps and considerations in planning marketing communications.
- As in all of the areas of the marketing mix, developments in technology and particularly the growth of the Internet are having major effects.

Further study and examination preparation

Now do these questions:

Question 7.5

Explain what is meant by:
  1. 'push' strategies;
  2. 'pull' strategies.

Question 7.6

Identify and briefly explain the elements of the promotions mix.

Question 7.7

What are the issues to be considered about the promotions mix for an industrial/technical product in relation to a consumer product?

Question 7.8

Briefly identify and critically appraise a response hierarchy model.

Question 7.9

Explain the recent impact of information technology for marketers planning a promotional campaign.

Previous examination question

Question E7

a. Using a consumer product or service of your choice, identify and comment upon each stage in planning a promotional campaign.

(12 marks)

b. Why might the selection of promotional tools differ for a campaign for an industrial product?

(8 marks)
(20 marks in total)

Bibliography

P. Bickerton, M. Bickerton, U. Pardesi, *Cybermarketing 2nd Edn*, Butterworth-Heinemann, 2000.

D. Chaffey, Maher, Johnston, Ellis-Chadwick, *Internet Marketing*, FT/Prentice-Hall, 2000.

Holtz, Shel, *Public Relations on the Net*, AMA, New York, 1999.

G. Lancaster, L. Massingham, R. Ashford, *Essentials of Marketing: 4th Edn,* Chap 11, McGraw-Hill, 2002.

Further reading

F. Brassington, S. Pettitt, *Principles of Marketing: 2nd Edn.* Chaps 14, 15, 16, 17, 18 and 19, 2000.

S. Dibb, L. Simpkin, W. Pride, O. C. Ferrell, *Marketing Concepts and Strategies: 4th European Edn.* Chaps 15, 16 and 17, Houghton, Mifflin, 2000.

Objectives

By the end of this unit you will:

- Understand the importance of service as an element of the marketing mix (3.14).

- Understand the factors that contribute to the delivery of service quality (3.14).

- Understand the relationship between service quality and the broader concept of customer care (3.14).

- Understand the role and importance of customer care and how to plan and implement a customer care policy (3.14).

- Understand the importance of people and a company's staff in contributing to customer care and effective service delivery (3.13).

Study guide

In this unit we shall look at the inter-related aspects of service and service quality in satisfying customer requirements and the ways in which the notion of customer service has expanded to encompass the broader area of customer care. Within these areas of service and customer care we shall look at the role that people, and particularly an organization's staff, play in service and customer care delivery. We shall look at why service and customer care have become increasingly recognized critical factors in the success of a business, whether it is concerned with providing services or selling products. Service delivery, customer care, and the all-important people element of an organization on which they are based have become the focus of a new approach for organizations providing products as well as services. In some ways for marketers this is familiar territory. Many marketing pundits have long argued that the delivery of extra 'added value' through the service, customer care and people dimensions are critical competitive factors in market places that are becoming more crowded and more competitive by the day. In fact we have already seen that it is these augmented product dimensions that are often the most important factors in choice for customers. As we saw in the Unit 'The marketing mix: product' decisions the augmented level of the product is sometimes the only way in which a company can differentiate itself from competitors. Increasingly, customers are looking for good service delivery and quality and will often, in addition, respond to high standards of customer care from the marketer. It is to these increasingly important areas of the marketing mix that we turn our attention in this unit.

The importance of service in satisfying customer requirements

Customers have become increasingly demanding in terms of what they require from the marketer. It is no longer sufficient for the marketer simply to provide a satisfactory product at a competitive price which is distributed and promoted in such a way as to make it readily available and known to the customer. Customers are demanding additional elements of service from the marketer. These additional elements can, as we have seen, be considered as part of the augmented product and can include any number of factors which the marketer can use to attract and hold customers. At one time, these elements might have been considered simply as product 'extras' including, for example, after sales care, technical advice, complaint handling, repairs and maintenance, etc. But increasingly service elements also encompass virtually every aspect of the marketing mix tools such as, for example, ordering systems and facilities, delivery services, credit and financial services for customers, enquiry lines, and so on. There are many reasons for this growth in the importance of these service elements of the marketing mix including the fact that customers have come to expect high levels of service in increasingly competitive markets. From the marketer's point of view, however, service represents one of the most potentially enduring ways of obtaining a sustainable competitive advantage. In time even the best protected product designs and technologies can be copied, competitive prices matched and effective promotion and channel arrangements emulated. One of the most difficult elements of competitive strategy to match, at least in the short term, however, are those which deliver high levels of customer service. The reason why customer service is so difficult to copy is that effective customer service in turn demands a customer care philosophy to be present throughout an organization. Building such a philosophy can take a long time and require substantial commitment from a company. Not only does it require effective systems and procedures, but above all it requires the right staff and attitudes in the organization. All factors which take time to build. Originally, the service element of the marketing mix, and particularly the people element on which, as we have already said, effective service delivery is built, were considered to be a special and additional part of the mix for service products and markets only. Certainly, in our final unit we shall return to the additional elements of the mix in service contexts, but it is now recognized that all markets require good service delivery, strong service quality backed up by effective customer care philosophies and systems and based on people. Because customer service delivery is so strongly linked to the broader concept of customer care, it is to this area we now turn our attention. We shall start our next section in this unit by reminding ourselves how customer service and customer care relate to our discussion of the augmented and potential product levels.

The nature of customer care

Definition

Augmented product

Augmented product refers to the extra elements aiming to provide additional customer satisfaction – helpful and well-trained sales people, range of products provided, guarantees of delivery and responsiveness to customer needs, having 'just the right' flavour, colour, price, etc.

Customer care is a widely used term, yet definitions of precisely what it covers vary quite a lot. Sometimes the term is used interchangeably with 'customer service' – a more familiar term but one that has never acquired the same cachet. Customer service developed from a focus on 'order-cycle' related activities into a much more general and all-embracing approach, which covers activities at the pre-, during- and post-transaction stages.

Customer care is the preferred term when we are forced to consider activities outside the realm, beyond direct contact with the customer. One commentator describes it as 'the ultimate marketing tool', and a critical factor in the process of differentiating products or services, to develop a competitive edge. It calls for what some have called the management and identification of 'moments of truth' – contacts between companies and customers where a firm's reputation is at stake. Interaction is still a critical dimension, and the focus has moved away from specific activities to look in general holistic ways at customer satisfaction.

An important aspect of customer care is attitude, covering every aspect of customer/supplier relationships. Customer care is aiming to close the gap between customers' expectations and their experience. Customer care is also, by common assent, a policy and a set of activities.

Activity 8.2

Summarize what you take to be the main characteristics of the 'customer-care' concept. When you have completed your own summary, compare it to that shown in the debriefing.

An important point to remember about the customer-care concept is that it is not simply a matter of responding to what customers perceive to be shortcomings but also a matter of anticipating what is often referred to as the 'delight' factor, and the difference between this product and its competitors.

Customer care and corporate culture

Most commentators see customer care as necessitating a culture change within a business. It is not an adjunct to company strategy but a core value that must form the basis for all policy-making and strategic thinking.

The difference between the Unit 'Customer care' and the more traditional notion of 'customer service' seems to lie in the degree of centrality this is given within the process of formulating corporate policies, objectives and strategies. Often it is part of programmes that set themselves the task of transforming the operating procedures of a business under the rubric of a 'quality' or 'customer-orientation' programme.

Various descriptions of customer care, then, agree that customer-impinging activities in policies or as a guiding concept form the core element in the implementation of customer care within a company.

Most practitioners would agree that modern strategic marketing begins and ends with the consumer, yet customer care may well be overlooked in the pursuit of broader, more abstract objectives. It is important to be aware of the dangers in programmes with broadly *similar aims and overlapping objectives,* but slightly different *perspectives and priorities.*

Activity 8.3

Referring back to the Unit 'The development of marketing and marketing orientation', list the ways in which the customer care concept is

- similar to,
- distinct from

the marketing concept.

The marketing concept expresses a particular business philosophy and provides an analysis of the nature of consumption, consumers, and markets today, placing a central importance on the formulation of strategies that take account of their characteristics. It is, in that sense, focused on consumers as they exist within their environments and as target groups.

The customer-care concept is a principle to guide the formulation of processes and practices within the organization that can unify and integrate the activities of all organizational members. In a sense, the customer-care concept expresses as a corporate mission the strategic objectives of a marketing orientation.

The importance of quality within the customer-care programme

Quality has been thought to be the critical differentiating factor between British firms and their successful foreign competitors, and, as a consequence, the pursuit of quality has become a major preoccupation of British companies. A by-product of the attempt to compete with successful foreign firms making inroads into domestic markets was a modernization process, which led, in many cases, to cuts in investment, downsizing, wage cuts and so on – and also to poorer service to customers. Such was a consequence of the search for higher levels of productivity and output, greater commitment and flexibility from the workforce, and a broad 'culture change' in the organization concerned.

As many studies showed, perceptions of quality and service in British products fell significantly, and customer satisfaction levels were also poor, representing a sure recipe for disaster in a situation where foreign competition was meeting targets for quality improvement.

Activity 8.4

Using a product with which you are familiar, compare those dimensions that differentiate a very good brand from a very poor brand. Use that list to derive a formulation of 'good quality'.

One of the main reasons for the success of Japanese and German competitors is an ability to create organizations dedicated to the pursuit of total quality, i.e. organizations focused entirely on the delivery of quality to customers. This seems to go hand in hand with a customer-care concept, to the degree that it makes very little practical sense to talk of one factor without the other also being given high priority.

Another reason for foregrounding customer needs has been the growing significance of services within the economies of advanced societies. Here the consumption of services has become more and more important over the past 20 years, as increasing affluence generates demand for the provision of people-based enterprises. In the 'Service Age' competition depends on quality being delivered, whether this is in catering and fast food, leisure provision, hospitality, entertainment or nowadays in medicine and other public services such as education.

Many universities, for example, have now included a customer-care element in their organizational mission statements. Once the preserve of the purely commercial organization, customer care and customer-care programmes are now being increasingly adopted in not-for-profit and public service sectors.

The Total Quality Management approach to such businesses uses customer care to deliver better service, or 'to meet customer requirements first time, every time'.

Customer Care and TQM, then, are closely related. Quality programmes, however, cover many topics other than dealing with customers. Customer-care programmes focus on gaining deep knowledge of customers, and aim to identify their needs and improve care provided for them. Care is the outcome of this process, and 'satisfied customers' are the focus of customer care programmes. The challenge is to maintain this emphasis throughout a quality process. While customer care should be focused on the way in which customers experience the delivery of the product or service, it is quality programmes that direct the processes constituting the services or products to which they are experiencing and responding.

A good example of a company which has put a lot of emphasis on customer care and TQM underpinned by effective quality programmes is Virgin Plc. This is a company which has put the concept and practice of customer care at the heart of all its businesses from mobile phones to air transport.

How quality programmes affect customer care, and what objectives TQM can have and what it can do, then, are clearly important issues for marketers interested in the implementation of customer care programmes.

Activity 8.5

Describe what you would expect to be the common elements in TQM and Customer-care programmes. Compare the list you produce with the following sections.

The preceding section should lead you to identify the following core elements:

- An emphasis on process.
- An emphasis on the details of the system.
- The need to establish fundamental changes in attitude, focus, and orientation.
- The idea of a 'core philosophy' that transforms practice.
- The derivation of the concept of quality for this particular product/service from customer perceptions, attitudes, expectations and needs.

Total quality management (TQM)

Briefly, 'quality' in management can be defined as combining the satisfaction of customer needs with the achievement of company objectives. That the two are intimately and inextricably connected is an article of faith for all who discourse on the subject.

The following areas are connected, within the terms of this analysis, in systems aiming to achieve success and profitability by placing the customer at the centre of all enterprise activities through providing the right amount of the following:

- Quality.
- Availability (at launch and afterwards).
- Service.
- Support.
- Reliability.
- Cost/value for money.

By common assent, such programmes must be 'total', reaching forward to distributors down the chain, and back to suppliers in the case of manufactured goods, to ensure the quality of raw materials and the condition of the product that reaches the ultimate consumer. Hence, Total Quality Management.

TQM is now widespread throughout many companies. At first it tended to be the larger manufacturing companies such as, for example, Ford and IBM which practised TQM, but as mentioned earlier the recognition of the importance of value of TQM in an organization has meant that, irrespective of the type of company, its size, or target market, TQM is increasingly practised.

The customer-supplier relation is very important indeed within the TQM philosophy. This relation is one of a long chain of such customer-supplier relations, with each customer being a supplier to someone further down the chain, so that it makes no sense to differentiate one role from the other. Rather than pursuing self-interest, and creating an adversarial relationship, the aim of TQM is to expand the pie the relation is concerned with dividing, in traditional terms.

The establishment of such programmes has been the foundation for startling corporate success stories, such as those enjoyed by Jaguar motors and, as a result, Ford – who, of course, now owns Jaguar. When consumer surveys showed large numbers of faults in the components bought in from outside suppliers, quality programmes installed as a consequence used testing systems that were installed with suppliers, and implemented extensive quality studies and audits. The subsequent improvement in quality and performance within the market place has been widely admired and analyzed.

Quality and customer care

As with quality programmes in general, TQM gives central place to the customer. Satisfying them is the first principle of TQM, since they are the guarantee of the organization's continued existence. Gaining custom means winning a competition for the patronage of each individual or corporate buyer, and satisfying the particular needs of that individual is the competitive edge that wins survival and prosperity rather than extinction.

Customer-driven quality is recognized in the US as a core value of the Malcolm Baldridge National Quality Award. The guidelines for its winners state 'Quality is judged by the customer'. All products and service attributes that contribute value to the customer and lead to customer satisfaction and preference must be the foundation for a company's quality system. Value, satisfaction and preference may be influenced by many factors throughout the customers' purchase, ownership and service experiences.

Activity 8.6

List as many companies as you can in which, in the course of business, there are avenues for gathering information about customer attitudes and beliefs regarding the company, or which provide readily accessible means to register either approval or dissatisfaction with the companies' service or products. Describe those companies that seem particularly good or particularly bad at these things.

Three principles guide customer-supplier relationships under TQM:

- Recognition of the strategic importance of customers and suppliers.
- Development of win-win relations between customers and suppliers.
- Establishing relations based on trust.

These principles are translated into practice by:

- Constantly collecting information on customer expectations.
- Disseminating this information widely within the organization.
- Using this information to design, produce and deliver the organization's products and services.

TQM programmes require the following conditions to be fulfilled.

Total commitment from staff

This is another way of talking about a structural or a cultural change being essential for the achievement of a quality programme. Often these schemes are presented as 'a philosophy of life' or a 'total way of thinking' rather than just another technique for management. It is a peculiar feature of these systems that they have a religious, or messianic, quality – advocates are spoken of as 'evangelists' or, more commonly, 'gurus'. It is perhaps unsurprising that the generation that toyed with transcendental meditation and flower power in the sixties should focus on gurus of a different kind in the nineties!

For this system to work, however, it is a practical necessity for all staff to participate. Those best placed to make quality work are the people who actually deliver products or services. Partial quality improvements will constantly face the problems created by those parts of the system that have not been reformed, when staff are trying to improve the quality of what they deliver to customers.

A customer orientation

As suggested above, each internal group in the quality chain is composed of a customer and/or supplier to other internal groups, and in some cases to the market. Although programmes can start at any point in this chain, even if the quality of the supply to a group is low, the group should aim to build up its own quality before addressing the shortcomings of its own supplier.

Note how a 'customer orientation' under TQM focuses not just on the external customer but on the customer-supplier relation that is a general feature of marketing processes. Customer-care programmes, although focused on external customers, are important influences on the way in which such processes are conceived and practised.

Defining customer requirements and obligations

From the viewpoint of an organization, customers can be thought of as an agglomeration of **requirements and obligations**. Customers may be external customers, employees, shareholders, top management, government and so on. Requirements will be fitted to resource constraints and the objectives of the organization, and must be realistic and obtainable. Obligations need to be clearly defined, and requirements need to be quantified and accepted by both sides as reasonable. If a customer-care programme is to be effective, the relations must be clearly specified on both sides.

An example of an organization which practises this wider view of the range of customers, or perhaps we might say 'publics', in addressing customer care-programmes is the Open University. The Open University have realized that customer care encompasses not just students but also their employers, tutors, local communities and even governments.

Activity 8.7

Explain:

- What effect focusing on customers and suppliers has on the formulation of strategy.
- The value of a 'win-win' relation in this context.
- The importance of trust in these relationships.

Measurement

This is extremely important for any quality programme, and, in relation to customer care, measurements must be continual and ubiquitous. Required performance needs to be clearly specified in terms that can be measured, and mechanisms must be instituted to provide clear indicators that these have been achieved. These must be in place before programmes are instigated.

Customer-care programmes will require survey data on internal and external customers, on customer behaviour, and on the degree to which customer needs are being satisfied. These should permit the application of techniques such as key ratio and trend analysis, and fit into a cycle of assessment, planning, implementation and monitoring.

Commitment from the top management

Top management needs to ensure that the programme is delivered, and also that it provides the cash payoff from improved quality in customer service.

Adherence to standard processes and procedures

Processes and procedures that are developed and specified as an end product of a TQM customer-care programme are intended to be followed. Such directions are intended to reproduce proven consistent quality, and should specify administered processes, timing, responsibility and areas of expertise, and gathering of feedback data. When these directions are adhered to, the output remains consistent, processes are appropriately monitored, and the data provide the basis for learning and consistent improvement.

Paying-customer objectives

The end product of any programme must be to satisfy the needs of the paying customer in order to accomplish particular commercial, financial or strategic objectives. To that end, all analysis within customer-care programmes, and the development of any processes and procedures within such programmes, must relate to these objectives. Examples of such objectives would be:

- Increasing sales and profits.
- Lowering prices of service provision.
- Improving customer perceptions of service.
- Shortening waiting lists and giving priority to customer needs.

The *mission* of the organization, and the corporate values that underlie corporate objectives, must always be clearly and directly related to the formulation of such objectives. If they are not, then TQM programmes will not accord with the strategic direction that has been agreed.

Activity 8.8

Using the example of an organization with which you are familiar, identify those parts, or aspects of its operational procedures, which seem likely to pose the most problems when TQM is being introduced. Why should managers or workers resist the introduction of TQM?

The idea of the activity is to make you think about the contrast between the ideals of TQM and the actual circumstances within many companies that might wish to introduce it. Who would lose, or consider that they would be likely to lose, when this system was brought in?

Customer care, a comprehensive approach to working with customers

The close relation between the 'customer orientation' that lies at the heart of marketing and the notion of customer care is readily apparent. Customer care can be seen as a perspective that focuses on working with customers at every stage of the planning and implementation process. This is important in marketing all types of product and service. It is a *service component* and, as such, shares the *characteristics* of service marketing. It is, for example:

- People-based.
- Perishable.
- Dependent on high customer involvement.
- Based on perceptions.
- Sensitive to images.
- Heavily dependent on consumption context.
- Delivered over time.

While marketing is, as we have seen, fundamentally based on customer orientation, it is possible, in the pursuit of marketing objectives, to lose sight of the things that will satisfy customer needs.

Following a marketing plan in the delivery of a service can result in customer-care shortcomings in the following ways:

- *As a result of an unrealistic corporate mission* – when those in charge of the company are making promises the company cannot possibly deliver. When the company is aiming to deliver the wrong level of care to the customer, or when the company is, for example, turning customers away.

- *As a result of poor information about customers and the market* – ignorance of customer needs, and consequent mismatch of care levels to needs can produce a lack of customer care. This may come about because the information system fails to identify those areas in which customer needs must be given priority, focusing instead upon general aspects of customer satisfaction. Business priorities, e.g. carrying out the processes of delivering a service, can be out of line with customer priorities. Tom Peters emphasizes this aspect of customer satisfaction constantly: good products or services that are perceived as failing because customers' small but important needs (being able to get coffee in a hotel in the early morning; having a space on which to place food or small items that may be needed quickly in an expensive car) are neglected.

- *Poor timing* – when information that has been gathered in the past about what it is that customers want is used for too long, a mismatch can occur. Customer priorities are changing, and it may be that, for example, selling on price, or on functional product attributes, becomes inappropriate as products become mature, competition increases, and differentiation is more problematic. In addition, good marketing may seek to identify needs of which some customers may not be fully aware; in marketing a product to satisfy these needs we are adding even more value to a product, by raising customer awareness of the needs it can meet that they do not, initially, anticipate.

- *Poor staff communication* – in the delivery of services particularly it is vital that staff should be aware of the needs suppliers require them to satisfy. When staff are not fully trained, or perhaps inadequately informed of the aims of a marketing programme, they may well fail to deliver the appropriate levels of service. Local improvisation will cause inconsistencies, and variations in the quality of product and service delivered will arise. Often staff will react to problems by falling back on a 'defence' of the systems they are operating.

- *Poor staff motivation* – when staff are not properly informed, trained or committed to delivering customer care, they will be inadequately motivated. This will invariably be communicated to customers.

- *Poor control* – systems of control are essential to the establishment and maintenance of customer-care standards throughout an organization. When such systems are absent or inadequate, levels of quality of customer care will vary. In some cases such variation may well take the form of very damaging inconsistencies, which may well undo the effects of good practice taking place in other parts of an organization, or at other times with the same staff or customers.

- *Confused priorities* – when staff are following through the delivery of, for example, specific practical aspects of service delivery, such as progressing an order or carrying out a task for the customer, they may find that there are too many priorities for them to pursue effectively. Attention to marketing tasks, or attendance to customer relations, is perceived to be an 'extra' in some organizations, and is strongly at risk of being sacrificed.

- *Organizational confusion* – many structures do not effectively delegate responsibilities for marketing or customer care. In principle, it should be part of everyone's job, but, at the same time, it must be expedited, and responsibility for the establishment and delivery of the systems that promote these priorities must be clearly defined within the organization.

- *No acceptance of marketing and customer care* – when staff are pressurized into delivering too many difficult practical aspects of their jobs – meeting efficiency or productivity targets, delivering increased levels of output – they may well feel that concerns over meeting customer needs are not something they should be greatly concerned about.

- *Short-term emphasis* – this is even more the case when the feedback, or the benefits of satisfying such needs, arise in the long rather than the short term. In this case distortions in the delivery of services or products may arise because only behaviour (satisfaction of needs) which brings short-term rewards to the supplier is being reinforced by positive feedback from the customer.

- *Power conflict* – inconsistencies will also occur when there are imbalances between the power at the disposal of different functions within an organization. Here, the level of care customers are offered varies according to which parts of the organization customers contact. When customers require to contact more than one part of the system, they are highly likely to experience inadequate service levels.

Activity 8.9

Think of the ways in which the implementation of a marketing plan can frustrate the delivery of customer care. For each of these areas, think of strategies in which problems could be overcome by modification or replacement of particular aspects of the marketing plan.

Your answer to the activity should bring out the contrast between the width of focus in these plans. Clearly marketing plans often have implications for customer-focused activities, and may imply conflicting, or contradictory, aims, e.g. over the price, quality, or assortment in the product range. The important point to grasp is that company policy requires that these issues should be confronted and resolved by creative tension between these objectives. They must inform each other, rather than be treated as separate and isolated.

Delivering adequate levels of customer care

Produce an adequate definition of the corporate mission

Without clear definition of corporate goals, the business will always be wasting resources and effort through lack of a clear focus and consistent goal. A mission statement has as one of its fundamental aims, however, the communication of purpose to each member of the organization – it must be easily understood by every participant – and it must also inform individuals how their roles within the organization contribute towards the achievement of this mission. It therefore has a key role in motivation, and if it is not clearly and effectively formulated the chance of establishing a customer-care ethos or 'culture' within the organization is seriously diminished. The line between mission statements and customer care is so important that we shall return to this area again shortly.

Activity 8.10

Formulate a mission statement for:

- Yourself.
- Your family.
- The leader of your country.

Use up-to-date and reliable information

Assumptions about what it is that customers want, and notions that it is 'obvious' which product attributes are most important to the customers, are all too common, and frequent causes of dissatisfaction. Information about customers should come from customers, or from those who are closest to them in delivering a product or service. Information about competitive activity, about changes in market conditions and even about the performance and perception of the company itself, should come from sources that are in touch with the recent reality of the situation, and not dependent on remote or potentially partial individuals or organizations.

Unless the company places a very high priority on the gathering, analysis, and dissemination of information to inform decision making, and also engenders a culture in which information flows freely and is available in a form that can be readily used by decision makers at all levels, it is difficult to see the organization developing the degree of openness and responsiveness that is such an integral part of the customer-care concept.

Use information to inform decisions and planning

Too much information is gathered ritualistically or simply because it seems like a good or useful thing to do. When information about customer needs is gathered, it must be used to make effective decisions, and placed at the heart of the planning process. If the information being gathered is not used in this way, the organization needs to ask why it is being gathered at all. An important part of this informational system are the mechanisms by means of which this information can be gathered, stored, analyzed, disseminated and rendered into forms that decision makers can relate to their particular concerns. Since customer care is essentially founded on 'listening' above all else, but also on 'measuring' and 'reacting', or learning from what our information can tell us about what customers think and want, decisions must be information-based in the case of even the most experienced and able managers.

Activity 8.11

Describe what information would be needed by:

- the managing director,
- the store manager,
- a sales person,

to meet the needs of customers in a store selling clothes to very large men. Are they the same, or are they different? Why?

How far can information be shared? How relevant is, say, economic data to a sales person? Should it be? How far can we take the process of 'flattening' an organization, and distributing skills across the workforce?

Act quickly

Information decays quickly. Failing to act on the basis of information that is available now, and acting after the information has ceased to be relevant, are equally damaging and inappropriate. Customer needs and standards change very quickly in some markets, and when action is needed, it should be taken as quickly as possible.

Use written plans that are understandable and achievable, and provide motivation for staff

Written plans should aim to meet communication objectives. If they are written for staff to implement, they should aim to provide a basis on which practical actions can be taken, effects can be identified and measured, and staff achievements can be formulated. Plans are counter-productive if those who are required to live by them feel that they cannot realistically be met, or that meeting them engenders no commitment and offers no reward or sense of achievement if their challenges have been met.

There is another school of thought about the notion of written plans. Arguing against the (traditional) idea of MBO (management by objectives), one author says that the creation of such objectives actually inhibits progress and militates against the achievement of high-quality service and products. The objectives set have to be achievable, and so the 'ceiling' on quality is fixed in advance. Setting such targets becomes increasingly difficult, and has less effect as time goes on, since it depends on setting 'realistic' goals, which are also built on goals that have just been achieved. In that sense written plans can provide a brake on potential improvement, or, as the quality movement refers to it the 'continuous improvement process'.

It is argued that a system in which excellence, quality and responsiveness to customer needs are ingrained into the corporate culture is far preferable; in that case striving for quality and seeking to find new ways to add value and satisfy customer needs becomes a constant, endemic feature of the operation of the organization, at every level, and in every process. Rather than planning for customer care, every employee sees it as a natural feature of the job. This does of course call for careful analysis of procedures, and specifications of what happens in every process, based on observation, description and analysis. In that sense written plans and clear definitions of procedures are essential bases for any programmes seeking to make beneficial change.

Produce regular progress reports on the implementation of the marketing plan

These must be reliable and detailed, and not simply reports on results. Constant attention to progress, adjustment as necessary to changes in conditions and new customer needs, and changes in perception, all require that the marketing plan being followed should form the background to what is done.

Make measurement central to the process of implementation

Scores and systems of measurement provide invaluable benchmarks of progress, and provide targets that can be seen to be met, or not.

Activity 8.12

Think of trying to improve the customer-care element of the service provided in a travel agency. Write down which aspects of service encounters can be measured, briefly indicating the kind of instrument used, e.g. a survey questionnaire. In addition, say which aspects would be difficult or impossible to measure – and why.

Compare your list with that shown in the debriefing.

Disseminate a marketing philosophy, but also assign clear responsibility for the marketing function.

If everyone's job has marketing aspects, trouble can occur if no one is actually responsible for making it happen. There must be clearly defined responsibilities here, as well as a core commitment to building it into the way in which the organization functions at all levels.

Activity 8.13

Describe what activities you believe to be required in order to establish customer care for:

- A car salesroom.
- A supermarket.

Customer care within the marketing process

Marketing calls for a structured approach and applying information about customer needs in order to achieve strategic objectives; typical steps include:

- Defining corporate mission, corporate objectives and strategies.
- Analysing the environment.
- Setting marketing objectives.
- Developing marketing strategies.
- Devising action plans.
- Measuring results.
- Reacting to results.

Within each of these steps customer-care issues arise and must be met. Often consideration of these issues will materially influence the ways in which the objectives of the marketing process are pursued. We consider them in more detail in the following section.

Defining the business mission

While definition of what business the enterprise is in, who is being served, and how this will be accomplished, seem incontestably essential questions for anyone in business, the simplicity they propose as the foundation of business activity is difficult to achieve. As the size of an organization and its tasks increase, so does their complexity, and the possibility of being diverted from central issues.

In defining the business mission, looking at who our customers are, and how we see ourselves as serving their needs, we need to take a large number of factors into account. Initial explorations of what customers want may actually reveal that this cannot be met by what the enterprise has to offer – in which case markets have to be redefined.

Mission statements that fail to accommodate the establishment of customer loyalty and the promotion of customer care as primary aims are bound to fail. Likewise, it is essential that mission statements espouse and promote effective plans to maintain high levels of caring for customers within the operating framework of the enterprise.

A good example of where a company's mission statement explicitly recognizes the importance of customer care and incorporates this into the company philosophy is that of the Interflora worldwide flower delivery company. The aims of the Interflora organization, particularly as regards customer care, are encompassed in its mission statement which is as follows:

> *Our mission is to ensure that Interflora will always be the consumer's first choice for flowers and appropriate gifts. This means: recognizing and responding to our customers' changing needs; providing a seamless service to our customers; leading our industry in innovation and design; continual improvement in quality, service, processes and costs and enabling our employees and associates to give their best.*

The marketing audit

The marketing audit must attempt to identify and define factors within the external environment that promote customer satisfaction and generate loyalty. This calls for comparisons between different policies, evaluations of the different degrees to which they actually promote customer loyalty, and analysis of why differences occur.

The audit should also evaluate the performance of the different factors within the enterprise that promote customer satisfaction, and identifying sources of dissatisfaction should play a major part in the marketing process.

Action plans for the formulation of the marketing mix

Problems, from the point of view of customer care, arise when such plans focus on short-term objectives, particularly sales and the promotion of improved margins. These very often prove antithetical to the main objectives of strategies based on customer care, which aim for the long term, not just winning custom, but winning customers by promoting good ongoing relationships, and looking for substantial long-term profits by sustaining customer loyalty.

Action plans to formulate marketing operations

Problems here have to do with the efficacy and efficiency of marketing procedures, e.g. the cost-effective and efficient delivery of beer to a public house, rather than with the perception and response of customers to the end product, e.g. an unfavourable comparison between product delivered in natural, old-fashioned wooden barrels, and that delivered in modern, cost-effective aluminium kegs – with a consequent attribution of many undesirable product characteristics, such as chemical taste, additives, poor quality, etc.

Results

When too much emphasis is placed on tracking sales and profit, rather than customer inventory movements, results may not be providing the most effective form of feedback for the organization to make long-term plans.

Activity 8.14

Give an example of a customer-care issue at each of the six stages listed.

When this framework is followed, attention is effectively focused on the delivery of customer care. What is also required, of course, is a clear idea of what customers want from the organization. This requires a systematic approach to the gathering and evaluation of information about what may actually be a number of different types of customer, since the product portfolio of many companies extends over different types of market for the same type of product, or of course different brands and product types.

Identifying customer needs and perceptions of the company

To use a strategy based on customer care successfully, two questions need to be answered:

- What policy of customer care is most appropriate for our company?
- How far should this policy affect our operations?

In order to succeed, knowledge of customer needs is vital. What expectations should the company aim to meet? In the real world these expectations will be related to the way in which the company is perceived. There are, for example, limits to the expectations a reasonable person has, and these are related to the realities of what resources a company has at its disposal, and how these must sensibly be employed.

The customer believes minimum rights should be respected, independently of such constraints, for they are the *sine qua non* of customer care. All customers have the absolute right to:

- A basic minimum level of customer care.
- Common courtesy from staff.
- Responsive and effective response to complaints.

Customers' requirements in terms of care are likely to vary according to the significance, as they perceive it, of each transaction with the supplier. When customers perceive a contact with the supplier to be important, they have higher expectations of the level of care they should receive.

Many products are bought as a package, of which customer care is a greater or smaller part. Among the factors that may be important are the following:

- Time taken.
- The importance of the service element of the package relative to other elements at different times in the relationship.
- How important it is for the customer to be in control.
- The degree of dependency on the supplier.
- The importance of the service to the customer.
- The degree of risk that is felt to attach to the supply of the service.
- The dependence of the service on staff or equipment.
- Contact with staff.

- Degree of control perceived in staff.
- Contact with other customers.
- Skill/expertise expected of staff.
- Degree of routine in encounters.
- Number and complexity of stages and service encounters.
- Emotions anticipated and experienced by customers at different stages.

The mix of factors is also affected by the characteristics and experience of individual customers. As a consequence, different individuals will view the same service in different ways. What is new and potentially stressful for one individual is routine to another, perhaps experienced, user of a service or product.

Given this important element, it appears likely that the role of the customer in the 'service-production' ('servuction') system can be increased according to the experience or number of occasions in which the customer makes use of the service or buys the product.

Levels of customer care may well be influenced thereby. While customers invariably expect minimum levels of care, they probably also have a desired level, which is influenced by the degree of experience they have of the organization. The greater experience they have, the more likely that they will entertain a perception of the level of care they receive.

These perceived levels contrast with actual levels, i.e. the levels the supplier says are provided in terms of customer-care activities. Perceptions of the levels of care are the strongest influence on satisfaction levels.

It is extremely important to define the 'minimum' levels of care expected by the customers. In many aspects these can be quantified very effectively, e.g. time taken to respond to a request for a repairman. Regular users will have a clear idea of desired and minimum standards, but how these are perceived will obviously vary across a group of customers. It is important for the company to identify minimum and 'optimum' levels. This would avoid the wastefulness and potential harm created by over-provision of certain aspects of customer care, e.g. having staff who are constantly pestering customers with offers of help.

Identifying the bands within which customer-care levels must be provided is particularly important. It is known that experience with the company providing the service or product, or with a competitor, provides a benchmark against which expectations are formed and delivery evaluated.

Identifying and analysing customer requirements are based on:

- Choosing customers.
- Researching and modelling needs.
- Determining care levels.
- Building flexibility in.

Activity 8.15

Briefly outline the issues and the problems that might arise if you were trying to collect information to determine customer requirements with regard to service levels for a wine bar in a busy city centre.

Compare your outline with that shown in the debriefing.

An outline of the practical steps in establishing a customer-care programme

It is very important to establish practical processes for achieving desired levels of customer care. Some of the most important practical steps are now summarized.

Identify customer needs and perceptions

This first step in establishing a customer-care programme illustrates, once again, that the start point is customer needs. We must clearly establish what these are and how our customer-care programme needs to be designed to meet them. We must also evaluate the perceptions that current and potential customers have with regard to our company and its standards of customer care.

Establish a mission statement

The mission statement was referred to earlier in the unit; the approach to customer care and its importance in the company must be a key part of this statement. We also need a widely accepted mission statement for the approach to customer care itself.

Set service level standards and specifications

Clear standards must be set for levels of customer care and the key elements to be included. Examples include standards for courtesy, credibility, communication, responsiveness, empathy with customer and confidentiality.

Establish management processes and communicate this to all staff

There should be clear specifications of how jobs should be done with regard to achieving customer-care objectives. This should include, for example:

- Who does what, and when – formal allocations of tasks and progress reviews.
- Information flows and systems required to implement customer-care programmes.
- The motivation, monitoring and control of people in the customer-care programme.
- Obviously responsibilities, and information on processes and procedures to be followed must be communicated to all staff.

Define tasks according to time factors

These factors include timing of recurrent work, seasonal factors, etc. This process should be accurately and comprehensively catalogued, and the programme of customer care must create systems by which the work can be handled according to the objectives of satisfying customer needs, and by using resources efficiently and cost effectively.

Establish a basic minimum level

Although customer-care programmes should be built around customer needs, wherever possible levels of customer care should meet the highest standards. However, it is also important to establish a baseline for standards of customer care, below which levels of customer care should not drop.

Ensure systems for effective response to complaints

Although the idea of a customer-care programme is to reduce complaints, and indeed to remove the need for them altogether, it is unlikely that all complaints can be removed in this way. The customer-care programme therefore must have clear systems and procedures for ensuring effective responses to customer complaints.

Secure management commitment

As stressed several times already in this unit, it is important to ensure commitment to customer-care programmes. It is especially important that this commitment is established, throughout all levels of management, but especially at the head of the organization.

Implement effective and continuous measurement and control systems

Again, we have stressed several times the importance of measuring and controlling the customer-care programme. It is pointless paying lip service to customer care, it must be supported by objective and rigorously enforced measurement and control systems.

Successful customer-care programmes

If programmes are to work, the following conditions must be met. Staff must be:

- Clear about the programme and their role in it.
- Committed to the programme.
- Well trained in programme needs.
- Sufficiently resourced to carry out their roles.
- Sufficiently skilled to carry out their roles.

The programme must:

- Provide clear benefits for the staff.
- Be reinforced by top management action, with effective implementation regimes, clear priorities, and sanctions and rewards.

Management must be:

- Informed about progress and effectiveness of staff performance.
- Provided with regular and appropriate information.
- The process must support marketing objectives and facilitate the work of staff towards its achievement.

Benefits of an effective customer-care programme

There is a range of clear benefits of an effective, long-term customer-care programme which marketers and top management should appreciate. We have touched on several of these benefits already but again, to summarize, an effective customer-care programme provides the following benefits:

- Helps to establish standards for customer care.
- Minimizes organizational confusion about what is required and why.
- Potentially offers a competitive edge.
- Helps to establish TQM quality control.
- Offers value added to customers.
- Promotes better understanding of customers.
- Can be very motivating to staff.
- Helps build customer relationships and improves customer retention.

Although all of these benefits are significant, the role of customer care in the last point in our list, namely building customer relationships and therefore improving customer retention, is, as we have already seen now accepted by marketers as being increasingly important. Because customer service delivery and the broader aspect of customer care are so powerful in helping build relationships and thereby retaining customers, customer service and customer care are vital aspects of relationship marketing. We shall return to this shortly in the unit.

Service delivery, customer care and the extended marketing mix

We have already touched on the fact that the marketing of service products is different to marketing physical products. We suggested that one of the major differences for the services marketer is the three additional marketing mix elements of 'people', 'physical evidence', and 'process'. Although we shall consider these further in the Unit 'Marketing in context' it is important that marketers understand the implications and the interplay between service delivery, customer care, and these three additional marketing mix elements. Some of these are outlined below.

- *People (internal staff)* It is important that there is commitment from all staff to customer care and that they are motivated. The 'people' element is central to effective service delivery and overall levels of customer care and it is vital therefore that there is investment in staff in terms of training and development in order to achieve predetermined levels of service delivery and customer care. Employee selection and motivation become central considerations, not just for the personnel department now, but for the marketer. If an organization's staff are badly trained, poorly selected, demoralized and unmotivated they cannot support good customer service delivery and they are unlikely to be interested in supporting adequate levels of customer care. More often than not, poor service delivery and customer care can ultimately be traced to weaknesses or problems in the people element of an organization's marketing mix. So, for example, staff should be guided into what represents an appropriate level of courtesy to customers. In order to ensure total quality management (TQM) internal quality groups should be devised and managed.

  Many of the market leaders in different industries have recognized the importance of the people element in providing effective customer care and again reflect this recognition in their mission statements.

- *Process* Processes should consider the customers' needs and perceptions with regard to adequate levels of service delivery and customer care. There should be customer support systems, TQM systems and good communications. Specifications should be written to ensure specific responses to customer complaints, to ensure minimal waiting times, minimize bottle-necks, etc.

  A good example of a company paying careful attention to the process element and its effect on customer care is McDonalds, which has designed its processes to ensure standardization with a view to minimizing waiting times, bottlenecks, etc.

- *Physical evidence* Elements such as good signage, staff uniforms, informative communications, must be planned and implemented to ensure that effective customer service delivery is maintained and a customer care ethos is achieved.

  Again, Interflora is a good example here. Although Interflora consists of 58,000 florists, effectively trading through their own trade association (which Interflora is), i.e. each business is an independent floristry business, elements of physical evidence are standardized throughout the world including, for example, the use of the Interfora logo, shop image, staff appearance, and so on. Even Interflora's trademark depicting the Roman god Mercury, serves to act as a common element of physical evidence, thereby forming a common bond between the worldwide network of florists which comprise Interflora whilst at the same time offering the customer the reassurance of a worldwide trademark.

In summary then, the integration of these three extended marketing mix elements is important to maximize the benefits of customer service delivery and customer-care programmes. In turn, and ultimately, these determine levels of customer satisfaction and the all-important levels of customer retention so important to relationship marketing.

Service delivery, customer care and relationship marketing

Remember, for any organization it is more efficient to keep customers rather than to keep finding new ones. We noted in the Unit 'The development of marketing and marketing orientation' that this is one of the key reasons for making relationship marketing so important. Put simply, a happy customer will come back for more. On the other hand, the evidence suggests that nearly 70% of most people will go elsewhere if they feel they are receiving indifferent levels of customer service. There are clear links then between customer service and customer care and the important relationship marketing concept. In particular:

- Organizations need to view any transaction as part of a long term goal.

- If the customer is satisfied with the product/service they have received for the price they have paid, they are more likely to return.

- A short-term outlook with lower levels of customer service might make higher short-term profits, but in the long run is likely to be less profitable.

- Trust is particularly important in relationship marketing, and hence it should be an important component of customer service. If a customer trusts an organization they are more likely to return. We must not forget, however, that trust is a two-way process. Not only must the customer trust the organization not to take advantage of them, but the business must also learn to trust its customers.

Customer service, by underpinning better relationships between an organization and its customers, helps to transform exchange relationships into 'win-win' rather than 'win-lose' ones.

Service delivery, customer care and new technology

As we have seen throughout, technology is changing marketing and marketing practices. Of particular importance with regard to service delivery and customer care in this respect, is the fact that many of the technological developments in marketing are meaning that relationships with customers often take place with no direct physical contact of any kind, but rather are relationships which operate via the ether of the Internet or perhaps some of the direct marketing channels such as direct response television.

Given that amongst the strongest relationships individuals have with other parties are those which are based on personal relationships involving direct contact, for example, and certainly direct communication, the less personal nature of some of contemporary marketing in some ways makes service delivery and customer care more problematical. Rather than thinking about developing customer care through these personal relationships with customers the marketer must think of other ways to ensure adequate levels of customer service and care and to develop long-term relationships with customers. Information on customers and particularly databases can be extremely useful here.

Databases and customer care

A customer database is a record system of information on customers. Increasingly, of course, these record systems are held on computer. This record system will include information such as, for example, customer purchases, expenditure, credit ratings, complaints, and so on. This information obviously can help in developing effective marketing mix programmes, but is particularly useful in developing systems of effective customer service delivery and customer care. The database can be central to a customer care programme and in particular where relationships with customers are themselves based on the Internet for example.

The database can help with customer service and customer care in the following ways.

- The database can be used to keep a record of customer contacts and any complaints.
- The database can be used to assess what customers want so that marketing programmes, for example, can be more closely targeted towards customers.
- We can use the database to keep ahead of customers and their needs by, for example, forecasting their future requirements.
- Data can be analyzed to discover any patterns, e.g. product faults, customer profiles, etc., thereby making it possible to improve the customer's experience of the exchange process.

International aspects of service delivery and customer care

Clearly, companies which operate in international markets want to develop similar standards of customer service delivery and customer care throughout their operations. Note how our Interflora example illustrates how a company-wide commitment to customer care throughout different markets in different parts of the world can help build the image of a company, develop more effective relationships with customers and serve as a standard for operating procedures for all staff. If a customer has a satisfactory experience with a company in one country then it is much more likely that customer will seek to use the same company when he or she purchases elsewhere in the world. On the other hand, if a customer experiences different levels of service and customer care from the same company in different parts of the world this is likely to lead to the customer being apprehensive and anxious about using the same supplier. However, customer-care programmes, including the selection of the level of customer care necessary and appropriate, are amongst the most difficult areas of the marketing programme to standardize. There are several reasons for this, but amongst one of the most important are differences in cultural practice in different parts of the world with regard to what is expected in terms of customer service and customer care. Almost without exception, the American customer expects, and in America largely gets, extremely high standards of customer service and care. In parts of Europe, however, including the United Kingdom, customers may not expect, and in fact positively dislike, some of the elements of customer service and care which are considered normal in the United States of America. In designing customer service and customer care programmes therefore, the marketer has to consider these cultural differences and reflect them in the design of customer service and customer care programmes. Notwithstanding this though, the international marketer should try to ensure consistent approaches to customer service and care in different parts of the world. Again, people, process and physical evidence are all important here. In designing an international effective customer-care programme many of the issues and steps for planning a purely domestic customer-care programme are to be found. In essence, and by way of reminding you of some of these issues and steps, the following should be considered:

- Identify customer needs and perceptions for each market.
- Establish a mission statement.
- Set service level standards and specifications reflecting individual country requirements but guided by an overall customer charter which reflects the mission statement and outlines measurable criteria/standards to be attained.
- Establish management processes and communicate these to all staff.
- Define specific tasks as regards customer-care elements for each country.

- Establish basic minimum levels of customer care.
- Ensure effective response systems for identifying, tracking and responding to complaints.
- Ensure management and staff commitment to programmes through for example, effective training and remuneration programmes.
- Ensure effective and continuous measurement of the customer-care programmes.

Summary

In this unit you have learned about the importance and scope of customer service and the broader concept of customer care of which customer service decisions form but a part. We have seen that:

- Customer service is an increasingly important element in customer choice and hence the marketing mix.
- Customer care is an all-embracing approach, which encompasses customer service but covers activities at the pre-, during-, and post-transaction stages of dealing with customers. Customer care needs to be part of the corporate culture.
- Total Quality Management is a key part of customer-care programmes.
- Adequate levels of customer service and care should be carefully related to marketing objectives and strategies.
- Customer service and care programmes need to be based on information about customer needs and requirements.
- The implementation of a customer service and care programmes should follow a series of pre-determined steps and stages.
- There are substantial benefits to be gained by all parties from the establishment of effective customer service and care programmes.
- The extended marketing mix elements are particularly important when it comes to considering customer service and care.
- Developing programmes for international levels of customer service gives rise to additional complexities, but in particular the marketer must consider differences in cultural circumstances and factors in designing and implementing customer-care programmes in international markets.
- Effective customer care can also be problematical when using some of the newer technologies and channels to market to customers such as for example, the Internet.
- There is considerable overlap and inter-relationship between customer service and customer care programmes and the increasingly important aspects of customer retention and relationship marketing.

Further study and examination preparation

Now do these questions:

Question 8.1

Identify the main reason for poor customer care.

Question 8.2

What are the main steps involved in planning a customer care programme?

Question 8.3

What are the main benefits of a successful customer care strategy?

Question 8.4

Explain the importance of total quality management.

Question 8.5

What are the three extended services mix elements and what is their significance in relation to customer care?

Previous examination question

Study tip

This question is taken from Fundamentals of Marketing paper December 2000 Question 5. Remember, you can access the full specimen answer for this question on the following website addresses: www.marketingonline.co.uk or www.bh.com/marketing.

Question E8

You work for an airline company and you have just been approached by a business traveller who has a complaint about the level of service which she has just experienced. The customer was delayed by one hour on an outward domestic flight and also by one hour on the return journey later that day. The main emphasis of her complaint was the lack of information about these delays.

    a. What are the practical approaches which could be undertaken by this organization to improve its standard of customer care.

(8 marks)

    b. Explain the practical steps in establishing an effective customer care programme.

(12 marks)
(20 marks in total)

Bibliography

F. Brassington, S. Pettitt, *Principles of Marketing: 2nd Edn*, Chap 18, 2000.

Further reading

D. Chaffey, Maher, Johnston, Ellis-Chadwick, *Internet Marketing*, FT/Prentice-Hall, 2000.

S. Dibb, L. Simpkin, W. Pride, O. C. Ferrell, *Marketing Concepts and Strategies: 4th European Edn*, Chap 1, Houghton, Mifflin, 2000.

G. Lancaster, L. Massingham, R. Ashford, *Essentials of Marketing: 4th Edn,* Chap 13, McGraw-Hill, 2002.

Objectives

By the end of this unit you will:

- Understand the importance of contextual setting in influencing the selection of, and emphasis given to, marketing mix tools and the additional mix components in appropriate contextual settings (4.1, 3.3).

- Understand the differences in the characteristics of various types of marketing context (4.2).

- Be able to compare and contrast the marketing activities of organizations that operate and compete in different contextual settings (4.3).

- Understand some of the key contemporary contextual factors affecting the marketing mix including information and communication technology, international and global dimensions, and the existing and potential impacts of the virtual market place (3.15, 4.4, 4.5).

Study guide

In many ways this unit seeks to draw together some of the key issues and concepts that we have considered in previous units. We shall see that, although of necessity we have to consider the individual elements of the marketing mix separately, in practice, it is vital that the marketer ensures these individual elements are combined and co-ordinated in planned marketing programmes. Many factors influence what is an appropriate combination and use of the marketing mix elements in marketing programmes including many of the factors considered in our unit 'Marketing Planning' encompassing, for example, opportunities and threats, company strengths and weaknesses and the selection of marketing strategies including the selection of target markets and positioning strategies. In addition, however, it is now recognized that the use and combination of the marketing mix elements is greatly influenced by the context in which these tools are applied. These contextual settings for marketing encompass in particular FMCG contexts, business to business (supply chain) contexts, large or capital project based contexts, services contexts, voluntary and not-for-profit contexts and small and medium enterprise (SMEs) contexts. We shall therefore compare and contrast the marketing activities and particularly the use of the marketing mix tools of organizations that operate and compete in these different contextual settings.

In this unit we shall also take the opportunity to explore some of the more recent contemporary developments affecting marketing activities and marketing mix decisions. In particular we shall draw together some of the main effects of information and communication technology which have been considered throughout the units in the coursebook and which are affecting the development and implementation of the marketing mix in organizations. We shall also, however, be considering the existing and potential impacts of the so-called 'virtual market place' on the pattern of marketing activities in different contexts.

We would expect you to take about 4 hours to work through this Unit and suggest you allow a further 3 to 4 hours to undertake the various activities suggested. Other than your notebook and writing equipment, you will not need anything further to complete this unit.

The nature and importance of contextual settings for marketing

As you would expect in a marketing fundamentals programme much of what we have considered in the units of this coursebook with regard to the tools and techniques of marketing and their application, the basic principles of marketing, if you like, are the same irrespective of the type of organization or market. So, for example, the basic elements of the marketing planning process, the importance of marketing objectives, effective segmentation, targeting and positioning etc. are the same for all organizations and markets. However, again as you would expect, there are differences with regard to the practice of marketing according to the context in which marketing activities take place. Of particular importance with regard to different contexts are the different types of markets and organizations in which marketing is practised and applied. This is particularly true with regard to the selection of and the emphasis given to the different marketing mix tools and their use and combination in different market and organizational settings. Suggesting this, however, raises the issue of what are the key types of marketing context, and in particular how can we classify these contexts into different types so as to be able to explore and discuss how the selection and emphasis given to the marketing mix tools may differ between these different contexts. Although there are various ways of classifying contextual settings the following represent some of the key and accepted classifications of contextual settings with regard to marketing.

- Fast moving consumer goods (FMCG).
- Business-to-business.
- Large or capital projects.
- Small and medium-sized enterprises (SMEs).
- Voluntary and not-for-profit organizations.
- Services.

Study Tip

You will note that these are the different contextual settings identified in the syllabus for marketing fundamentals. For obvious reasons then we have organized our discussion on the different contexts in this unit around these.

Fast moving consumer goods (FMCG)

Our first contextual setting is that of fast moving consumer goods markets (FMCGs). Consumer goods markets are markets where the customer is purchasing products and services for their own or perhaps their family's use. The principle motives for purchase, therefore, are personal in nature. This type of customer then may be contrasted with those buyers who are purchasing primarily for their organizations or institutions and hence are business-to-business customers purchasing, for example, raw materials and components etc. in the supply chain and/ or large or capital project based products and services for organizational motives.

In fact, fast moving consumer goods represent only a sub-element of consumer goods purchasing and marketing. FMCG contexts are where customers are purchasing products or services for personal reasons but are products and services which generally involve relatively low financial outlays, are bought frequently and are generally non-durable. They include, therefore, products such as toothpaste, confectionery, grocery products, some of the more frequently purchased electrical items such as, say, batteries, light bulbs, and so on. FMCGs therefore may be contrasted with, for example, durable consumer goods such as refrigerators, cars, computers and even non-durable consumer purchases which involve large infrequent outlays such as, for example, holidays, houses, and so on. We have to be careful, therefore, in discussing how the marketing mix tools may vary within the broad category of consumer goods as there are so many different types of consumer goods contexts. However, it is fair to say that within the consumer goods category, fast moving consumer goods marketing involves probably the most distinct differences in the use and application of the marketing mix tools compared to, for example, our business-to-business and large or capital project based contexts. Put another way, FMCG marketing lies at the extreme, if you like, of consumer goods marketing when it comes to the application of the marketing mix tools. Bearing this in mind, the following represent some of the key characteristics of the FMCG context and the implications for the application of the marketing tools.

As already mentioned, FMCG contexts involves marketing to customers who are buying generally low financial outlay products, bought frequently, and with little information search or alternative evaluation by customers. In this type of context, although again we find all sorts of different combinations of the marketing mix according to an individual company's positioning strategy and so on, as a generalization when it comes to the mix elements we might expect to find the following:

Aspects of the product element of the mix which are particularly important in FMCG contexts include branding, packaging, and logos and design. Branding and brand image in particular are important as these provide reassurance for a customer and facilitate relatively easy brand choice. With regard to the promotional element of the mix there is likely to be heavy emphasis on advertising rather than personal selling. Advertising will generally be aimed at the mass market and will again tend to stress brand image and persuasive advertising messages rather than detailed factual messages. The importance and role of price in FMCG marketing varies enormously across different products and markets, but value for money is likely to be particularly important and predominate in customer choice. Negotiation between buyer and seller regarding price is likely to be used infrequently in FMCG markets. Nor is tendering widely used, though the importance and prevalence of negotiation will depend upon the culture in a market. In some cultures therefore, negotiation is the order of the day even for fast moving consumer goods. The availability of credit and payment terms may be important facets of pricing in consumer markets generally, but are less likely to be important in the case of FMCG markets due to the relatively low outlays involved. Many FMCG products and brands have short product lifecycles, often due to fashion influences or consumers simply becoming bored. New product development and innovation is important in FMCG markets then, if only by way of, for example, repositioning, repackaging etc. so as to keep customers interested. Distribution for FMCG goods will often need to be intensive and will normally take place through intermediaries and particularly of course, retailers. Although relationship marketing, particularly through the brand element of the marketing mix, may still be important in FMCG markets, the degree of brand switching in this type of market often means that relationships are difficult to develop and maintain with customers. Finally, although we should not dismiss it entirely, customer service plays a less important role in FMCG marketing than it does in, for example, business-to-business markets, large or capital project-based marketing, or of course services marketing.

In planning the marketing mix in FMCG markets, as indeed in all marketing planning, it is important to understand the nature of the consumer buying decision process and the factors which affect this. With regard to this decision process and the factors which affect this for fast moving consumer goods, a simple model is useful.

Problem recognition
↓
Information search
↓
Evaluation of alternatives
↓
Purchase decision
↓
Post purchase behaviour

Figure 9.1   A model of consumer buyer behaviour

- *Need recognition*   This is the start point of the buying process for a fast moving consumer good. Purchasing is essentially a problem solving process. So unless the consumer perceives there is a problem, then no purchasing will take place.

  The marketer therefore needs to understand the process of problem recognition and sometimes will attempt to prompt it. So, for example, advertising and promotion may be designed to convince customers that their current products and brands could be improved. Remember, in fast moving consumer goods markets advertising and promotion are amongst the most heavily used elements of the marketing mix.

- *Information search*   Having recognized that they have a problem, the next step in the purchasing process is to search for information regarding products and brands which may offer a solution to this problem. Information search can be based on existing information in the consumer's memory for example, but sometimes the customer will search for information from a variety of sources including, e.g. friends, relatives, sales persons, magazines and other forms of marketer dominated sources of information.

  Obviously the marketer of fast moving consumer goods must ensure that the customer is provided with sufficient information in order to make a decision and obviously will be concerned to ensure that this information causes the customer to prefer the marketer's product and brand offerings.

- *Evaluation of alternatives*   The information collected through the process of search will be used to evaluate the various alternatives on offer. Essentially this is part of the process where the customer makes a choice.

  The marketer must understand how alternatives are evaluated and particularly the choice criteria in this process. Evaluation criteria are amongst the most important facets in the buying process affecting the selection of the marketing mix tools. Obviously if customers are primarily interested in price in choice then the marketing mix must reflect this.

- *Purchase Decision*   This is the stage of the process where the customer actually makes the purchase choice. It may be felt that by this time the customer is beyond the reach of the marketer in as much as the decision is made. However, the marketer can still influence the customer at this stage. So, for example, a customer may have decided on the product and brand to be purchased, but if this is out of stock due to, say, poor distribution, then the customer may still make a different purchase choice at this stage.

- *Post-purchase evaluation*   Having made the purchase the customer must then evaluate this. So, for example, the customer will assess if they are satisfied with the decision. We know that often customers will be anxious about whether they have made the right choice or not. Every effort, therefore, must be made by the marketer to assure the customer that they have. One way of doing this, for example, is to write to the customer assuring them that they have made the right choice and reminding the customer that, if they have any problems or worries about the purchase, these can be discussed with the supplier.

Study tip

The extent to which the customer will pass through each and every stage of this buying process varies considerably. It is useful to remember that there are three types of decision making or purchasing situation. ***Extended decision making*** involves all the steps in the purchasing process outlined above and is normally associated with expensive and/or risky purchases such as the purchase of a new car. The second type of decision making is ***limited decision making.*** Here, although the customer may pass though all the stages, they may only spend comparatively little time and effort at some of the stages in the process. So, for example, the customer may spend comparatively little time searching for information and/or evaluating alternatives. This type of purchasing decision making often occurs where the customer has some experience of the product or service in question, or for other reasons is not prepared to spend a long time making the purchase. Finally, the third type of decision making process is ***routine response behaviour.*** Usually associated with frequently purchased low-cost items, here the purchasing process is almost automatic. Very little time, if any, is spent searching and evaluating alternatives, rather the customer here goes straight from problem recognition to choosing, for example, a favourite brand. Most fast moving consumer goods fall into the routine response behaviour.

What factors influence FMCG purchasing behaviour?

In addition to understanding the steps in the purchasing decision process for fast moving consumer goods, the marketer must understand the factors affecting purchasing behaviour. The problem here is that potentially very many factors can come into play. However, some of the most important influences on FMCG buying decisions are as follows.

- *Personal factors*   These factors include factors such as demographics, e.g. age, sex, race, income. They also encompass situational factors such as, say, the amount of time available to the consumer when making the purchase decision. Finally, personal factors include the level of involvement and commitment the individual has when making the purchase.

- *Psychological factors*   Psychological factors include a whole host of factors pertaining to an individual's overall and purchasing behaviour. We know that some of the more important of these factors include: perceptions, motives, learning, attitudes and personality. Essentially, these factors operate internally but they can be influenced, or at least taken account of by the marketer. So, for example, we know that personality influences both product and brand choice. The extrovert personality is more likely to choose a different brand to the introvert.

- *Social/cultural factors*   These factors too are extremely important in influencing the purchasing process and product and brand choice. Amongst the most important social factors known to influence consumers are roles and family influences, reference groups, social classes, culture and sub-culture. We know, for example, that the choice of a newspaper is heavily influenced by social class as are products such as holidays, cars, cosmetics, etc.

Social/cultural factors in purchase choice are important in many markets but are particularly so for the international marketer.

Nestlé for example, adapt their coffee brand products to social/cultural factors in different parts of the world. In the United Kingdom where coffee and coffee drinking tends to have strong socializing overtones, coffee brands are advertised in social settings or situations, such as, for example, friends gathering together for a drink. In Germany and France, however, although obviously there are still social aspects, culturally the emphasis in coffee choice and drinking tends to be on the taste of the coffee.

These, then are some of the major considerations which stem from the contextual setting for FMCG markets. We can now turn our attention to the business-to-business context.

Business-to-business

As you already know here the marketer is targeting other organizations or institutions as customers. Remember that the business-to-business market customer differs from the consumer market customer in as much as they are primarily purchasing for organizational purposes and motives rather than personal ones. As with FMCG marketing, and for that matter any marketing context, in planning marketing mix programmes the marketer can benefit from an understanding of the nature of the customer and in particular the buying process and the factors which affect this. As we suggested with FMCG marketing then, it is useful, indeed essential for the marketer to understand the behaviour of business-to-business customers. In achieving this understanding the marketer can usefully address the following questions with regard to business-to-business buyer behaviour.

Who is involved in the buying process?

In contrast to FMCG markets there are often many people involved in the buying decision making process in business-to-business markets. Of particular importance are the different roles which these different people may play.

In order to help you understand these different roles better we shall use the example of the purchase of a new piece of production machinery by a business customer.

- *Initiators*　These are the persons who start the process of buying. So, for example, the buying process may be initiated by, say, the production department in the organization who feel that an existing piece of production machinery is near to the end of its useful life.

- *Influencers*　Influencers can affect the buying decision in different ways, e.g. technical people may have helped in a major or minor way to develop the product specification for the new piece of machinery.

- *Deciders*　These are the people who make the actual buying decision. In this case, the deciders might be, for example, the production director or even the chief executive.

- *Buyers*　These people have the authority to sign orders and make the actual purchase in the organization. They may also help to shape the specification but their principal role is in supplier negotiation and selection. In our case, and indeed in most situations, this is likely to be the purchasing department.

- *Users*　Users are the people who will be working with, or using, the product or service purchased. In our example, users are the machine operators. It makes sense for a purchasing organization to ask operatives what problems they have had in using a particular piece of machinery and what features of a proposed new piece of equipment would help them perform their jobs more effectively.

We can see then that buying behaviour in business-to-business settings can involve several individuals and roles which combine to effect what is essentially a group purpose. It is very important, therefore, for the marketer to identify the individuals and/or functions comprising this group and performing the range of roles outlined above. In marketing we refer to the individuals/functions involved in the buying process as the *decision making unit* (DMU).

Business-to-business marketers should be clear about the members of the DMU and direct their marketing efforts accordingly.

How do they buy?: a model of industrial buyer behaviour

As with FMCG purchasing, purchase decisions in business-to-business markets can usefully be looked at as a series of steps or stages in a problem-solving process. These are shown in Figure 9.2.

Problem recognition

↓

Develop product specification to solve problem

↓

Supplier search

↓

Supplier evaluation relative to specifications

↓

Supplier selection

↓

Product ordering/purchase

↓

Performance review

Figure 9.2 *A model of business buyer behaviour*

We can see that this process is very similar in nature to that described for consumer product purchasing. However, there are more steps in the process and the process itself is usually more formalized. Again, though, the marketer, by understanding the steps in the process, is able to develop appropriate marketing strategies for each stage. So, for example, it is important to know what product specifications have been set by the business purchaser and wherever possible, to try and influence this in favour of your particular products and services. Similarly, we need to understand again how purchasers search for products and suppliers and the criteria used to evaluate them.

Study tip

As with consumer product purchasing, not all industrial purchasing processes involve all of the steps or at least to the same degree. You will recall that we earlier distinguished between extended decision making, limited decision making and routine response types of purchasing in consumer markets. The industrial equivalents of these different types of purchasing processes are: ***new task*** purchasing; ***modified rebuys;*** and ***straight rebuy*** purchases.

Why do they buy?

You will recall that we have already stressed the fact that a key difference between business and consumer buyers is the fact that business buyers buy in order to further their organization's objectives and plans. The motives for purchase, therefore, for the business buyer are somewhat different. Generally speaking, the business buyers' motives are much more rational than their consumer counterparts with, for example, little or no impulse purchasing. Similarly, because the business buyer is often interested primarily in costs and profit, price and negotiation on price and terms is likely to be much more important.

What factors affect?

If anything, the range of factors affecting business buyers is greater and more complex than for the consumer purchasing process. This is principally because, although individual and psychological factors are likely to be less important, the business purchasing process takes place in the context of an organization, thereby introducing several new factors into the buying process. The most important factors affecting the business buying process which the marketer must seek to analyse and understand through marketing research are as follows:

- *Environmental factors* The range of uncontrollable factors which affect all marketers also affect their customers. These include political factors, regulations and laws, economic factors and technological factors. So, for example, new legislation may affect the specifications which customers need a supplier to meet.

  A good example of this is in the car industry where engine component suppliers must meet increasingly stringent legislation regarding, for example, emission levels.

- *Interpersonal factors* The notion of a decision-making unit means that very often relationships amongst the people in this unit can have a key influence on purchasing. So, for example, conflict between, for example, marketing and production functions in the purchasing organization may affect the choice of a supplier.

  As an example of the sources of such conflict the marketer in an organization may prefer to use a supplier who can supply the latest technology, which may give the marketer's company an opportunity to develop a competitive edge over other companies in the market place. On the other hand, the production management of an organization may prefer a supplier who, though not at the cutting edge of technology, can supply products and services using tried and tested technology.

- *Organizational factors* The fact that purchasing takes place in the context of an organization means that the marketer must assess and understand things such as an organization's purchasing policies and systems. For example, some organizations may require suppliers to initially tender through a closed tender system for business.

  Amongst some of the best examples of such organizations are government or institutional buyers such as, for example, those that buy for, say, defence related products where closed tendering is the norm.

- *Individual factors* Finally, although business buying is by its very nature, much more constrained and formal than its consumer counterpart, we must not forget that industrial customers are also individuals and are therefore affected by things such as their education and background, personal preferences regarding suppliers and their sales persons, etc.

These factors are likely to be particularly important where there is a strong professional network. Examples would include marketing products to the medical industry or to, say, the legal profession.

These differences in the nature of business buyers and the purchasing process allied to the different motives for purchase give rise to several differences when it comes to applying the marketing mix tools in business-to-business markets. These are outlined and discussed below.

The marketing mix elements in business-to-business markets

In business-to-business markets, the following are likely to be more significant in supplier and brand choice: quality assurance, delivery, speed and reliability, price and after-sales and technical service. The reliability of the product, together with the degree of back-up service being offered is a crucial part of the marketing mix in business-to-business markets. In terms of the promotional element of the mix, much more emphasis is likely to be placed on personal selling as opposed to the advertising element. We have to be careful not to assume that business-to-business products are always bought on price. They are not. It is value that counts. However, obviously price is always going to be a key factor in the marketing mix. Prices are much more likely to be negotiated in the business-to-business market and we may get different processes for pricing and particularly quoting prices, such as, for example, tendering. Finally, in business-to-business markets, although intermediaries are used, particularly in export and international markets, often distribution is direct.

Before we move on to discussing our other contexts for marketing it might be useful to summarize our discussion of FMCG and business-to-business marketing by reiterating some of the key differences between these two marketing contexts and the implications of these for the use of the various marketing mix tools.

A brief summary of some of the suggested differences between marketing in FMCG versus business-to-business markets is shown in Table 9.1.

Table 9.1 *FMCG and Business to business markets compared*

FMCG markets	Business to business markets
Buyer/buying situations	
Individual/family	Group/organizational
Personal motives	Organizational requirements
Often unplanned/less rational	Planned/rational
Not specialist buyers	Trained/professional
Less informed	Well informed
Little power	Substantial power
Marketing mix Product	
Often standardized	Often customized
Less technical	More technical
Less service	More service
Price	
Less important	More important
Rarely negotiated	Frequently negotiated
Few tenders/bids	Often tenders/bids
Promotion	
Emphasis on non-personal	Emphasis on personal
Place	
Less direct	Usually direct
Logistics important	Logistics vital

Activity 9.1

Try to find an example of a product that is marketed in both business and consumer markets, e.g. a cleaning product, writing paper and envelopes, coffee, etc. Compare and contrast the ways in which this product might be marketed to each of these different markets, with particular respect to the use of the marketing mix.

Large or capital project-based contexts

A considerable amount of marketing activity centres around the marketing of large or capital project-based products. In fact the marketing context here is essentially our business-to-business context already outlined and discussed. Many of the factors that affect the business-to-business marketer then including the complexity of the decision making process, group influences and the motives for purchase also affect the marketer concerned with large or capital project-based products. However, when marketing large or capital project-based products, if anything, heightens and emphasizes some of the differences we have described in the marketing mix elements between FMCG and business-to-business markets.

So for example, in this context personal selling as an element of the promotional aspect of the mix becomes even more important and critical. Most large or capital-based projects require substantial expertise and both technical and commercial skills on the part of the sales person. Although advertising and particularly corporate advertising and PR may still play a role, it is personal selling which will dominate. In addition, price negotiation again is even more important. After all, here the customer is considering substantial outlays which commit his/her organization to long time scales. Because of this, the customer will be concerned to ensure long term continuity of, for example, service backup from the supplier. Related to this, full contract or turnkey services may be expected by the customer whereby the supplier will undertake to make all necessary arrangements to for example, plan, install, and service and maintain machinery and buildings etc. The service element will be particularly important even though the customer may be specifying highly technical products. Distribution will almost certainly be direct in this marketing context.

Small-and medium-sized enterprises (SMEs)

Although there is perhaps an understandable tendency to think of marketing being applied in large organizations, we should not forget that in many countries the smaller company is the predominant business unit. In addition, it is increasingly recognized that the small to medium sized new entrepreneurial business often represents the large multinational of the future. Many governments, therefore, are interested in helping SMEs to become established and eventually grow.

Until relatively recently, however, SMEs have been slow to take up and use the concepts and tools of modern marketing. To be fair, this has been due in part to a perhaps unwitting attitude in many textbooks, where the application of marketing is often only discussed in the context of the large company. If anything, however, the small company needs to be even more marketing-oriented than its larger counterpart, and certainly there is nothing in marketing that the smaller organization cannot adopt. The basic concept and tools of marketing are essentially the same whether applied to the one-person business or the large multinational. However, it would be unrealistic to expect that these tools would be used in precisely the same way in both types of organization. The following are some of the considerations in applying marketing tools and in particular the marketing mix in SMEs. We first list some of the limitations inherent in most SMEs compared to their larger cousins, followed by the implications of these limitations for planning and applying some of the tools of marketing we have discussed so far in earlier units of the coursebook.

Financial limitations

Clearly the absolute amount of finance available to the smaller business is often very restricted. In turn this means, of course, that extensive and expensive market research or advertising campaigns are out of the question. The smaller business simply cannot afford, for example, national TV advertising or a full test market, and you should therefore be careful to take account of this where appropriate in, say, mini-case questions.

Staff/specialist limitations

In the larger company specialization is the order of the day. Marketing functions are broken down into more and more specialized areas, with specialist marketing, researchers, corporate planners, distribution specialists and so on. In the smaller business only one person may be responsible for all these functions and, in the case of the one-man business, for all the other functions as well.

This means that the smaller business has much more restricted internal access to specialist marketing expertise, and may therefore have to make more use of outside help and advice for planning and control.

Competitive limitations

Clearly many small businesses compete with larger ones. Again the small businesses simply do not have the resources to compete head on with their larger rivals. Particularly when it comes to competing on price, the smaller business is at a disadvantage, but also the smaller business, as we shall see, is often restricted in the range and types of market in which it can compete.

None of these limitations mean that the smaller business cannot be just as successful and profitable through the use of effective marketing as a large one. As you have already seen, the smaller business has a number of built-in advantages. However, the limitations do mean that a slightly different approach to the application of some of the marketing tools discussed in earlier units has to be adopted.

Activity 9.2

Before proceeding, see if you can think of any examples of how the application of the marketing tools might have to differ, owing to the limitations of the small business.

Market analysis and research

Although the elements of market analysis and research are similar for the smaller business, both finance and marketing expertise (as regards techniques of research) may be severely restricted. However, this does not mean that marketing analysis and research should not be carried out – indeed they are vital. Even without expensive and sophisticated marketing research, the smaller business can do much to improve its market intelligence. Here are some of the more useful sources and techniques for the smaller company.

The smaller business in particular must make the fullest possible use of secondary sources of data. In the larger business the use of desk research is often the first step in analysing a marketing problem. In the smaller one it may be the only one.

Examples of useful sources of marketing research information for the smaller business include:

- Internal sources: sales statistics, customer information, accountancy information, sales reports, etc.
- Central libraries.
- Yellow Pages and trade directories.
- Chambers of commerce, local authorities, banks.
- Local colleges/universities.
- Government sources.

In fact, in most countries government sources of information are likely to be the most important and potentially most useful sources of secondary information for the smaller business.

Syndicated research

Syndicated research occurs where a group of research buyers share the cost and fundings of research among themselves. Because of this, syndicated research is of particular relevance to the smaller business that cannot afford its own tailor-made research study but needs information over and above that available from secondary sources. The majority of such syndicated research services are in fact conducted by the larger marketing research agencies, and the results are sold to whoever will buy. In the UK syndicated research services include:

- Retail Audits (A C Nielsen Company).
- Target Group Index (British Market Research Bureau).
- National Readership Survey (Research Bureau Ltd).

Activity 9.3

These are examples of syndicated research organizations available in the United Kingdom. If you are not from the United Kingdom, see if you can find examples of similar syndicated research services in your own country.

In recent years a number of market research companies have begun to produce specialized 'multi-client' research, in which a report is prepared for a limited number of companies that are prepared to commission and share the research between them.

Shared research

This type of research can be particularly cost-effective for the smaller company. Here some of the costs and field work are shared by a number of companies but the results are not. 'Omnibus' surveys are regular research surveys undertaken by the use of a predetermined sampling frame and methodology. A smaller business can 'buy a seat' on the omnibus by adding its own questions.

Omnibus research has the major advantage of low cost, as the field-work costs are shared by all participating companies. The number of questions that can be added to an omnibus is, however, generally limited to between six and ten and, because the respondents will be asked questions about a variety of products in the same interview, questions are best kept short and factual to avoid respondent fatigue.

Product decisions

Even in a small business product decisions are still among the most important that the company will take.

Once again financial limitations will normally prohibit expensive research and development programmes, but the smaller business can develop ideas for new products from a number of sources. For example:

- Customers.
- Competitors.
- Trade publications.
- Patent brokers.
- Product-licensing information services.

As with marketing research, government help is often at hand. For example, in the UK the Department of Trade and Industry will help with innovation or the introduction of new technologies.

Pricing decisions

The small business must price its products so as to achieve long-run marketing and financial objectives. Again, the general consideration and approaches to pricing strategies are the same in the small as in the large business but the smaller company can tend to neglect one or two basic pointers, namely:

- As we have seen, prices should be related to the market and not solely to costs. Smaller companies often rely too heavily on cost-based approaches to pricing.

- Although the smaller business may have fewer overheads than its larger counterpart, under-pricing is dangerous. The evidence suggests that more companies fail from under-pricing than over-pricing. The smaller business should be looking for ways in which to charge a premium price, e.g. for better delivery, after-sales service, and so on.

Promotional decisions

It is in this element of the marketing mix that we can observe some of the greatest differences between small and large businesses. Once again these differences stem largely from the small business's limited financial resources. In the smaller business all the elements of a co-ordinated promotional mix – personal selling, public relations and publicity, advertising and sales promotion – can and should be used. However, as previously noted, the smaller business simply has not the financial resources to undertake expensive promotional campaigns. Television advertising and some of the more expensive magazine and colour supplements are simply out of the question. Wherever possible, the smaller business needs to make use of more focused campaigns and media, together with the use of 'free' promotion that well-organized public relations can bring. Below are listed some of the more appropriate forms of promotion and media for the smaller business:

- Local newspapers.
- Local commercial radio.
- Trade magazines and directories.
- Yellow Pages.
- Sponsorship of local events, sports teams, etc.
- Exhibitions.
- Press releases.
- Direct mail.
- Websites.

Place decisions

In terms of the place element of the promotional mix the small business may find that it has to make more use of 'agents' and 'dealers' rather than employing its own sales force.

Marketing strategies for SMEs

There is now substantial evidence to show that marketing strategy is dependent on each firm's size and position in its industry. Understandably, large firms can implement certain strategies not affordable by small ones.

As far as the small business is concerned a focus strategy is usually by far the most effective. Rather than trying to achieve lower costs or highly differentiated products, the smaller business is better focusing on specialist market segments where it can compete effectively.

This type of strategy is also called 'niche marketing', where the company concentrates on smaller, more specialized parts of the market that larger companies are likely to ignore. Such niche marketing allows both more efficient operations and the development of customer goodwill and loyalty.

Question 9.2

In what ways, i.e. on what bases, might the SME choose to specialize in niche markets?

Voluntary and not-for-profit organizations

Marketing is increasingly being applied outside of the traditional profit-making sector. Hospitals, charities, museums and so on are all examples of voluntary and not-for-profit organizations using the tools of marketing. Often the marketing mix in such organizations is combined and applied in very different ways to their profit-making counterparts. Perhaps one of the most obvious differences in the marketing mix for these organizations is the absence of price in the marketing mix. Many do not actually set prices for their products and services, although of course there is always a cost and someone must pay for them. Very often the voluntary and not-for-profit organization will emphasize organizational or corporate image as opposed to, say, brand image in the promotional mix. Finally, many of these organizations 'sell' direct to the customer and hence have very different channels of distribution.

Obviously, voluntary and not-for-profit organizations primarily exist to achieve objectives other than the conventional business objectives of profit, return on capital, etc. This description, however, includes a very wide range of diverse types of organization, e.g. public organizations such as the army, local fire services, local authorities and so on, through to hospitals, charities, churches and religious causes, and political parties. Understandably, with this range of organizations we can expect to find differences in their approaches to marketing and their use of the marketing tools. However, most of the concepts and tools discussed in earlier units can be applied to these organizations. Some of the special characteristics of such organizations that need to be considered in developing marketing plans and programmes are the following:

- Like services, the products provided by such organizations are often intangible and therefore are different when it comes to marketing them.

- 'Customers' may be more difficult to identify than in the profit-making organization. Very often there are several diverse groups that will need to be targeted. It is often more appropriate to define a target public or a range of stakeholders than target customers.

- The marketing objectives of voluntary and not-for-profit organizations are generally set in terms of achieving a desired response, such as a financial contribution, increased use of the service, a vote, etc.

The following is a brief outline of how these characteristics of the voluntary and not-for-profit organization give rise to differences in the application of the tools of the marketing mix:

- *Products* are usually intangible and may be an idea or service.

- *Price* is often difficult to define and may often be associated more with the exchange of things such as time and effort to help a charitable cause or a political party rather than financial exchange.

- *Place* is less concerned with the movement of goods and more with the communication of ideas. Marketing channels tend to be short.

- *Promotion* in some ways is the most important element of the mix for voluntary and not-for-profit organizations. All the promotional tools are likely to be used, although there may be less emphasis on personal selling.

Services

We earlier suggested that many of the concepts regarding products and their management are similar for both physical products and service products. Because of the growth and importance of services marketing together with the special characteristics of services, the marketing mix for service products needs to be extended to include an additional 3 marketing mix elements, namely the additional 3Ps of people, process, and physical evidence. We shall look at these three additional elements therefore in this part of the unit, but we shall also consider the application of our conventional 4Ps to services.

It would be useful to start by looking at the growth of service sectors and the distinguishing and special characteristics of service products. This will enable us to look at the issues that arise in planning marketing strategies for services, and in particular how these relate to the special characteristics identified. This will enable us to look at the combination of our marketing mix elements to services including our additional 3Ps.

The growth and scope of the service sectors

As you probably know, the service sector has been one of the fastest growing parts of many economies. Indeed, a considerable number of the developed economies of the world can now be termed 'service economies', in that the service sector contributes the greater part of economic activity. For example, currently in the United Kingdom the services have grown to account for some 65 per cent of total UK output, with a consequent decline in the relative proportion accounted for by manufacturing and agricultural industries. This trend has continued as economies continue to move towards post-industrial societies.

Definitions and distinguishing characteristics of services

As is so often the case, virtually every marketing text offers a different, if related, definition of what constitutes a service. Unfortunately there is still no one accepted definition of the term 'service'. Nor, indeed, given the enormous diversity of types of service, should we expect one. For our purposes we shall take what is perhaps one of the more concise definitions.

Definition

Service

A service is any activity or benefit that one party can offer to another that is essentially intangible and does not result in the ownership of anything.

Again, remembering the wide diversity of service industries and products, this definition underlines what are recognized as being some of the key distinguishing characteristics of services. Such characteristics set them apart from their physical-product counterparts, and may give rise to additional and different considerations with respect to planning and controlling their marketing.

These suggested 'special' characteristics of services are shown below:

- Perishability.
- Intangibility.
- Variability.
- Inseparability.
- Non-ownership.

In order to explain these further we can compare and contrast services against physical products with respect to each characteristic. These are shown in Table 9.2.

Table 9.2 Services and physical products contrasted

Now let us consider each of these characteristics in turn.

- *Perishability*   Perhaps of all the suggested special characteristics of service products this is one of the most difficult to appreciate. You will note that in Table 9.2 services are shown as being highly perishable compared to physical products. But how could, for example, the services of, say, an airline be considered to be more perishable than, say, fresh food and vegetable products?

    The reason is that, unlike most physical products, many services cannot be stored. For example, if an airline does not sell all the seats on a particular flight, then those seats, or rather the sales revenue the filling of them would have carried, has immediately and irreversibly gone.

- *Intangibility*   Think back to the last time you visited your local store or supermarket to shop. The products will probably have been on open display. You probably picked them up in your hands, felt the weight of them, perhaps even sniffed at them, before deciding whether or not to buy.

  Compare this with the choice of the services of, say, an insurance policy. You can't touch, see or smell the product before choosing, although clearly you can make some assessment based on past experience, word of mouth, or even the location and decor of the insurance office. The intangible nature of most services gives rise to special problems both for suppliers and consumers.

- *Variability*   In the production and marketing of physical products companies have increasingly paid attention to ensuring consistency in quality, features, packaging, and so on. More often than not the customer can be sure that every tin of Heinz baked beans he buys, even in a life-time of purchases, will not vary. The provision of services, however, invariably includes a large measure of the 'human element'. Indeed with many services we are purchasing nothing else but the skills of the supplier. Because of this, it is often very difficult for both supplier and consumer to ensure a consistent 'product' or quality of service.

- *Inseparability*   A key distinguishing feature of service marketing is that the service provision and provider are inseparable from the service consumption and consumer. For example, we cannot take a hotel room home for consumption; we must 'consume' this service at the point of provision. Similarly, the hairdresser needs to be physically present for this service to be consumed. As we shall see, this has implications both for channels of distribution and scale of operations.

- *Non-ownership*   The final distinguishing feature of a service is that, unlike a physical product, the customer does not secure ownership of the service. Rather the customer pays only to secure access to or use of the service. Again the hotel room is a good example. Similarly with banking services, although the customer may be given a cheque book, credit cards, etc., they serve only to allow the customer to make use of what he or she is actually buying, namely, bank services.

Marketing issues associated with services

Although the basic principles of a marketing concept and marketing management are essentially the same as for physical products, the characteristics of services give rise to a number of important issues when one considers marketing services.

Activity 9.6

For the characteristics of services we have just outlined, try to assess what might be some of the marketing implications associated with each of them. For example, what do you feel might be some of the marketing implications of the fact that services are intangible etc.? When you have done this, compare your assessment with that shown in the debriefing.

The marketing mix and services

We can now look more closely at how the marketing mix may be applied to service products. We shall look first at our conventional 4Ps and then at our additional three mix elements in services marketing.

The service product

The 'product' element of the marketing mix for service products requires that decisions be made on the following:

- The type and range of services.
- The quality and attributes of the services.
- Warranties, after-sale facilities, etc.

As regards product life cycle management and new product development, all the tools and concepts of physical-product marketing apply, although, as mentioned previously, given the intangible nature of services, concept testing of new ideas for services takes on particular significance and can be extremely difficult to conduct.

Pricing of services

Again the basic methods of price determination and alternative pricing strategies, such as market skimming versus market penetration, apply equally to services. You will recall, however, that the perishability of services means that the careful matching of demand and supply is crucial. Because of this, we should expect to find that a much more flexible approach to pricing and margins is appropriate for services.

You should also note that the intangible nature of service products also tends to heighten the use by customers of price as an indicator of quality.

Place and services

Remember that the perishable nature of service products stems from the fact that they cannot be stored. This means that with one or two exceptions physical distribution is not a key problem. As regards channels, we have also noted that inseparability demands that many services are sold direct by producer to consumer. However, some type of agent or broker is often used to market financial or travel services, for example, and increasingly franchising has become an important method of widening the distribution and market spread of many types of service, particularly in the fast-food market.

Promoting services

Once again we find that the intangible nature of service products raises special consideration for their marketing. You will recall that the marketer of service products needs to stress the benefits rather than the features of his service. So, for example, a college needs to promote, say, the job prospects for its graduates as much as the details of the courses it offers.

Personal selling is particularly important in the promotional mix for services. Often the customer is purchasing the personal qualities and skills of the service provider, so that an ability to develop close relationships and win customer confidence is crucial.

You should also note that some service providers are either reluctant, or prohibited, from advertising their services. This is the case, for example, in some areas of the UK medical profession, where the code of ethics in this service industry prevent advertising being used.

Additional marketing-mix elements in service marketing

In addition to the conventional '4Ps' of the marketing mix outlined above, we have suggested that in the case of service marketing this list needs to be extended to include three further Ps, namely people, physical evidence, and process.

- **People**, owing primarily to the intangible and inseparable characteristics of service products, a key factor in how the customer perceives the service and the degree of satisfaction received by the customer is the person(s) actually providing the service at the point of contact. Often the extent to which a customer is happy with a service is due to the attitude, skills and appearance of the people the customer comes into contact with when consuming the service. In fact, very often a customer will purchase a service primarily because of the people they deal with.

For example, many people will use a particular hair salon primarily because of the hairdresser. Similarly, although one might be able to have one's teeth filled by any dentist, we usually go back because we are happy with a particular dentist.

The importance of the people element of the marketing mix for services cannot be overestimated. Because of this, it is important that this element of the mix is planned. Time and resources should be spent on factors such as staff training, appearance, selling skills and so on.

- **Physical evidence**, a somewhat unusual term, relates to those factors that can help to shape the customer's perception and image of the service provider. For example, you have probably noticed that many hotels these days provide writing paper, pens, entertainment information and so on in their hotel bedrooms – thus producing an image of caring and quality. Similarly, many of the fast-food outlets take great care over the design and layout of the outlets and how they are furnished.

  Increasingly service marketers are focusing their attention on the design and provision of a total service concept designed to create a pre-planned atmosphere or image.

- **Process**, the final element of the marketing mix for services, is based on the idea that the ways in which the service is provided, e.g. systems of delivery, are also important. A number of factors can be included under this element of the marketing mix, including systems of order processing, processes for dealing with customer queries and complaints, parking facilities, booking systems, and systems for dealing with excess demand.

These then are the 7Ps of the marketing mix for services. In fact, it is now increasingly recognized that all products have a service component; and indeed for many physical products this service element is the most important in customer choice. Because of this, some of the notions of service marketing, including some of the mix elements, are now being applied to the marketing of physical products. For example, many forward-looking companies have developed total systems of customer care and quality, covering every aspect of their marketing and dealings with customers. We looked at such customer care and service elements in the Unit 'The marketing mix: people, service and customer care'.

Contemporary and further issues in the marketing context

As we have seen throughout the units of the coursebook, both marketing thinking and marketing practice continue to develop and change. Marketing takes place in a very dynamic environment. Moreover it is through marketing activities that the opportunities and threats presented by these dynamics are responded to. In this final part of the unit we consider what are probably two of the most important developments affecting the context in which marketing and marketing mix decisions in particular take place.

The first of these developments relates to the continuing application of new technology to marketing practice. We have touched on some of the applications and implications of new technology already as we have worked through the units. Here we draw together some of the key strands of these developments and underline a gradual but increasing move towards the development of what many have termed a 'virtual' marketplace. In doing so, we shall reiterate some of the key effects of information and communication technology on the development and implementation of the marketing mix.

Our second key development related to contemporary and further issues in the marketing context is the increasing importance of the global dimension in marketing as companies continue to expand their planning and marketing horizons by focusing their attention on the international marketing setting.

The effects of information and communication technology on marketing: the move towards the virtual marketplace

As already mentioned at several points throughout the units we have noted the increasingly important effects of developments in information and communication technology and marketing. There is no doubt that these developments are rapidly changing the face of marketing and particularly the development of marketing plans and the application of the marketing tools. We have already alluded to some of these effects with respect to each of the major elements of the marketing mix earlier. Outlined below, however, in more detail are some of the more important issues which developments in information and communication technology and a move towards a virtual marketplace are giving rise to.

The growth of electronic commerce (e-commerce)

One of the most important areas affected by advances in technology has been the growth of electronic commerce. Often referred to as 'e-commerce' or alternatively, 'e-business'. E-commerce is a collective term to describe a variety of commercial transactions which make use of the technologies of electronic processing and data transmission.

Definition

Electronic commerce

The use of electronic technologies and systems so as to facilitate and enhance transactions between different parts of the value chain.

This definition highlights the fact that, irrespective of the type of electronic commerce, its purpose is to improve the transaction processes which are so central to marketing. E-commerce would not have grown to the extent it has and will continue to do had it not offered enhancements to the process of marketing. Often these enhancements, as already stated, will be in the form of cost reductions for the marketer, but much more important are those enhancements which accrue to the customer. Put another way, the growth of e-commerce would not have been possible without the growth of the 'e-customer'. Remember, the marketing concept states that marketing is about identifying and satisfying customer needs. If customers, therefore, did not perceive a need for e-commerce then the various e-commerce technologies would simply have withered and died. Finally, our definition points to the fact that e-commerce and the technologies which underpin it can, and do, relate to the total value chain including not only customers but also intermediaries, suppliers, and other external agencies such as, for example, advertising and market research companies. In fact, again, as we shall see, the ability to link and co-ordinate all the members of the value chain is one of the major reasons for the growth of e-commerce. Furthermore, it is broad enough to encompass any electronic technology and system which can be used to do this.

E-commerce encompasses many of the individually most significant developments in technology affecting marketers, which will therefore be covered shortly in this unit, such as, for example, the Internet, electronic data interchange (EDI), the intranet and the extranet, the World Wide Web, database marketing and so on.

The first stages of the e-commerce revolution began over twenty years ago when companies began to use their computers for more effective delivery and supply systems. Initially, it was primarily in business-to-business transactions that this development took place, where effective customer and supplier relationships have always been felt to be particularly important. From manual systems of ordering and supply, gradually the computer enabled 'automation' of these processes to take place. This automation was built around the ability of the computer to exchange information electronically with regard to supply and delivery between customers and their suppliers. Eventually, this developed into fully automated systems of electronic data interchange (EDI) systems. Such EDI systems enabled, for example, an automatic order for, say, components to be sent to a supplier when the computer-based stock system in the customer's company monitored a minimum stock and re-ordering level. The required order would be sent via direct computer links to the supplier's computer, which would then automatically check the stock availability, delivery schedules, etc. At the supplier's end the customer's order would be dealt with electronically and the order confirmed, invoice sent, etc., again electronically, back to the customer. Such EDI systems are now widespread in business-to-business markets, but perhaps more importantly, in the context of the development of e-commerce, this development together with advances in the facilitating technologies spawned a whole new approach to business and marketing incorporating new electronic ways of doing business.

Obviously, as already mentioned, given that e-commerce is a collective term for all electronically based systems and techniques of doing business, it encompasses a huge variety of specific technologies and applications each with their attendant advantages with regard to facilitating the marketing process. With this in mind, however, below are listed some examples of the advantages which e-commerce technology can give rise to and therefore some of the reasons for its rapid growth.

Some advantages of e-commerce

Remember again that the specific advantages to be derived from the application of a particular e-commerce technology depends upon that specific application. In general terms, however, some of the advantages underpinning the growth of e-commerce include, e.g:

- Better communication between marketers and customers.
- Faster and more flexible transactions.
- Ability to reach and serve geographically disparate customers.
- Facilitates better control and co-ordination of all value chain activities.
- Improved relationships with customers.
- Related to above, increased customer retention and loyalty.
- Increased speed of doing business, ability to anticipate and react to increasingly rapid change.

Of course, many of these advantages are those that accrue to the marketer's organization. Needless to say, e-commerce has only grown to the extent that it has because it also offers significant advantages to the customer. Examples of advantages of e-commerce to customers include:

- One-stop shopping.
- More convenient purchasing, e.g. from home.
- The ability to compare and contrast product offerings from different suppliers and therefore get the best value.
- Faster and more flexible purchasing.
- The opportunity to communicate directly with suppliers regarding, for example, needs, terms, complaints.

Examples of markets/products affected by electronic commerce

Some examples of areas of consumer marketing where e-commerce is being applied include:

- Travel/holidays.
- Financial services – banking, insurance, etc.
- Music/entertainment.
- Food/wine.
- Books.
- Computer hardware and software.
- Event tickets.
- Restaurant bookings.
- Cars.
- Toys.

We can see, even from this illustrative list, that the range of industries and markets now affected by e-commerce is diverse and, moreover, the list is growing all the time. From its original business-to-business market usage the effect of e-commerce and the technologies which under-pin it are becoming more and more widespread.

Activity 9.7

Try to list other examples of products/markets where e-commerce techniques and activities are being used.

When you have completed your list compare it with the debriefing.

Clearly, e-commerce and new technology is having significant effects on marketing and markets, so let us now consider some of the e-commerce and new technologies further including the increasingly ubiquitous internet, intranet and extranets.

The Internet

Probably the most significant e-commerce tool and technology is the Internet.

Definition

Internet

The internet is a network of computers which are linked together such that the computer user may communicate with the other computers in the system.

Originally developed so that academics and scientists in different geographical locations could communicate with each other quickly and easily, the Internet has now developed into a global network of linked computers through which individuals can perform any number of different activities. Using the Internet, an individual can investigate what is on offer to purchase from any company in the world which is connected to the network and is offering products and services on this network. Individuals can visit company websites, order products from virtual shopping precincts, book tickets for concerts, holidays and aeroplane flights, transfer information, ideas and money electronically and so on. From the point of view of the marketer the Internet offers the opportunity to reach customers anywhere in the world. Moreover, as we shall see, the Internet increasingly allows the marketer to communicate directly with individual customers, build up a powerful database on customers' needs and wants, and develop very effective relationships with customers. The Internet means that no longer does a company have to be large to operate in global markets. Increasingly, therefore, the Internet facilitates more and more competition. There is no doubt that the Internet is changing both consumer and therefore marketing practices and habits considerably. Increasingly, customers will shop for and buy products and services from home using their PCs. This has implications for virtually every facet of marketing, such as, for example, product development, pricing, promotion and distribution. Marketing via the Internet is probably the fastest growing area of marketing now with the growth of the so-called 'dot.com' companies and gradually we are moving more and more towards what can only be termed the virtual marketplace.

However, perhaps what many do not realize, is that in fact it is probably the more established companies that have been responsible for the move towards this virtual marketplace in most countries. Indeed the much vaunted so-called 'dot.com' companies have so far proved to be extremely disappointing in terms of their lack of success and profitability. There are many reasons for this perhaps, but one of the most important is probably the fact that customers generally feel safer using the Internet to deal with and buy from companies that have well-established brand names and long-established records of trading, albeit in the past using more traditional methods. For example, some of the major retail banks have been amongst some of the first and most successful protagonists of the virtual marketplace. Most conventional marketers in developed economies now at least have websites which customers can visit to find information, but increasingly these companies now have some facility for at least a degree of on-line shopping. Those companies that have seen the potential and the importance of the Internet now often offer all of their products for sale over the Internet, obviously combined with suitable methods of payment and delivery and distribution.

Study tip

If you do have access to the Internet try visiting a few company websites to find out how they are designing their Internet offerings and services. Make notes on those that impress you from a marketing point of view and those that do not. What are the differences between the two groups?

Perhaps an interesting phenomenon with regard to some of the early dotcom companies is the fact that some of these companies have moved from purely being Internet-based marketers to actually developing their own retail distribution outlets to market their products, i.e. the movement in this area is in two directions – many conventional retailers etc. are becoming more involved in Internet marketing for their products and services, but at the same time some early virtual marketers are establishing more conventional marketing channels and techniques.

A good example of this is the dotcom company 'Think Natural dotcom'. Originally an Internet marketer this company has been successfully selling health-related products through its website for two years. Partly as a result of this success, however, it has now negotiated a deal with

Superdrug, a conventional retailer in this area, to include the stocking of many of its products and brands in Superdrug retail outlets throughout the United Kingdom.

This illustrates that increasingly we must think of on-line/virtual marketing and conventional marketing not as being dichotomous alternatives but as being a set of marketing approaches and techniques which are increasingly being used together by companies. The Internet, then, is just another tool in the marketing process, albeit a powerful and increasingly important one. This, in turn, means that the Internet activities of a company's marketing must be planned as part of the overall marketing strategy and marketing mix of the company and not, as it so often has been in the past, simply be tagged on as an afterthought or an extra.

A further facet to consider with regard to the growth of the Internet and virtual marketing is that it is increasingly changing the conventional boundaries and structures of markets and the competition within them. The British Sky Broadcasting Group (BSkyB) is, as its name suggests, essentially a communications company primarily, of course, in television. But increasingly, in the future the growth of its interactive services may begin to transform this company into a potential major competitor for conventional retailers as it increasingly sells products and services through its Internet facilities to customers directly in their own living rooms.

Increasingly, therefore, no marketer in the future will be able to ignore the Internet even if – as is increasingly unlikely – their companies are not actually marketing via the net.

By providing direct links with customers, suppliers and distributors and by facilitating transactions, processes and information transfer, the Internet will radically transform the way marketing is done.

The Internet can be used in a vast number of ways for marketing purposes. It can be used as an external research tool to access market and competitor information. It can be used as a direct marketing channel and a home shopping site. It can be used to raise awareness and support other communication tools for specific campaigns. For example, a leading manufacturer of white goods is currently about to use its Internet site as the main promotional tool when launching its new products because it is felt that the Internet can provide more crucial information which the customer will require before making a decision.

The Internet can also be used by organizations to communicate with other organizations in business-to-business marketing via e-mail. As the ownership of personal computers grows, mobility improves and the cost of Internet use declines, more consumers will also be contactable directly via e-mail instead of using mailshots.

The intranet

> **Definition**
>
> **Intranet**
>
> The intranet is an electronic system of internal communication throughout an organization.

Similar to the Internet but operating within an organizational system, the intranet connects functions and activities within an organization thereby facilitating rapid and effective internal systems of communication. Intranets allow, for example, employees to access information from other parts of the company though obviously some of this may be restricted. This allows greater management of communication and can be used to advantage for relaying, say, information on important developments from outside an organization such as, say, competitor actions, etc. The intranet may also be used to advantage for internal promotional material such as company newsletters, etc.

The extranet

Definition

Extranet

The extranet is a system of electronic communication which connects members of a value/supply chain network together.

The extranet links together value chain companies such as, for example, material/component suppliers, producers, distributors and intermediaries, and in some cases, customers. The development of EDI networks and marketing referred to earlier are an example of the extranet application. The extranet allows much closer and more sophisticated relationships to be developed between the members of the value chain, and the access and use of such information should allow for mutual economies and enhanced communication. This strategy also encourages trust and commitment between two organizations, such as a supplier and a customer. For example, the extranet may be used to allow a customer on-line access to some of its internal information sources. The extranet is used in a growing number of organizations where such access to information has helped in planning sales and logistics down the line. Obviously there are some potential problems which relate to the level of investment required to allow for this system to work effectively. One must also consider the problem of access to information when one organization wishes to terminate the relationship.

Databases

Strictly speaking, databases are not a technology but rather bring a number of technologies together to increase and enhance customer information which a company can then use in its marketing. Databases, however, are so important in contemporary marketing, and particularly in the move towards the virtual marketplace that we consider these further here.

Definition

Database

A database is a store of customer information which can be used to develop marketing strategies.

Remember that central to the marketing concept is the need to know your customers. Developments in information collection, storage, and analysis are now making information one of the most important competitive assets a company can have.

A customer database can be built from many sources. So, for example, information can come from customer orders, subscription lists, guarantee return forms, loyalty cards, company sales persons, customer complaints, customer enquiries, traditional market research and outside companies that specialize in providing customer information. We can see from this list that information on customers can come from a wide variety of sources, both from inside and outside the organization. Coupled with the ability to store and manipulate large amounts of data, the plethora of customer data sources means that all too often it is possible to be overwhelmed by data. In order to avoid such information overload, whilst at the same time ensuring that valuable information about customers is not overlooked or lost, database management needs careful planning. The essence of successful database marketing requires careful attention to the following:

- Specific objectives for the database, including types of information required and why.
- Effective systems for data capture including strategies for this.
- Appropriate systems for data storage including effective database maintenance.
- Effective systems of analysis and interpretation of data based around providing information for marketing decision making.

Without careful attention to the objectives and uses to which the database is to be put, it is all too easy to collect data just for the sake of it. The marketer and database planner need to work carefully together to determine precisely what data is required in the context of being useful for decision making. Data capture involves systems for providing and collecting data for the database and encompasses many of the sources already mentioned such as market research, loyalty cards and so on. Companies have become much better at data collection with often very sophisticated methods for providing data. It is important to remember that there is considerable legislation relating to the collection and use of data on customers. The most important legislation is enshrined in the Data Protection Act of 1998 which covers both manual and computer systems and protects customers' rights in several respects with regard to data on them. It is particularly important in building a database that valuable sources of customer data are not ignored. Many companies suffer from the fact that the different departments in the organization each have their own databases which are often never used by the rest of the organization. Increasingly, companies are using what is referred to as 'data warehousing' to deal with this problem.

Definition

Data warehousing

Data warehousing is the process of collecting all the data on customers and centralizing this into a single pool within a company.

Activity 9.8

List examples of the sorts of data on customers which functions other than the marketing function in an organization might generate in the course of performing their functional activities in an organization.

When you have completed your list you should compare it with the debriefing.

Once the database is established, the next step is to use this data in order to improve our marketing. This involves ensuring that the data is analysed and manipulated so as to provide information for marketing decision making. Again, developments in information technology and computing power in particular have facilitated much more sophisticated analysis and interpretation of data for this purpose. Sophisticated statistical analysis and modelling techniques allow the marketing manager to look for important patterns of cause and effect between various data elements. This is sometimes called 'data mining'.

> **Definition**
>
> **Data mining**
>
> Data mining is the process of analysing and manipulating data so as to provide new and more powerful insights into customer behaviour patterns in order to improve marketing decisions.

Such database analysis and manipulation has enabled the marketer to use database information in much more powerful ways in recent years including, for example, segmentation and targeting strategies, the development of relationship marketing strategies, customer retention and loyalty strategies, improved promotional and particularly direct mail strategies. Some of these applications of databases are considered in more detail later in the unit.

In managing the customer database it is particularly important to ensure that the database is regularly maintained, or as it is sometimes referred to, cleaned. Obviously, customers and information on them is changing all the time. If the database contains inaccurate information we run the risk of making the wrong decisions. For example, many companies waste money sending direct mail material to customers who have long since moved on. Worse still, there are examples of companies sending out marketing literature to customers on their database who are no longer living. Clearly, using inaccurate data at best wastes money, and at worst risks alienating customers or potential customers. It is not possible to describe in detail the techniques for ensuring clean databases, but many companies for example now reference their data against third-party lists to ensure its accuracy. Other companies use external consultants to ensure that the database is maintained. At the very least, companies should regularly check the information held on databases to try to ensure that the database is as up to date and accurate as possible.

Digital communications

Again, not a single technology but rather one which underpins several of the technological advances now affecting marketing, including, for example, many of the e-commerce developments. Digital technology developments, and particularly those which underpin recent developments in communications, are important enough to consider in their own right.

Digital technology is changing many facets of marketing activity and is set to change them even more in the future. This is particularly true in the area of communications. For example, digital technology is changing the face of television and therefore things like home shopping, which will increasingly be digitally based.

A growth area in the last few years has been the development of direct response television advertising (DRTV). This allows marketers to make very effective use of promotional campaigns which are designed to elicit an immediate response from the customer in the form of an enquiry, or more often than not, an order.

One of the most exciting developments in this area is the growth of interactive television which is based on the new digital technologies. Not only does this allow customers to shop from home but in the future will increasingly be used for access to the web and associated activities such as e-mail services. There are those who believe that the television rather than the computer will be the interactive market of the future.

Similarly, we have seen the growth of multi-media, including, for example, CD-ROMs, and DVD systems, which are changing areas such as advertising and promotion in marketing and leading to the development of entirely new products, especially in the music and entertainment industries. Of course, marketers do not necessarily need to be experts in digital technology but they do need to recognize that increasingly marketing will make use of this technology, as indeed will the rest of society.

Wireless communications/mobile technologies

Related to developments in digital communications is the growth of wireless technologies and the mobile technologies and communications which are associated with them. Increasingly, the marketer, for example, will be able to communicate with customers and customers with marketers irrespective of where they are and what they are doing anywhere in the world. Although the Internet allows communication globally with customers, currently customers must have access to a computer. Admittedly, this can be a laptop computer but most Internet usage is in the home. In the future, wireless technologies will mean that, for example, the marketer and consumer will be able to communicate via a mobile phone. Already the new generation of mobile phones allows direct access to the Internet and facilities such as the sending and receiving of e-mails. There is no doubt that this application of technology and its importance to marketers will grow in the future and hence will be another contributory factor in the move towards a virtual marketplace.

Further examples of the effects of information and communication technology (ICT)

Remember, we are looking at the area of information and communication technology and advances in these because they are fundamentally changing the process and application of many marketing activities. Indeed, this is the reason for including this area in the CIM's syllabus for this subject. We have already considered, therefore, some of the main effects of developments in ICT and particularly the growth of the internet and the move towards the virtual marketplace. The effect of developments in ICT are so ubiquitous however that virtually every facet of marketing activity is being affected and in some areas transformed. Clearly, it is impossible to detail all the possible effects and implications in this area, but in addition to the effects already outlined, here are some more of the effects of ICT on marketing practice.

Application of the marketing concept

Developments in ICT are enabling marketers to apply the principles of the marketing concept to much greater effect than before. There are many reasons for this but essentially ICT and particularly the marketing research and database elements already referred to are enabling the marketer to understand and respond to customer needs and requirements much more effectively than ever before.

The marketing planning process

We discussed the impact of new technology and technological developments on the marketing planning process in our Unit 'Marketing Planning'. We noted that virtually every element and step in the marketing planning process ranging from the marketing audit to evaluation and control is being impacted by developments in technology.

Marketing research

In some ways perhaps the most obvious example of the potential for technological advances. The advances in IT have been very helpful to marketing researchers and in particular has made the often difficult process of international marketing research much easier. It has also made much secondary research far easier and economical. Below are some of the ways in which these advances in IT are being used in marketing research.

Secondary research

External secondary data sources are now available in a range of different technological formats in addition to print. Researchers can now access Internet-based sources and websites. On-line format allows the researcher to access and manipulate data with appropriate software; the data usually available on a subscription basis. Such sources are often very much more up to date than printed formats. A number of good universities have websites which provide an extensive listing of Internet-based information sources.

Internal secondary data sources, and particularly the databases referred to earlier, are also becoming increasingly powerful information sources. Remember, internal databases enable the market researcher to identify and analyse customer behaviour in some depth. Again, such information can be rapidly updated.

Primary research

Again, the use of information technology can help the research in a number of ways.

For example, in terms of gathering information, quantitative data using a research instrument or questionnaire can be posted on the Internet on a particular site. It can also be e-mailed to potential respondents easily – so long as e-mail addresses are available. Quantitative information can also be collected via on-line scanners as an observation tool to assess purchasing behaviour. Scanners and electronic equipment can be used to monitor instore traffic flows. Digital television will increasingly allow the researcher to gather further quantitative information directly from respondents. As regards qualitative information, chat rooms or discussion areas on the Internet are particularly useful.

Like many things to do with the Internet, the initial excitement regarding the potential for it as a new research tool has died down a little, with marketers becoming more realistic about what the Internet can and cannot do with respect to marketing research. Slowly but surely, market researchers are learning that using the Internet possibly requires new marketing research tools and certainly new attitudes and approaches to marketing research. Marketing research companies and marketing managers are only just beginning to learn how to use the Internet in this respect. But as they do so, this tool will become increasingly useful to marketers.

Information technology developments are also helping in the analysis stage of market research. For example, during interviews, the responses can be entered directly into laptop computers which can ensure that the information is ready to analyse instantaneously. This can also be undertaken for telephone interviews. Increasingly powerful computer packages can be used to analyse the information effectively. There are now a number of different software packages that can also help to analyse qualitative data.

Promotional campaigns and the promotional mix

Advances in technology and particularly ICT developments have, and will continue to have, a major effect on the promotional elements of the marketing mix. Consider the following examples of uses and applications in this area of the marketing mix.

Advertising

Direct response television advertising (DRTV) has allowed advertising to achieve more than just awareness. Data can be captured and responses can lead to converts. The introduction of satellite television and digital technology has allowed for more sophisticated targeting via traditional advertising. The use of the Internet site as an advertising window or banner advertising on other linked sites has been evident in the last five years. The use of the Internet as a vehicle for advertising is growing rapidly.

Activity 9.9

In what ways does satellite television allow for more sophisticated targeting with respect to advertising?

List any reasons you can think of and then compare your list with that shown in the debriefing.

Sales promotions

The sophistication of databases and the direct mailing of sales promotions has been very powerful for some organizations. The use of the website and the 'free downloadable program or screen saver' has allowed the marketer to become more creative.

Personal selling

As we shall see later in the unit, automated customer-handling technology has begun to erode some of the elements of personal selling. Indeed, some believe that new technology will mean that the role of personal selling will decline. Certainly, new technology and the growth of, for example, the use of call centres by companies can significantly reduce selling costs. However, and again as we shall see later, one has to be careful when diminishing the role of personal selling not to erode the service to the customer. New technology is certainly facilitating greater control over sales-force activities in the field. The obvious examples are the use of mobile phone networks, e-mails through laptops, etc. Intranet technology, by allowing speedier and more flexible communication with sales staff, can, if used properly, increase sales force motivation and effectiveness in dealing with customers. Satellite and digital technology enable video conferencing thereby allowing sales conferences to be held even where sales staff are globally scattered. Obviously, access to powerful and cheap computing power enables very rapid analysis of response to sales data and sales performance which can be fed through to head office from a modem operated by each sales person at the end of the sales day.

Public relations

New technology is also affecting the PR element of the promotional mix. The use of the website as a relationship-building tool has been very effective for some organizations. For both internal (staff) and external audiences (customers, journalists, community, etc.) it has been easier to communicate using the intranet, the Internet and mobile technology. For example, internal newsletters can be communicated on the intranet and press releases to journalists can be e-mailed instantly with digital pictures using satellite technology. The web is proving to be a particularly useful communication tool for crisis management such as disasters, accidents, tampering and pollution scares, etc. when accurate and rapidly changing information to the public is crucial.

Direct mail

Advances in technology have had a major effect on the direct-mail element of the promotional mix. In particular, of course, the growth in databases and a marketer's ability to increasingly improve both the accuracy and the complexity of information held on such databases is allowing the marketer to use direct marketing, and direct mail in particular, much more effectively. So, for example, the marketer can use the database to identify key target customers based on data regarding their purchasing habits, interests, and attitudes and opinions. By using databases in this way, the marketer is able to target the direct mail campaign to the right people thereby reducing the cost whilst at the same time increasing the response rate.

Websites are often thought of as just another selling device, but the website can be used much more actively, in particular to develop better relationships with a company's customers and publics.

Customer relations

A well designed and operated website allows for very effective communication with customers. If customers can easily find the website and access information on it, and if they find that these visits are rewarding in the sense of offering more than simply information, the customer is likely to be favourably impressed with regard to the company and its offerings.

Media relations

The website can also be dedicated to developing media relations. This can be one of the most potent public relations tools as, for example, reporters can access information which they may need at any time of the day or night, and if prepared carefully, in a format that is ready to use.

Investor relations

As the financial community is increasingly used to using the Internet, a corporate website can also be important for investors accessing information. This would include the annual reports being posted on the site.

Community relations

The website can also be used for developing community relations. This site could include information relating to the promotion of local joint projects, contributions to arts and culture, invitations to open days and educational pages.

We can see, therefore, that the strategic design and use of the website is growing in importance in today's market place and this must be considered as part of an integrated communications strategy.

New product development

As with marketing planning the impact of technological developments and ICT in particular on this area of marketing were discussed in earlier units.

Customer relationship management (CRM)

As we have mentioned several times in this coursebook, an important development in both the theory and practice of marketing has been the move towards so-called 'relationship marketing'. Remember that we said that relationship marketing is based on the building of trust between the organization and its customers. Rather than viewing exchanges between the organization and its customers as one-off individual transactions, relationship marketing is based on the notion of building long term between both parties to the exchange. As such, customer relationship management (CRM) places increased emphasis on co-operation, co-ordination, and communication between the members of the value chain. It also places much greater emphasis on the importance of developing customer loyalty and therefore retaining customers. Although effective relationship marketing requires, first and foremost, the right attitudes, philosophy, and culture in an organization, the translation of these facets into effective relationship marketing programmes is increasingly facilitated by advances in technology.

For example, the use of sophisticated databases and the use of direct communications can enhance the relationship which can be built with a customer. The financial services sector and now many FMCG organizations are becoming more effective at using electronic methods to ensure that their relationship with their customers is more robust and effective in terms of securing mutual benefit. Indeed, they use technology and other marketing techniques to endeavour to build loyal customers with the intention of retaining them for a lifetime. Using the database, the marketer can, for example, develop loyalty schemes such as those used initially by many supermarket retailers, but now spreading into consumer durable goods marketing.

You will recall that relationship marketing was primarily initially used in business-to-business markets where it continues to grow. The extranet coupled with EDI systems, both outlined earlier in this unit, allows the different members of a value chain accurate and instant information which they may wish to use for planning purposes. This use of the extranet can be used to build and maintain very strong bonds between the members of the value chain and therefore can help to build customer loyalty and retention. The extranet not only allows for greater flow of information which facilitates cost economies, but it also communicates trust and commitment between customers and suppliers.

There are now many companies who specialize in CRM management. Most of these companies use sophisticated information and database technology in developing and implementing CRM systems for their clients. A good example is the company 'Software for Sport' which, amongst its other activities, supplies CRM software and systems to football clubs. This application of CRM shows in fact how far relationship management has come in marketing. At one time, many would have argued that CRM has little application in football, where, for example, someone is unlikely to switch from supporting one club to another, i.e. most fans are loyal to their favourite football clubs. However, the clubs have realized that unless they make efforts to retain even brand-loyal customers there are dangers in, say, people switching from watching their favourite club live to watching them on, say, Sky TV. They may also switch from one sport to another as the newer sports, for example, ice hockey, appear to be more exciting. In other words, even in this bastion of brand loyalty, companies cannot afford to become complacent about their relationships with customers. Software for Sport brings together information on, for example, season ticket holder data, club shop transactions, visits to club amenities, etc. into a single database. By doing so, football clubs are able to build up information on fans and corporate customers to help them market their clubs and facilities. In addition to this software for databases some football clubs are also using smart card technology, which helps to improve the ticket application process and can be used to monitor data on season ticket holders.

These are just some examples of how technology is being used to facilitate CRM. Most of the modern CRM systems require sophisticated information technology. Overall, this technology gives far greater market and customer knowledge based on sophisticated databases which in turn allow far higher levels of service and targeted marketing efforts to increase customer loyalty.

Customer service and customer care

Finally, in our examples of applications and uses of technological advances in marketing, is the area of customer service and customer care. Examples of ways in which advances in technology are impacting this area include:

- By effectively removing physical distance between customers and marketers, customer and company come closer together.

- Improved databases facilitate the tracking of customer satisfaction and the following up of any complaints thereby potentially improving customer service.

- The interactive nature of many of the new technologies allows customers potentially much greater involvement in the development of marketing programmes to satisfy their needs. Technological advances in information technology facilitate the ease with which customers can evaluate and purchase products and services such as, for example, home banking and shopping, etc. all help to improve levels of customer service.

Automated customer-handling operations

An example of how new technology is affecting customer service is the growth of automated customer-handling operations.

Automated customer-handling operations have been in existence for a number of years now. Such systems enable the organization to handle large numbers of customer enquiries and complaints. Most of these systems are based on automated voice and push button instructions when customers telephone the organization. By pushing a series of buttons in response to automated voice prompts, the customer is directed to the right department or person in the company and/or to the source of the information required.

As an example, Barclays Bank now allows customers to access information about their accounts twenty-four hours a day by telephone. The customer can access this information by keying in on the telephone their membership number and pin number, and by push-button technology they can, for example, access account balances, order cheque books, transfer money, etc. New technologies are allowing organizations to offer a level of service which might not have been available previously, and typically this is related to out-of-hours access to information and services.

Having said this, a company must be very careful to ensure that it is introducing new technology for the right reasons when it comes to customer care. So, for example, in some cases, automated customer handling operations are introduced primarily to save costs for the company rather than with the objective of improving customer care. In addition, there is now an increasing concern that far from improving customer service, some of the automated customer handling operations lack the human interface which many customers seek. In addition, the amount of time lost during what can be often long and laborious push-button processes can be very annoying to customers. Therefore, in considering technologies which enable a greater degree of automation in customer handling operations, organizations need to be careful that such systems do not alienate their customer base and indeed erode levels of customer care rather than enhance them.

Activity 9.10

Try to list any reasons that you can think of why many customers increasingly feel that automated customer handling operations are annoying and frustrating.

The whole area of e-commerce and the applications of new technology to commerce and marketing is now very much a hot issue. You can expect, therefore, to come across a considerable amount of information and reports on developments in this area in textbooks, newspapers, reports and, needless to say, on the Internet itself. You should be constantly looking for information in this area and particularly examples of developments and applications of technology in marketing. Finally, remember this is a huge area of study in its own right and therefore you should consider at least one of the textbooks recommended in this area in the CIM syllabus.

International and global dimensions

Our second major development in the context of marketing which in turn has given rise to major implications for the nature of marketing undertaken by organizations including their use of the various marketing mix tools is the increasingly important international and global dimensions of marketing practice.

Study tip

As you are no doubt aware international and global marketing is an area of study in its own right. It is not possible but thankfully nor is it essential to encompass every facet of the international and global dimensions of marketing in this unit even if we confine ourselves to just examining the implications of the international and global context on the marketing mix tools. What follows, therefore, are just some examples of the ways in which international and global dimensions impact this area of marketing in order to illustrate the importance of these dimensions in contemporary marketing.

Extending knowledge

With reference to our study tip above, you are advised to consult a good basic text which covers the area of international marketing. We recommend G. A. Lancaster, L. Massingham and R. Ashforth, Essentials of Marketing, 4th Edition, 2002, Chapter 14.

Here then are just some ways in which international and global dimensions affect some of the areas of marketing, and particularly the elements of the marketing mix which we have discussed throughout the units.

International issues in products and packaging

The international and global marketer faces additional complexities and decisions when it comes to products and packaging compared to the purely domestic marketer. The STEP factors in particular are very important determinants affecting product and packaging decisions. To the extent to which these STEP factors are likely to differ between different countries, therefore, the marketer must take these into account in products and package areas of the mix. So, for example, when it comes to packaging design some countries are much more stringent with regard to recyclability regulations. Similarly facets such as the product lifecycle stage for a product differ between different countries. Obviously, decisions about aspects such as product features, design, components and so on, of a product will have to reflect individual country requirements. Perhaps one of the most significant issues facing the international marketer in this respect is the extent to which it is possible and desirable to standardize the product for different international markets. The other side of the coin being of course the extent to which the product needs to be modified or adapted to different countries. In fact this standardization/adaptation issue runs throughout the marketing mix decisions for the international and global marketer, but it is particularly important when it comes to products and packaging. The main reason for this is that on the one hand standardization in the product and packaging areas of the marketing mix probably represent some of the largest potential cost savings available to a company. Put simply, the more a company can standardize its products, the more economies of scale it will gain. Offset against these gains, however, are the potential barriers to and disadvantages of product standardization. So, for example, consumers in many of the African markets simply don't want, can't use, or can't afford many of the features and design attributes of products marketed to the Western European or Northern American markets. So, for example, a much more basic washing machine or television is much more appropriate. Put simply, there can be major barriers to product and packaging standardization. The successful marketer must strike a balance between standardization versus adaptation bearing in mind the costs of adaptation compared to meeting the needs of customers in individual markets.

When it comes to branding we have seen the emergence of global brands in recent years. Again this is a result of many factors, for example, consumers are much more cosmopolitan these days and exposed to a much wider range of global influences. Within this environment, backed by the resources and efforts of the multi-nationals, global brands have flourished. All the advantages associated with effective brands and brand management outlined in the Unit 'Product decisions' apply equally as much, if not more so, when set in an international/global context. Global brands allow consumers to buy their favourite brands with equanimity anywhere in the world giving them confidence and security. The marketer benefits through lower costs of brand support, although admittedly supporting global brands can and does require substantial investment and resources, particularly in advertising and promotion.

With regard to the new product aspects of marketing activities, increasingly, new products are being developed with global marketing in mind. It is much easier to build in requirements for adaptation to meet the needs of other markets at the early stages of product development rather than adapt them later on. This means that the marketer must be aware of factors in international markets which must be considered when considering product specifications for new products. In particular, any regulatory and legal factors must be considered. Needless to say, however, it is differences in buyer requirements which are likely to cause major changes to the product development programme. Returning to our standardization adaptation issue, many companies have attempted to develop global new products. So, for example, the Ford Motor

Company have attempted to design and build a 'world car'. The basic concept of this product is to have a standardized core design for things like chassis, engines, and so on, which can then be modified to meet the needs of individual markets or regions in different parts of the world. Understandably developing global products is not easy and requires, for example, global inputs from marketing research.

Pricing in international markets

The techniques, inputs to, and strategies for pricing apply whether considering purely domestic or international markets. So, for example, the primary inputs include areas such as costs, demand, competitors, customer and company considerations. Pricing can be cost, demand or competitor based and pricing strategies can involve skimming or penetration. However, as in other areas of the marketing mix there are additional complexities and considerations when pricing in international markets. Some of these additional complexities and considerations are listed below:

- The marketer must consider any additional costs due to, say, tariffs and duties as a result of trading across international boundaries.

- Linked to the above, international marketers often face the issue of 'price escalation' for their products in international markets, i.e. there are forces which drive up prices such as tariffs, but also increased costs of transport and distribution.

- The international marketer also faces the problem of having to take account of different currencies and, related to this, changes in exchange rates. In some circumstances even small differences in exchange rates can have a major effect on profitability.

- The international marketer has to consider the terms and conditions which each party agrees to when considering price and delivery arrangements. So, for example, prices can be set at, say, a free on board price (f.o.b.) where the price includes delivery onto the customer's ship, say, for transport. On the other hand, a price may be set which includes carriage, insurance, and freight (cif) i.e. all the costs to the customer's factory.

There is no doubt, then that pricing in international markets is more complicated, however, as we move more and more towards global markets and free trading blocks some of these complexities may well reduce.

International aspects of channels and physical distribution

As with the price element of the marketing mix, and indeed each of the other elements of the mix, the underpinning principles, issues and management of channels and physical distribution are the same for both domestic and international markets. Again, as with price, however, these basic principles and decisions are made more complex when planning the place element for international markets. In addition, there are one or two considerations and complications which the international marketer faces in planning place which are simply not encountered when planning for purely domestic markets.

Some of the added complexities and considerations for international place decisions include the following:

- Perhaps for obvious reasons, the distances involved for physical distribution are often much greater in international channels. This makes planning some of the logistical and physical distribution elements that much more important. So, for example, for products often travelling long distances, including by sea and by air, physical protection of the products during transit is much more important.

- International channels involve several types of intermediaries often not found in purely domestic marketing. So, for example, we have export agents of various types, international forwarders and freighters, specialist government intermediaries, etc. The international marketer needs to be aware of, and be able to plan for and work with a wider variety of types of intermediaries.

- Linked to the points above, the international marketer must take much greater care over decisions such as responsibilities and payments between the different parties in the chain, for example, who takes title to goods, and at what point in the channel.

- Channel arrangements which are used satisfactorily in the domestic market simply may be unavailable in international markets. The UK, for example, has one of the most highly concentrated and developed retailing sectors in the world. Such channel arrangements are simply not available in many other countries and particularly developing ones.

- Finally, and again as with all marketing decisions for international markets, the market, competitive and macro environment factors are often very different in international markets, which may have a major effect on the selection of channel and physical distribution arrangements. For example, even within Europe the competitive market structure for car distribution is very different across the different countries of Europe. In the United Kingdom, for example, car distribution is still very much controlled by the major car manufacturers with things like prices being more manageable from the manufacturer than in other parts of Europe due to different distribution arrangements.

International aspects of promotion

There are several additional considerations when considering the use of the promotional tools in international markets. Again, many of these are similar to those affecting the tools of Product, Price and Place already discussed. The main considerations are as follows:

- Because many aspects of promotion, including areas such as message design, media availability, and more recently, technological considerations such as access to Internet and communication technologies, are substantially affected by political, economic, social, cultural and technological considerations, and because these are often substantially different in other geographical areas of the world, it is vitally important to consider these differences when planning international promotional campaigns.

- Having said this, international communications, again underpinned by developments in information technology, are becoming more global in nature. It is now much more realistic to plan global promotion and communication campaigns in international marketing.

- As in all of the areas of the marketing mix, a key consideration for the international marketer when planning international promotion is the extent to which it is possible and advisable to use standardized versus adapted promotional campaigns. Many factors affect this decision including, for example, the nature of the product, target market countries, the resources available, and perhaps above all, the similarity or otherwise of customer needs and behaviour. Overall, however, there has been a trend towards trying to standardize the tools of marketing by international marketers. This is particularly so with respect to at least some elements of promotional campaigns, and in particular elements such as brand names, corporate image, and central messages relating to company positioning and business missions. Companies like Coca Cola and McDonalds have tried to build promotional campaigns which span the globe with only changes in language in advertising etc. and media due to differences in availability. Obviously, standardization offers many advantages including:

1. The development of a consistent corporate and brand image.
2. The potential for economies of scale in the production of promotional material, for example, advertising campaigns.
3. The potential to appeal to what is an increasingly global customer.

These potential advantages, though, need to be compared and assessed against the individual needs and circumstances in particular markets.

International aspects of customer care

Clearly, companies which operate in international markets want to develop similar standards of customer care throughout their operations. Note how our Interflora example illustrates how a company-wide commitment to customer care throughout different markets in different parts of the world can help build the image of a company, develop more effective relationships with customers and serve as a standard for operating procedures for all staff. If a customer has a satisfactory experience with a company in one country then it is much more likely that that customer will seek to use the same company when he or she purchases elsewhere in the world. On the other hand, if a customer experiences different levels of service and customer care from the same company in different parts of the world this is likely to lead to the customer being apprehensive and anxious about using the same supplier. However, customer-care programmes, including the selection of the level of customer care necessary and appropriate, are amongst the most difficult areas of the marketing programme to standardize. There are several reasons for this, but amongst one of the most important are differences in cultural practice in different parts of the world with regard to what is expected in terms of customer care. Almost without exception, the American customer expects, and in America largely gets, extremely high standards of customer care. In parts of Europe, however, including the United Kingdom, customers may not expect, and in fact positively dislike, some of the elements of customer care which are considered normal in the United States of America. In designing customer-care programmes therefore, the marketer has to consider these cultural differences and reflect them in the design of customer-care programmes. Notwithstanding this though, the international marketer should try to ensure consistent approaches to customer care in different parts of the world. Again, people, process and physical evidence are all important here. In designing an international effective customer-care programme many of the issues and steps for planning a purely domestic customer-care programme are to be found. In essence, and by way of reminding you of some of these issues and steps, the following should be considered

- Identify customer needs and perceptions for each market.
- Establish a mission statement.
- Set service level standards and specifications reflecting individual country requirements but guided by an overall customer charter which reflects the mission statement and outlines measurable criteria/standards to be attained.
- Establish management processes and communicate these to all staff.
- Define specific tasks as regards customer-care elements for each country.
- Establish basic minimum levels of customer care.
- Ensure effective response systems for identifying, tracking and responding to complaints.
- Ensure management and staff commitment to programmes through for example, effective training and remuneration programmes.
- Ensure effective and continuous measurement of the customer-care programmes.

International implications of technological advances in marketing

Technological advances in marketing have affected many areas of international marketing operations. Once again, however, it is primarily developments in ICT which have had, or are having, the most profound and far-reaching implications. The speed with which information can be obtained and accessed, both by customers and by companies, has led to, for example, much greater and increasingly global competition. When a customer can access information and purchase products from anywhere in the world simply by clicking a button on their keyboard and entering the World Wide Web, obviously this means that companies are exposed to potentially global competition. As we saw in an earlier unit when we discussed the effect of the Internet in this respect, this means that the marketer must consider a much broader range of competitors and expect customers to shop for the best value and service.

Obviously, increased global competition because of developments in technology can be both an opportunity and a threat. In the case of developing and launching new products, technology, and again particularly information technology, is presenting major opportunities and advantages for marketers these days. New technology can help cut the costs and increase the speed for developing and launching global new brands particularly through the use of new technology based marketing research techniques.

New technology is also facilitating the ease of communication where companies have different operating divisions throughout the world. So, for example, marketing managers can be kept informed of company and market developments much more easily and intelligence on markets can be shared. In this sense it is probably as much the intranet as well as the extranet which is presenting opportunities and advantages for the global marketer.

As already mentioned, ICT in particular is helping to facilitate at least pan-regional and in some cases global marketing, including the development of global brands.

Some companies are now launching pan-regional or even global websites. One example of a company which has just launched its first pan-European website is the Schweppes company with a website which gives details of bars throughout Europe, including their facilities, prices, etc. This website encourages customers who have visited a bar listed on the site to use 'word of mouse' to rate these and spread their experience and views about a particular bar to other members of the website. In effect, if you like, it is along the lines of a consumer guide to bars and drinking throughout Europe. In the future we can expect many more companies to use their international websites in similar ways to this, responding with pan-global technology to pan-global customers.

These, then are some of the major additional considerations and implications with regard to the application and management of our various marketing mix elements in the context of international and global markets. Remember again we have only covered a small proportion of the issues in this area and again you are reminded therefore to read at least one, and preferably more, chapters from the texts recommended for this syllabus by the CIM.

Summary

- In this unit we have explored the importance of contextual setting in influencing the selection of, and emphasis given to, the marketing mix tools.
- We have explained the differences in the characteristics of various types of marketing context and their impact on marketing mix decisions.
- We have compared and contrasted the marketing activities of organizations that operate and compete in different contextual settings.

- We have seen the effects which information and communication technology and the move towards a virtual marketplace are having on the development and implementation of the marketing mix.

- We have seen that marketers that operate in an international and global context need to take account of this with respect to the use and application of the different marketing mix tools.

Further study and examination preparation

Now do these questions:

Question 9.3

Using examples explain the importance of contextual setting in influencing the selection of, and emphasis given to, the marketing mix tools.

Question 9.4

Briefly outline the seven marketing mix elements in Services marketing.

Question 9.5

Using examples, explain how the marketing mix elements may have to reflect differences between countries when the marketer operates in an international environment.

Question 9.6

How can technological advances be used specifically within the promotional elements of the communications mix?

Question 9.7

Explain what is meant by the following terms and state how each might be used by marketers at a tactical level.
1. Internet.
2. Intranet.
3. Extranet.

Previous examination question

Study tip

This question is taken from Fundamentals of Marketing paper December 2000 Question 7. Remember, you can access the full specimen answer for this question on the following website addresses: www.marketingonline.co.uk or www.bh.com/marketing.

Question E9

a. Using a financial service of your choice, identify four differences between services and products and discuss the problems that these differences present to the marketer.

(8 marks)

b. Identify the extended marketing mix which a small service company (such as a management consultancy) would need to consider when marketing its services.

(12 marks)
(20 marks in total)

Bibliography

D. Chaffey, L. Mayer, L. Johnston, Ellis-Chadwick, *Internet Marketing*, FT/Prentice-Hall, 2000.

P. Bickerton, M. Bickerton, U. Pardesi, *Cybermarketing 2nd Edn*, Butterworth-Heinemann, 2000.

S. Dibb, L. Simpkin, W. Pride, O. C. Ferrel, *Marketing Concepts and Strategies: 4th European Edn,* Chaps 7, 20 and 21, Houghton, Mifflin, 2000.

G. Lancaster, L. Massingham, R. Ashford, *Essentials of Marketing: 4th Edn,* Chaps 12 and 14, McGraw-Hill, 2002.

Further reading

F. Brassington, S. Pettitt, *Principles of Marketing: 2nd Edn,* Chaps 22 and 23, FT/Prentice-Hall, 2000.

D. Jobber, *Principles of Marketing: 3rd Edn,* Chaps 14, 20 and 21, McGraw Hill, 2001.

Preparing for your examination

You are now nearing the final phase of your studies and it is time to start the hard work of exam preparation.

During your period of study you will have become used to absorbing large amounts of information. You will have tried to understand and apply aspects of knowledge that may have been very new to you, while some of the information provided may have been more familiar. You may even have undertaken many of the activities that are positioned frequently throughout your Coursebook, which will have enabled you to apply your learning in practical situations. But whatever the state of your knowledge and understanding, do not allow yourself to fall into the trap of thinking that you know enough, you understand enough, or even worse, that you can just take it as it comes on the day.

Never underestimate the pressure of the CIM examination.

The whole point of preparing this text for you is to ensure that you never take the examination for granted, and that you do not go into the exam unprepared for what might come your way for three hours at a time.

One thing's for sure: there is no quick fix, no easy route, no waving a magic wand and finding you know it all.

Whether you have studied alone, in a CIM study centre, or through distance learning, you now need to ensure that this final phase of your learning process is tightly managed, highly structured and objective.

As a candidate in the examination, your role will be to convince the Senior Examiner for this subject that you have credibility. You need to demonstrate to the examiner that you can be trusted to undertake a range of challenges in the context of marketing, that you are able to capitalize on opportunities and manage your way through threats.

You should prove to the Senior Examiner that you are able to apply knowledge, make decisions, respond to situations and solve problems.

Very shortly we are going to look at a range of revision and exam preparation techniques, and at time management issues, and encourage you towards developing and implementing your own revision plan, but before that, let's look at the role of the Senior Examiner.

A bit about the Senior Examiners!

You might be quite shocked to read this, but while it might appear that the examiners are 'relentless question masters' they actually want you to be able to answer the questions and pass the exams! In fact, they would derive no satisfaction or benefits from failing candidates; quite the contrary, they develop the syllabus and exam papers in order that you can learn and then apply that learning effectively so as to pass your examinations. Many of the examiners have said in the past that it is indeed psychologically more difficult to fail students than pass them.

Many of the hints and tips you find within this Appendix have been suggested by the Senior Examiners and authors of the Coursebook series. Therefore you should consider them carefully and resolve to undertake as many of the elements suggested as possible.

The Chartered Institute of Marketing has a range of processes and systems in place within the Examinations Division to ensure that fairness and consistency prevail across the team of examiners, and that the academic and vocational standards that are set and defined are indeed maintained. In doing this, CIM ensures that those who gain the CIM Certificate, Advanced Certificate and Postgraduate Diploma, are worthy of the qualification and perceived as such in the view of employers, actual and potential.

Part of what you will need to do within the examination is be 'examiner friendly' – that means you have to make sure they get what they ask for. This will make life easier for you and for them.

Hints and tips for 'examiner friendly' actions are as follows:

- Show them that you understand the basis of the question, by answering *precisely* the question asked, and not including just about everything you can remember about the subject area.
- Read their needs – how many points is the question asking you to address?
- Respond to the question appropriately. Is the question asking you to take on a role? If so, take on the role and answer the question in respect of the role. For example, you could be positioned as follows:

  'You are working as a Marketing Assistant at Nike UK' or 'You are a Marketing Manager for an Engineering Company' or 'As Marketing Manager write a report to the Managing Partner'.

  These examples of role-playing requirements are taken from questions in past papers.
- Deliver the answer in the format requested. If the examiner asks for a memo, then provide a memo; likewise, if the examiner asks for a report, then write a report. If you do not do this, in some instances you will fail to gain the necessary marks required to pass.
- Take a business-like approach to your answers. This enhances your credibility. Badly ordered work, untidy work, lack of structure, headings and subheadings can be off-putting. This would be unacceptable in the work situation, likewise it will be unacceptable in the eyes of the Senior Examiners and their marking teams.
- Ensure the examiner has something to mark: give them substance, relevance, definitions, illustration and demonstration of your knowledge and understanding of the subject area.
- See the examiner as your potential employer, or ultimate consumer/customer. The whole purpose and culture of marketing is about meeting customers' needs. Try this approach – it works wonders.
- Provide a strong sense of enthusiasm and professionalism in your answers; support it with relevant up-to-date examples and apply them where appropriate.
- Try to do something that will make your exam paper a little bit different – make it stand out in the crowd.

All of these points might seem quite logical to you, but often in the panic of the examination they 'go out of the window'. Therefore it is beneficial to remind ourselves of the importance of the examiner. He/she is the 'ultimate customer' – and we all know customers hate to be disappointed.

As we move on, some of these points will be revisited and developed further.

About the examination

In all examinations, with the exception of Marketing in Practice at Certificate level and Analysis and Decision at Diploma level, the paper is divided into two parts.

- Part A – Mini-case study = 40 per cent of the marks
- Part B – Option choice questions (choice of three questions from seven) = 60 per cent of the marks

Let's look at the basis of each element.

The mini-case study

This is based on a mini-case or scenario with one question, possibly subdivided into between two and four points, but totalling 40 per cent of marks overall.

In essence, you, the candidate, are placed in a problem-solving role through the medium of a short scenario. On occasions, the scenario may consist of an article from a journal in relation to a well-known organization: for example, in the past Interflora, EasyJet and Philips, among others, have been used as the basis of the mini-case.

Alternatively, it will be based upon a fictional company, and the examiner will have prepared it in order that the right balance of knowledge, understanding, application and skills is used.

Approaches to the mini-case study

When undertaking the mini-case study there are a number of key areas you should consider.

Structure/content

The mini-case that you will be presented with will vary slightly from paper to paper, and of course from one examination to the next. Normally the scenario presented will be 400–500 words long and will centre on a particular organization and its problems or may even relate to a specific industry.

The length of the mini-case study means that usually only a brief outline is provided of the situation, the organization and its marketing problems, and you must therefore learn to cope with analysing information and preparing your answer on the basis of a very limited amount of detail.

Time management

There are many differing views on time management and the approaches you can take to managing your time within the examination. You must find an approach to suit your way of working, but always remember, whatever you do, you must ensure that you allow enough time to complete the examination. Unfinished exams mean lost marks.

A typical example of managing time is as follows:

Your paper is designed to assess you over a three-hour period. With 40 per cent of the marks being allocated to the mini-case, it means that you should dedicate somewhere around 75 minutes of your time to both read and write up the answer on this mini-case. Some students, however, will prefer to allocate nearer half of their time (90 minutes) on the mini-case, so that they can read and fully absorb the case and answer the questions in the context of it. This is also acceptable as long as you ensure that you work extremely 'SMART' for the remaining time in order to finish the examination.

Do not forget that while there is only one question within the mini-case, it can have a number of components. You must answer all the components in that question, which is where the balance of times comes into play.

Knowledge/skills tested

Throughout all the CIM papers, your knowledge, skills and ability to apply those skills will be tested. However, the mini-cases are used particularly to test application, i.e. your ability to take your knowledge and apply it in a structured way to a given scenario. The examiners will be looking at your decision-making ability, your analytical and communication skills and, depending on the level, your ability as a manager to solve particular marketing problems.

When the examiner is marking your paper, he/she will be looking to see how you differentiate yourself, looking at your own individual 'unique selling points'. The examiner will also want to see if you can personally apply the knowledge or whether you are only able to repeat the textbook materials.

Format of answers

On many occasions, and within all examinations, you will most likely be given a particular communication method to use. If this is the case, you must ensure that you adhere to the requirements of the examiner. This is all part of meeting customer needs.

The likely communication tools you will be expected to use are as follows:

- Memorandum
- Memorandum/report
- Report
- Briefing notes
- Presentation
- Press release
- Advertisement
- Plan

Make sure that you familiarize yourself with these particular communication tools and practise using them to ensure that, on the day, you will be able to respond confidently to the communication requests of the examiner. Look back at the Customer Communications text at Certificate level to familiarize yourself with the potential requirements of these methods.

By the same token, while communication methods are important, so is meeting the specific requirements of the question. This means you must understand what is meant by the precise instruction given. **Note the following terms carefully:**

- **Identify** – select key issues, point out key learning points, establish clearly what the examiner expects you to identify.
- **Illustrate** – the examiner expects you to provide examples, scenarios and key concepts that illustrate your learning.
- **Compare and contrast** – look at the range of similarities between the two situations, contexts or even organizations. Then compare them, i.e. ascertain and list how activities, features, etc. agree or disagree. Contrasting means highlighting the differences between the two.
- **Discuss** – questions that have 'discuss' in them offer a tremendous opportunity for you to debate, argue, justify your approach or understanding of the subject area – *caution* it is not an opportunity to waffle.
- **Briefly explain** – this means being succinct, structured and concise in your explanation, within the answer. Make your points clear, transparent and relevant.
- **State** – present in a clear, brief format.
- **Interpret** – expound the meaning of, make clear and explicit what it is you see and understand within the data provided.
- **Outline** – provide the examiner with the main concepts and features being asked for and avoid minor technical details. Structure will be critical here, or else you could find it difficult to contain your answer.
- **Relate** – show how different aspects of the syllabus connect together.
- **Evaluate** – review and reflect upon an area of the syllabus, a particular practice, an article, etc., and consider its overall worth in respect of its use as a tool or a model and its overall effectiveness in the role it plays.

Source: Worsam, Mike, *How to Pass Marketing*, Croner, 1989.

Your approach to mini-cases

There is no one right way to approach and tackle a mini-case study, indeed it will be down to each individual to use their own creativity in tackling the tasks presented. You will have to use your initiative and discretion about how best to approach the mini-case. Having said this, however, there are some basic steps you can take.

- Ensure that you read through the case study at least twice before making any judgements, starting to analyse the information provided, or indeed writing the answers.
- On the third occasion read through the mini-case and, using a highlighter, start marking the essential and relevant information critical to the content and context. Then turn your attention to the question again, this time reading slowly and carefully to assess what it is you are expected to do. Note any instructions that the examiner gives you, and then start to plan how you might answer the question. Whatever the question, ensure the answer has a structure: a beginning, a structured central part of the answer and, finally, always a conclusion.
- Keep the context of the question continually in mind: that is, the specifics of the case and the role which you might be performing.
- Because there is limited material available, you will sometimes need to make assumptions. Don't be afraid to do this, it will show initiative on your part. Assumptions are an important part of dealing with case studies and can help you to be quite creative with your answer. However, do explain the basis of your assumptions within your answer so that the examiner understands the nature of them, and why you have arrived at your particular outcome. **Always ensure that your assumptions are realistic.**
- Only now are you approaching the stage where it is time to start writing your answer to the question, tackling the problems, making decisions and recommendations on the case scenario set before you. As mentioned previously, your points will often be best set out in a report or memo type format, particularly if the examiner does not specify a communication method.
- Ensure that your writing is succinct, avoids waffle and responds directly to the questions asked.

Part B

Again, with the exception of the Analysis and Decision case study, each Part B is comprised of six or seven more traditional questions, each worth 20 per cent. You will be expected to choose three of those questions, to make up the remaining 60 per cent of available marks.

Realistically, the same principles apply for these questions as in the case study. Communication formats, reading through the questions, structure, role-play, context, etc. – everything is the same.

Part B will cover a number of broader issues from within the syllabus and will be taken from any element of it. The examiner makes the choice, and no prior direction is given to students or tutors on what that might be.

As regards time management in this area, if you used about 75 minutes for the mini-case you should have around 105 minutes left. This provides you with around 30 minutes to plan and write a question and 5 minutes per question to review and revise your answers. Keep practising – use a cooker timer, alarm clock or mobile phone alarm as your timer and work hard at answering questions within the timeframe given.

Specimen examination papers and answers

To help you prepare and understand the nature of the paper, go to www.marketingonline.co.uk or www.bh.com/marketing to access Specimen Answers and Senior Examiner's advice for these exam questions. During your study, the author of your Coursebook may have on occasions asked you to refer to these papers and answer the questions. You should undertake these exercises and utilize every opportunity to practise meeting examination requirements.

The specimen answers are vital learning tools. They are not always perfect, as they are answers written by students and annotated by the Senior Examiners, but they will give you a good indication of the approaches you could take, and the examiners' annotations suggest how these answers might be improved. Please use them. You can also access this type of information through the Virtual Institute on the CIM website using your student registration number as an access code.

Other sources of information to support your learning through the Virtual Institute are 'Hot Topics'. These give you scope to undertake a range of associated activities related to the syllabus and study areas, and will also be very useful to you when you are revising.

Key elements of preparation

One Senior Examiner suggests the three elements involved in preparing for your examination can be summarized thus:

- Learning
- Memory
- Revision

Let's look at each point in turn.

Learning

Quite often students find it difficult to learn properly. You can passively read books, look at some of the materials, perhaps revise a little, and regurgitate it all in the examination. In the main, however, this is rather an unsatisfactory method of learning. It is meaningless, shallow and ultimately of little use in practice.

For learning to be truly effective it must be active and applied. You must involve yourself in the learning process by thinking about what you have read, testing it against your experience by reflecting on how you use particular aspects of marketing, and how you could perhaps improve your own performance by implementing particular aspects of your learning into your everyday life. You should adopt the old adage of 'learning by doing'. If you do, you will find that passive learning has no place in your study life.

Below are some suggestions that have been prepared to assist you with the learning pathway throughout your revision.

- Always make your own notes, in words you understand, and ensure that you combine all the sources of information and activities within them.
- Always try to relate your learning back to your own organization.
- Make sure you define key terms concisely, wherever possible.
- Do not try to memorize your ideas, but work on the basis of understanding and, most important, applying them.
- Think about the relevant and topical questions that might be set – use the questions and answers in your Coursebooks to identify typical questions that might be asked in the future.
- Attempt all of the questions within each of your Coursebooks since these are vital tests of your active learning and understanding.

Memory

If you are prepared to undertake an active learning programme then your knowledge will be considerably enhanced, as understanding and application of knowledge does tend to stay in your 'long-term' memory. It is likely that passive learning will only stay in your 'short-term' memory.

Do not try to memorize parrot fashion; it is not helpful and, even more important, examiners are experienced in identifying various memorizing techniques and therefore will spot them as such.

Having said this, it is quite useful to memorize various acronyms such as SWOT, PEST, PESTLE, STEEPLE, or indeed various models such as Ansoff, GE Matrix, Shell Directional, etc., as in some of the questions you may be required to use illustrations of these to assist your answer.

Revision

The third and final stage to consider is 'revision', which is what we will concentrate on in detail below. Here just a few key tips are offered.

Revision should be an ongoing process rather than a panic measure that you decide to undertake just before the examination. You should be preparing notes *throughout* your course, with the view to using them as part of your revision process. Therefore ensure that your notes are sufficiently comprehensive that you can reuse them successfully.

For each concept you learn about, you should identify, through your reading and your own personal experience, at least two or three examples that you could use; this then gives you some scope to broaden your perspective during the examination. It will, of course, help you gain some points for initiative with the examiners.

Knowledge is not something you will gain overnight – as we saw earlier, it is not a quick fix; it involves a process of learning that enables you to lay solid foundations upon which to build your long-term understanding and application. This will benefit you significantly in the future, not just in the examination.

In essence, you should ensure that you do the following in the period before the real intensive revision process begins.

*   Keep your study file well organized, updated and full of newspaper and journal cuttings that may help you formulate examples in your mind for use during the examination.
*   Practise defining key terms and acronyms from memory.
*   Prepare topic outlines and essay answer plans.
*   When you start your intensive revision, ensure it is planned and structured in the way described below. And then finally, read your concentrated notes the night before the examination.

Revision planning

You are now on a critical path – although hopefully not too critical at this time – with somewhere in the region of between four and six weeks to go to the examination. The following hints and tips will help you plan out your revision study.

*   You will, as already explained, need to be very organized. Therefore, before doing anything else, put your files, examples, reading material, etc. in good order, so that you are able to work with them in the future and, of course, make sense of them.
*   Ensure that you have a quiet area within which to work. It is very easy to get distracted when preparing for an examination.
*   Take out your file along with your syllabus and make a list of key topic areas that you have studied and which you now need to revise. You could use the basis of this book to do that, by taking each unit a step at a time.
*   Plan the use of your time carefully. Ideally you should start your revision at least six weeks prior to the exam, so therefore work out how many spare hours you could give to the revision process and then start to allocate time in your diary, and do not double-book with anything else.
*   Give up your social life for a short period of time. As the saying goes 'no pain – no gain'.

- Looking at each of the subject areas in turn, identify which are your strengths and which are your weaknesses. Which areas have you grasped and understood, and which are the areas that you have really struggled with? Split your page in two and make a list on each side. For example:

Planning and control	
Strengths	Weaknesses
Audit – PEST, SWOT, Models Portfolio analysis	Ratio analysis Market sensing Productivity analysis Trend extrapolation Forecasting

- Break down your list again and divide the points of weakness, giving priority in the first instance to your weakest areas and even prioritizing them by giving them a number. This will enable you to master the more difficult areas. Up to 60 per cent of your remaining revision time should be given over to that, as you may find you have to undertake a range of additional reading and also perhaps seeking tutor support, if you are studying at a CIM Accredited Study Centre.
- The rest of the time should be spent reinforcing your knowledge and understanding of the stronger areas, spending time testing yourself on how much you really know.
- Should you be taking two examinations or more at any one time, then the breakdown and managing of your time will be critical.
- Taking a subject at a time, work through your notes and start breaking them down into subsections of learning, and ultimately into key learning points, items that you can refer to time and time again, that are meaningful and that your mind will absorb. You yourself will know how you best remember key points. Some people try to develop acronyms, or flowcharts or matrices, mind maps, fishbone diagrams, etc., or various connection diagrams that help them recall certain aspects of models. You could also develop processes that enable you to remember approaches to various options. (But do remember what we said earlier about regurgitating stuff, parrot fashion.)

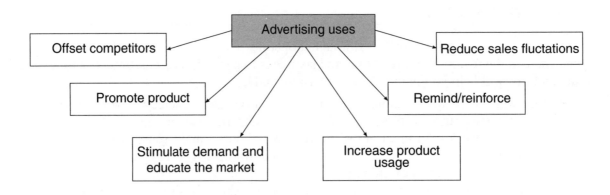

Figure A1.1 *Use of a diagram to summarize key components of a concept (Source: Adapted from Dibb, Simkin, Pride & Ferrell, Marketing Concepts and Strategies, 4th edition, Houghton Mifflin, 2001)*

Figure A1.1 is just a brief example of how you could use a 'bomb-burst' diagram (which, in this case, highlights the uses of advertising) as a very helpful approach to memorizing key elements of learning.

- Eventually you should reduce your key learning to bullet points. For example: imagine you were looking at the concept of Time Management – you could eventually reduce your key learning to a bullet list containing the following points in relation to 'Effective Prioritization:'

  - Organize
  - Take time
  - Delegate
  - Review

  Each of these headings would then remind you of the elements you need to discuss associated with the subject area.

- Avoid getting involved in reading too many textbooks at this stage, as you may start to find that you are getting confused overall.

- Look at examination questions on previous papers, and start to observe closely the various roles and tasks they expect you to undertake, and importantly, the context in which they are set.

- Use the specimen exam papers and specimen answers to support your learning and see how you could actually improve upon them.

- Without exception, find an associated examination question for the areas that you have studied and revised, and undertake it (more than once if necessary).

- Without referring to notes or books, try to draft an answer plan with the key concepts, knowledge, models and information that are needed to successfully complete the answer. Then refer to the specimen answer to see how close you are to the actual outline presented. Planning your answer, and ensuring that key components are included, and that the question has a meaningful structure, is one of the most beneficial activities that you can undertake.

- Now write the answer out in full, time-constrained and written by hand, not with the use of IT. (At this stage, you are still expected to be the scribe for the examination and present handwritten work. Many of us find this increasingly difficult as we spend more and more time using our computers to present information. Do your best to be neat. Spidery handwriting is often offputting to the examiner.)

- When writing answers as part of your revision process, also be sure to practise the following essential examinations techniques:

  - **Identify and use the communication method** requested by the examiner.
  - **Always have three key parts to the answer** – an introduction, middle section that develops your answer in full, and a conclusion. Where appropriate, ensure that you have an introduction, main section, summary/conclusion and, if requested or helpful, recommendations.
  - **Always answer the question in the context or role set.**
  - **Always comply with the nature and terms of the question.**
  - **Leave white space.** Do not overcrowd your page; Leave space between paragraphs, and make sure your sentences do not merge into one blur. (Don't worry – there is always plenty of paper available to use in the examination.)
  - **Count** how many actions the question asks you to undertake and double-check at the end that you have met the full range of demands of the question.
  - **Use examples** – to demonstrate your knowledge and understanding of the particular syllabus area. These can be from journals, the Internet, the press, or your own experience.

- **Display your vigour and enthusiasm for marketing.** Remember to think of the Senior Examiner as your Customer, or future employer, and do your best to deliver what is wanted to satisfy their needs. Impress them and show them how you are a 'cut above the rest'.
- Review all your practice answers critically, with the above points in mind.

Practical actions

The critical path is becoming even more critical now as the examination looms. The following are vital points.

- Have you registered with CIM?
- Do you know where you are taking your examination? CIM should let you know approximately one month in advance.
- Do you know where your examination centre is? If not find out, take a drive, time it – whatever you do don't be late!
- Make sure you have all the tools of the examination ready. A dictionary, calculator, pens, pencils, ruler, etc. Try not to use multiple shades of pens, but at the same time make your work look professional. *Avoid using red and green as these are the colours that will be used for marking.*

Summary

Above all you must remember that you personally have invested a tremendous amount of time, effort and money in studying for this programme and it is therefore imperative that you consider the suggestions given here as they will help to maximize your return on your investment.

Many of the hints and tips offered here are generic and will work across most of the CIM courses. We have tried to select those that will help you most in taking a sensible, planned approach to your study and revision.

The key to your success is being prepared to put in the time and effort required, planning your revision, and equally important, planning and answering your questions in a way that will ensure that you pass your examination on the day.

The advice offered here aims to guide you from a practical perspective. Guidance on syllabus content and developments associated with your learning will become clear to you as you work through this Coursebook. The authors of each Coursebook have given subject-specific guidance on the approach to the examination and on how to ensure that you meet the content requirements of the kind of question you will face. These considerations are in addition to the structuring issues we have been discussing throughout this Appendix.

Each of the authors and Senior Examiners will guide you on their preferred approach to questions and answers as they go. Therefore where you are presented with an opportunity to be involved in some activity or undertake an examination question either during or at the end of your study units, do take it. It not only prepares you for the examination, but helps you learn in the applied way we discussed above.

Here, then, is a last reminder:

- Ensure you make the most of your learning process throughout.
- Keep structured and orderly notes from which to revise.
- Plan your revision – don't let it just happen.
- Provide examples to enhance your answers.

- Practise your writing skills in order that you present your work well and your writing is readable.
- Take as many opportunities to test your knowledge and measure your progress as possible.
- Plan and structure your answers.
- Always do as the question asks you, especially with regard to context and communication method.
- **Do not leave it until the last minute!**

The writers would like to take this opportunity to wish you every success in your endeavours to study, to revise and to pass your examinations.

Karen Beamish
Academic Development Advisor

The answers that follow are indicative and are not intended to be complete. Some of the answers to the activities are embedded in the course materials, the essential text, in web sites or simply in the mind of the reader.

Unit 1

Debriefing Activity 1.2

So what conclusions did you arrive at from this activity?

Each statement is of course intended to capture the essence of the sort of differences in managerial attitudes and outlook we might find in organizations with each of the different orientations. Your answer should have been as follows:

Company A = No. 4 This company is product-oriented: the attitude is that a good product will sell itself.

Company B = No. 2 This company is sales-oriented: the attitude is that aggressive hard selling is required.

Company C = No. 1 This company is marketing-oriented: the attitude is that even though it is sometimes difficult, everyone in the company must try to satisfy the customer.

Company D = No. 3 The company is production-oriented. The attitude is characterized by an almost exclusive focus on production efficiency and effectiveness.

Debriefing Activity 1.3

Although you may have used different words, your answers should have indicated the following:

Factor	*Marketing-oriented era*
Demand	Latent demand low
Average disposable income	High
General level of education	High
Mass media/access to information	Well developed/high
Supply/industry capacity	Overcapacity
Competition	Severe/global

Debriefing Activity 1.7

Exam hint Use the initial letters APIC to help you remember the key tasks of marketing managers:

A: Analysis – The first stage in marketing management's tasks. Customers, markets, competitors, and company strengths and weaknesses must be analysed. Examples from recruitment advertisements include 'Market analysis'/ 'Building of customer database'.

P: Planning – Includes objective setting, choice of target markets, marketing strategies and tactics. Examples from recruitment advertisement include 'Develop long-range marketing plans', 'new product/service development', 'corporate identity'.

I: Implementation – Includes staffing, allocating tasks, budgeting and organizing. Examples from recruitment advertisement include 'handling hybrid staff/ line role', 'leading change process'.

C: Control – Evaluating progress against objectives and targets. Correcting any deficiencies. Example from Recruitment Advertisement includes 'Strong Bottom Line Orientation'.

Debriefing Question 1.1

The four consumer rights that President Kennedy referred to in his speech in 1962 were as follows:

- The right to safety.
- The right to be informed.
- The right to choose.
- The right to be heard.

Since Kennedy's speech outlining these four basic rights, the consumer movement has gathered pace, first in America and then in Western Europe. Consumers have become increasingly critical of what are admittedly sometimes questionable practices of a minority of marketers. They are also increasingly aware of their rights, and demand that these be protected. Many of the worst excesses of marketing in years gone by are now covered by legislation that protects consumers. Above all, consumers have become much better organized and skilled in protecting themselves. In the United Kingdom, for example, in addition to the legal protection afforded to consumers, a number of consumer organizations look after and promote consumers' interests. Some of these are official, such as consumer watchdogs set up to monitor marketing activities and particularly prices in the now privatized utilities of electricity, gas and water. Others are unofficial, such as local pressure groups that will respond to what they see as any infringement of their rights by local companies. There are even specialist consumer magazines, which report on the marketing activities of companies and in particular look at how customers can get the best value. Perhaps the best example of such a magazine in the United Kingdom is *Which?*, produced and published by the Consumers' Association.

Debriefing Activity 1.10

The results of consumerism have included an increase in various acts and legislation designed to protect consumers, and an increased awareness on the part of marketers of the need to ensure that consumers' views and welfare are protected. Enlightened marketers see consumerism not as a threat but an opportunity to respond to changing customer needs and requirements. The most successful companies have been those that have responded positively to the consumer movement and have been proactive in developing marketing programmes to take account of the movement.

There are plenty of examples of how the consumer movement has in one way or another affected how products are produced and marketed, and even if they are marketed at all. For example, in the interests of health, cigarette advertising in many countries is now at least severely constrained and often banned completely. Similarly, many food products are now marketed on the basis of the fact that they are healthier than their predecessors of several years ago. Consumers are demanding and getting healthier and safer products from marketers.

Debriefing Activity 1.11

Here are some examples of products and services whose marketing has been affected by an increased interest on the part of the consumer in health and safety:

- Lower tar tobacco products.
- Low fat products.
- Low cholesterol products.
- Exercise products.
- Sun blocks.
- Air bag crash protectors in cars.

Debriefing Activity 1.12

Here are just some examples of issues associated with marketing that are frequently raised as causing problems for the environment:

- Products that use/deplete scarce resources, e.g. hardwood forests.
- Products whose manufacture, use, or disposal of, pollutes rivers, etc.
- Products that endanger species.
- Products whose manufacture, use, or disposal of, pollutes the atmosphere.

Debriefing Activity 1.13

Examples of products that have specifically been marketed to take account of green issues and concerns include:

Unleaded petrol. Fake furs. Chlorine-free detergents. CFC-free aerosols and refrigeration. Biodegradable plastics. Recyclable packaging.

Wood products made from managed forests.

Debriefing Question 1.2

The basic view of marketing is that to succeed, a business requires satisfied and happy customers who return to the business to provide additional custom. It is about an exchange process for something of value, typically payment or a donation; the customers receive a product or service that satisfies their needs.

We can refer to three definitions which confirm this view:

1. Marketing consists of individual and organizational activities that facilitate and expedite satisfying exchange relationships in a dynamic environment through the creation, distribution, promotion and pricing of goods, services and ideas.

   Dibb, Simkin, Pride and Ferrell, 1997

2. Marketing means working with markets to bring about exchanges for the purpose of satisfying human needs and wants. It is a process, by which individuals and groups obtain what they need and want by creating and exchanging products and value with others.

   Kotler, Armstrong, Saunders and Wong, 1996

3. Marketing is the management process responsible for identifying, anticipating and satisfying customer requirements profitably.

   The Chartered Institute of Marketing

However, these definitions mainly refer to products and services, it must not be forgotten that marketing is also important for the not-for-profit organizations such as charities, etc., where profit is not the goal. In these organizations marketing is required for a range of other issues such as raising awareness, communicating messages which aim to change behaviour, etc. Take time to consider the exchange process for a number of organizations and clients/customers with which you are familiar.

Debriefing Question 1.3

Philip Kotler details the main differences between the following concepts as follows:

1. The *production concept* holds that consumers will favour products that are available and highly affordable and that the management therefore should focus on improving production and distribution efficiency.

2. Many organizations follow the *selling concept*, which holds that consumers will not buy enough of the organization's products unless it undertakes a large-scale selling and promotion effort.

3. The *marketing concept* holds that achieving organizational goals depends on determining the needs and wants of target markets and delivering the desired satisfactions more effectively and efficiently than competitors do.

Thus it can be seen that the organizations which are customer focused are practising the marketing concept and endeavour to achieve the maximization of customer satisfaction. However, the production or selling concepts can lead to 'marketing myopia' and short-term results.

Debriefing Question 1.4

The answer to this question will be based on your knowledge of different organizations, however, you should try to make a note of such organizations and try to identify their problems and reasons for not adopting a marketing concept. Some good current examples are some of the train companies within the UK.

Debriefing Question 1.5

The steps for introducing a marketing-oriented concept within an organization are as follows:

1. define and determine customers' needs
2. top management commitment for marketing orientation
3. invest resources and set up information systems
4. adapt the product/service and/or internal structures
5. communicate the philosophy of staff (customer-driven shared values) and establish a marketing-oriented culture
6. establish marketing strategy and set up customer care systems
7. measure and control.

Debriefing Question 1.6

Some of the main difficulties encountered when introducing a customer-oriented culture are as follows:

1. managers fail to realize or understand the true concept
2. the structure of the organization may require changing and this can lead to other manager's resistance and costs
3. people are frightened and reluctant to change
4. the power struggle between different departments within an organization can hinder the process e.g. the production department
5. in some organizations the responsibility for marketing strategy and implementation are separated and this may offer many problems.

Debriefing Question 1.7

The use of information technology can assist in the management of a customer-oriented culture in the following ways:

1. the sophisticated use of current databases to understand consumer behaviour
2. using the Internet as a marketing information system e.g. for gathering competitor intelligence information
3. using the world wide web to make products more accessible for consumers i.e. the use of on-line shopping, offering more information about the company or product
4. building customer care systems for customers/clients using e-mail and webcasting
5. considering segmentation and global niches from the observation of the use of current or specifically designed Internet pages.

Debriefing Question 1.8

According to Dibb, Simkin, Pride and Ferrell, 1997, for an exchange to take place, three conditions need to exist – two or more individuals must participate, each party must possess something of value that the other party desires, each party must be willing to give up its 'something of value' to receive the 'something of value' held by the other party. However, this process is very interesting when considering charities, as the 'something of value' for the 'customer' or donator is usually money or time to help the charity – the exchange item is the self-esteem and sense of well being received by the donator.

Debriefing Question 1.9

Within a service organization it is important to consider the characteristics of services as intangible, inseparable, perishable and variable. These characteristics mean that the organization will need to ensure that a marketing orientation is managed well.

Regular customer audits will need to identify the consumer's expectations and perceptions of the service quality and delivery. This means that the service quality must be managed well and includes the tangibles, reliability, responsiveness, assurance and empathy of the organization. Marketers need to therefore consider the extended marketing mix elements of people, processes and physical evidence.

Therefore, those developing a marketing-oriented service organization will need to consider the marketing strategy, the management style, structure of the organization, the information systems, skills and staffing and shared values of the organization, so that customer-driven service quality levels are paramount.

Debriefing Question 1.10

This is very similar to Question 5 and the main barriers are detailed within that answer. However, for this answer try to think of examples from any organizations with which you are familiar. You should get used to citing examples within your examination scripts as this will add to your discussion and demonstrate your understanding and knowledge of the theory to the examiner.

Debriefing Question 1.11

There are a number of issues which marketers must understand when considering their role. As we enter the new millennium marketers are much more aware of their responsibility towards society in terms of moral and ethical responsibilities of business. The recognition of the social and environmental impact of marketing must be appreciated, such as economic, legal and, importantly, ethical concerns. Society has become more concerned about factors such as the environment and safety issues, which have grown out of consumerism and green marketing issues. Consumers are demanding and getting healthier and safer products from marketers.

It is interesting to consider the concept of social responsibility relating to the marketing mix and the following offers some examples of these implications:

Products: safety, recyclable packaging and the use of environmentally friendly materials.

Promotion: accurate and reliable, the use of an ethical stance as a communication message (e.g. Body Shop).

Pricing policies: ensure fair and ethical pricing strategies.

Place: distribution using 'green' methods.

People: organizations' responsibility for their staff and the local community.

Process: consideration of the energy consumed and decreases in waste products.

Policies: companies consider the motivational aspects for their staff and how to add value to society in general.

Debriefing Question 1.12

One of the most recent changes in marketing management has been the concept of relationship marketing. Relationship marketing is where all the activities of an organization are used to build, maintain and develop customer relations, which should lead to customer retention. RM is concerned with getting and keeping customers by ensuring that an appropriate combination of marketing, customer service and quality is provided. It is concerned with the development of mutually beneficial long-term relationships with customers and suppliers. This leads to two-way communications and the development of personalized marketing strategies to ensure a unique sustained competitive advantage. The concept also considers all of the organization's partnerships – supplier, lateral, internal as well as the buyer/consumer. To ensure successful RM there needs to be a supportive organizational culture, internal marketing and a clear understanding of customer expectations. The use of information technology is also important to help manage the programme with the use of sophisticated customer databases.

Debriefing Question E1

First of all note the allocation of marks to each part of the question. In the examination you will need to allocate your time accordingly.

On the first part of this question you would need to first justify your business-to-business and non-profit organization which in your view have been successful in adopting the marketing concept. The examiner would be looking for examples and reasons such as: researching customer needs, adaptation of the marketing mix elements to meet these needs, and the implementation of a good customer care policy.

The second part, worth 8 marks does not require in-depth knowledge of Information Technology but does require some understanding of how this technology can help a company become more customer and marketing oriented. A good answer would include, for example, the use of databases to build more information on customers and their needs; using the world-wide web and the internet to make products more accessible and the use of, for example, e-mail technology to help communicate with customers and build better customer care systems. Lots of examples can be used in this answer and could equally well be applied to either the business-to-business organization selected or the non-profit organization.

Unit 2

Debriefing Activity 2.2

The following is a brief explanation of Porter's three core strategies and their implications:

1. *Cost leadership*
   This is a strategy based on having the lowest costs in the industry. It therefore requires the company to pursue ways of reducing cost, such as economies of scale, efficiencies in design and production, etc. Essentially it is not a marketing strategy as such, more a financial one. The problem with this approach is that it is not market/customer-oriented and can leave a company vulnerable to its more marketing-oriented competitors.

2. *Differentiation*
   This strategy is based on offering the market something distinct and different from competitors. For example, the differentiation may be based on, say, having the highest quality in the industry, or perhaps the speediest delivery. A more marketing-oriented approach than cost leadership but needs to be based on differences that are valuable to customers and can be protected from competitors.

3. *Focus*
   As implied by the title of this strategy, it is based on targeting specific segments of the market rather than adopting an industry-wide approach. Companies that focus can become specialists in supplying particular markets but can be vulnerable to market trends and larger competitors

Debriefing Activity 2.3

Examples of variables used to segment consumer and industrial markets are shown below:

- **Consumer bases**

    Demographics: e.g. age, sex, race, religion

    Socio-economic: e.g. income, occupation, social class

    Geographic: e.g. country, region, type of housing

    Personality and lifestyle: e.g. extrovert, introvert

    Purchase occasion: e.g. regular, special, distress

    User status: e.g. first-time, non-user, regular user

    Usage rate: e.g. heavy, light, medium

    Benefits sought: e.g. quality, service, economy

- **Industrial bases**

    Demographic: e.g. industry type, end use, company size

    Geographic: e.g. country, region

    Purchasing organization: e.g. centralized, decentralized

    User status: e.g. non-user, first-time, regular

    Usage rate: e.g. heavy, light, medium

    Benefits sought: e.g. delivery, quality, service, economy

Debriefing Activity 2.5

Some of the advantages and disadvantages of each targeting strategy are as follows:

- Undifferentiated targeting

    1. Advantages, e.g. low cost, economies of scale, simple
    2. Disadvantages, e.g. not customer-oriented

- Differentiated targeting

    1. Advantages, e.g. customer-oriented, spreads risk
    2. Disadvantages, e.g. potentially high cost

- Concentrated targeting

    1. Advantages, e.g. customer-oriented, specialized skills
    2. Disadvantages, e.g. high risk/vulnerable to market change.

Debriefing Question 2.1

It is important that marketing managers are able to understand the environment in which they are operating. This means that a systematic PEST analysis will need to be undertaken on a regular basis. The PEST analysis includes:

- *Political factors* such as a change in government and the ramifications of their strategies, e.g. tax levels, pollution policies and education issues.
- *Economic factors* such as the impact of the trade cycle, disposable income and inflation.
- *Social/cultural issues* such as the ageing consumer, increases in one-parent families, changing values and attitudes and beliefs to smoking.
- *Technological factors* such as the increased rate of computer capability production methods.

The environmental scanning or PEST analysis should help to identify the opportunities and strengths of an organization and its products/services. It is also important that a SWOT analysis is undertaken to help plan the marketing mix, which includes:

- *Strengths* of the product/service/organization.
- *Weaknesses* of the organization.
- *Opportunities* available to the organization (external factors).
- *Threats* which may come from the competitions or other external factors.

This analysis helps the marketer understand the environment in which the organization is operating and thus the marketing plan can be devised taking account of the issues identified.

Debriefing Question 2.2

In order to plan the marketing mix effectively, a systematic marketing planning process must be undertaken on a regular basis. The steps involved are as follows:

- Identification of *corporate mission and objectives*.
- *Marketing audit analysis*: marketing opportunities/trends; customers' needs and perceptions; the marketing environment and trends; competition and competitors' strategies.
- *SWOT analysis*.
- *Marketing objectives* set.
- Determine *marketing strategy*: growth strategies; overall competitive strategies; segmentation, targeting and positioning strategies.
- *Tactics* - plan marketing mix.
- *Implementation*.
- *Monitoring and control*

Debriefing Question 2.3

These issues have clear implications for marketers when considering the marketing mix.

Porter identified three core marketing strategies:

- *Cost leadership* companies can implement a cost leadership strategy by driving down their own costs such as production and transportation. Investment in technology is one of the key ways in which cost can be kept low and economies of scale achieved.
- *Focus strategy* – this is where the organization considers focusing on very specific segments. The strategy can be coupled with cost leadership or differentiation. To implement this strategy, there must be very good information about the specific segments and strong relationships will need to be achieved. The creation of a specialist reputation will be necessary.
- *Differentiation strategy* – this strategy relies on the ability to offer some unique and different benefits, such as the creation of a strong brand.

The marketing mix should reflect and support the broad thrust of these generic marketing strategies and a company pursuing cost leadership, for example, would probably have a very different marketing mix to one pursuing differentiation.

Debriefing Question 2.4

Ansoff has proposed a useful framework for detecting new intensive growth opportunities called a product/market expansion grid:

The company first considers whether it could gain more market share with its current products in their current markets – known as a market penetration strategy.

A second possible strategy is the development of new markets for current products – known as a market development strategy.

A third strategy that the company can consider is the development of new products for its current markets – a product development strategy.

Finally, a diversification strategy may be considered where it might develop new products for new markets.

Debriefing Question E2

a On the first part of the question the answer should have focused on explaining a SWOT analysis, in particular explaining that strengths and weaknesses stem from the internal part of the marketing audit and involve controllable elements whereas the opportunities and threats stem from the external audit encompassing the PEST factors and are essentially uncontrollable. The term 'realistic' in the question is intended for you to demonstrate that you realize that only some of the opportunities presented by the environment can be taken advantage of according to a company's profile of strengths and weaknesses.

b This second part of the question obviously requires an understanding of the role of marketing planning. Note that it is not intended to be turned into a question on new product development. The answer should encompass issues such as analysing the marketing environment and company strengths and weaknesses and the importance of identifying target segments for the new product together with objectives and strategies encompassing the marketing mix and backed up through implementation and control systems.

c Relatively straight forward, this, apart from it requires an overview of the whole marketing planning process ranging from the identification of corporate objectives through to monitoring and evaluation. Note the importance of using examples in discussing briefly each of the steps.

Unit 3

Debriefing Activity 3.1

Clearly, there are two different views here – customers are seeking to derive some kind of satisfaction whereas those who sell to customers seek to provide that satisfaction and in return for this require some kind of recompense. Although customers pay money for something specific and identifiable, they are in fact paying for something incorporating promotion, availability and perceived value. This has been termed a 'bundle of satisfactions', which can be tangible or intangible and Figure 3.1 explains this more fully.

Debriefing Activity 3.2

There are obvious answers here, e.g. fitted curtains ordered by the housewife are for privacy at night. However, curtains are also part of the furnishings of a room and in most cases they are purchased to co-ordinate with the decoration of the rest of the room. The decor of the room might then produce a feeling of 'homeliness'. The fitted curtains might come from a good quality yet expensive store, and if this is the case, the housewife might well be able to impress her friends with the purchase. There are many more possible 'bundles of satisfactions' that might be considered, depending upon the motives of the housewife.

A simple satisfaction might be in the case of the 8-year-old who has just purchased an ice cream, which might be simply the sheer potential delight of what is to come!

The important thing to remember is that satisfactions will differ according to the buyer behaviour of the individual making the purchase. In other words, buyers' motives for purchase will be different, and this indeed is what makes marketing interesting in terms of considering the complexities of human behaviour. You should then be able to work out many and varied need satisfactions for the other examples.

Debriefing Activity 3.13

It is important to note that products can be, and often are, at different stages of their lifecycles in different parts of the world. Obviously the international marketer in particular needs to consider this in using the notion of the lifecycle stages for planning strategy. This applies to every stage of the product lifecycle but if we consider, as we do here, the introductory stage, a good example of a product being at different stages in different parts of the world is the home computer or PC. In the United States these products are well into the growth stage with regard to diffusion in the market place. In the United Kingdom however, the PC has only just begun to enter this growth stage. In the Eastern Bloc countries and in many developing countries the home computer has only just entered the introduction stage of the lifecycle.

Debriefing Activity 3.14

With reference to our earlier comment regarding products being at different stages of the lifecycle in different countries, digital television is now in the growth stage in the United Kingdom but towards its peak of growth and even entering maturity in Japan.

Debriefing Activity 3.19

Taking the United Kingdom as the market, as mentioned earlier, the home personal computer is now moving into the growth stage of its diffusion. In the early stages of this process, the innovator categories who were the first to purchase their home computers were a relatively small group of consumers who had a high degree of technical knowledge and interest in computers. Put simply, they were 'computer freaks' who were more interested in the technical aspects of the product. As the product has begun to move through the market place however, we have begun to see the emergence of the early adopters and now the early majority group. The early adopters were often again technically oriented customers but many of this group were interested in the games aspect of PCs. The early majority, however, although still interested in these entertainment aspects, are beginning to use computers as tools to help them in their family and sometimes business lives. In short, this group are much more interested in more everyday uses for their computers. Eventually the late majority will enter the market as prices continue to drop whilst uses expand. Finally, the laggards will enter when eventually, and probably still with some reluctance, they begin to see the potential benefits of the home PC.

Debriefing Activity 3.20

Needless to say, and as you probably appreciate, there is indeed a relationship between the two. In fact, essentially they are opposite sides of the same coil - so as to speak. The adoption process effectively underpins the diffusion process and hence the product lifecycle. The product adoption process, however, relates to the steps and stages which an individual passes through en route to either accepting or rejecting a new product. Diffusion on the other hand represents a summary or collective view of the individual adoption processes. Quite simply, the more individuals who adopt a new product or service, and the quicker they do this the greater and speedier would be the rate of diffusion in the market. The diffusion process represents adoption over time and the product lifecycle model represents this on a cumulative basis.

Debriefing Activity 3.22

Obviously your answers to this activity will depend upon the examples you have selected, but in the case of your industrial product, the major functions of packaging are likely to be much more closely related to the more functional aspects of the package such as, for example, protection and ease of use. In the case of the non-food consumer product such as, for example, clothing, the functions of the packaging will again be protection and ease of use but in addition, if it is a clothing product, the packaging will also have to facilitate the handling of the product before purchase, and possibly information in terms of care of the product, etc. Finally, for our processed food item for sale in a typical supermarket, the packaging must again protect and these days prevent tampering, but also must facilitate stacking and display. Perhaps above all, the packaging must serve to differentiate the product and act as the 'silent salesperson'.

Debriefing Activity 3.23

There are many examples where marketers have prolonged the lifecycles of brands and kept them fresh, exciting and successful. Perhaps one of the best of these examples is the Lucozade brand. Initially positioned as a glucose drink primarily for the sick, eventually as consumers became more informed, the brand waned in this market. Recognizing this, the brand management team began to position and promote the brand as a 'pick me up' drink for the tired housewife midway through her morning chores. As lifestyles changed, and in particular as health and fitness became particularly important in the lifestyles of many consumers in developed economies, the brand was positioned even more strongly as an energy drink. Using well known sports people in their advertising, the brand managers of Lucozade have managed to establish the brand as one of the leading ones in the energy drink market.

Debriefing Question 3.1

In planning the product portfolio, the marketer needs to think through different levels of the product as each level adds more customer value and the total of all the levels constitute a customer value hierarchy. The fundamental level is the core benefit (such as 'knowledge' when buying a book), the second level is the basic product (e.g. the pages and cover). The third level is the expected product, as a set of attributes that the buyer normally expects and agrees to when they purchase the product. The fourth level is this augmented product. This is where the product must meet and exceed the customers' desires beyond their expectations. For example a book publisher can augment the product by adding enhancements via the Internet for only those who have purchased the book.

Today's competition mainly takes place at the product augmentation level. Product augmentation leads the marketer to look at the buyer's total consumption system. However, the marketer has to realize that the product augmentation strategy will cost money and the benefits can soon become expected benefits by the customer.

The fifth level is the potential product, which encompasses all the augmentations and transformations that the product might ultimately undergo in the future.

Debriefing Question 3.2

When considering the launch of a new product it is important to distinguish between the different categories of consumers with respect to the stage in the life cycle of the product at which they adopt the new product. We call these adopter categories. These are outlined below.

1. *Innovators*   These are likely to be younger, better educated and relatively affluent with a higher social status than other customers. They are likely to be broad-minded receptive people with a wide range of social relationships. Innovators are important because they are the first to adopt new products.
2. *Early adopters*   Early adopters are the next group after innovators to adopt new products. They possess many of the characteristics of innovators but tend to belong to more 'local' systems. They tend to be opinion leaders in their groups and are highly influential.
3. *Early majority*   The first group in the mass market to adopt new products, this group is slightly above average in socio-economic terms. They are heavily influenced by opinion leaders from the early adopter category and make extensive use of marketer provided information in their adoption decisions.
4. *Late majority*   As the term implies, this group adopt only towards the end of the life cycle. They are generally more conservative and are heavily influenced by social pressure and economic considerations.
5. *Laggards*   These are the most cautious of all the groups and hence adopt last. They tend to be older, with a relatively low socio-economic status, conservative in their tastes and risk avoiders.

Debriefing Question 3.3

Packaging is often referred to as the fifth 'P' of the marketing mix. Recently packaging has become a very effective and potent marketing tool with an increasing number of products which are sold on a self-selection basis at supermarkets, hence the growth of copy-cat packaging.

The role of packaging includes the following:

- Protection and preservation of the contents.
- Facilitation of mechanized handling.
- The display of legal and usage information.
- Offering an innovation opportunity.
- Silent salesman - attracting attention by size, shape and colour.
- Promote the product.
- Reinforce promotional messages and integrated with current advertising.

Debriefing Question 3.4

Each product has a life cycle, which portrays distinct stages in its sales - each posing different challenges to the marketer (see model in unit) and usually includes the development, introduction, growth, maturity and decline stages. The PLC concept is used to interpret product and market dynamics and is often used as a strategic planning tool. Kotler has identified the following characteristics for each stage.

Development	*Introduction*	*Growth*	*Maturity*	*Decline*
No sales	Low sales	Rapidly rising sales	High sales	Declining sales
High cost of R&D	Negative profits	Rising profits	High profits	Declining profits
Test market	Innovator customers	Early adopters	Middle majority customers	Laggard customers
	Few competitors	More competitors	Competitors start to decline	Smaller number of competitors

Debriefing Question 3.5

There are many criticisms of the product life cycle concept, which are as follows:

- The stages are not always easily defined.
- Not all products go through each stage, for example fad products such as 'cyberpets' (a children's toy).
- Strategic decisions can change the cycle, for example the repositioning of a product can have an impact on length of the stages.
- The life cycle varies in different industries.

Debriefing Question E3

a   On this part of the question, in fact the likely characteristics would be the same irrespective of the product/market in question. The examiner here therefore is looking for you to identify and discuss the characteristics of the decline stage of the plc including: dwindling sales and profits, saturated market place, customers' changing behaviour and perhaps late adopters and laggards entering the market; many competitors, and difficulty in differentiating competitive offerings.

b   Here, there is more scope for, and necessity of applying to the magazine market in the question. The examiner would be looking for you to demonstrate that you understood how to possibly extend the product lifecycle though you should also demonstrate that this really should be done before the decline stage is entered. Another alternative is to milk the product and eventually withdraw it from the market. In turn, the answer should demonstrate that if the company wishes to continue in business it should already have looked towards developing and launching new products.

Unit 4

Debriefing Activity 4.1

Your thoughts are probably centering around the product life cycle as a vehicle for longer-term planning, and the product mix for both long- and short-term planning. Perhaps too you have thought about the product adoption process, and where most customers might be in this process, in relation to short-term planning.

After you have gone through this unit, you should be able to cite more product tools that might be appropriate for inclusion when formulating your answer to this particular question.

Debriefing Activity 4.5

The accuracy of any model is only as good as the information upon which the model is based. A BCG matrix type model requires a great deal of accurate market and company information before the model can be used as a meaningful management tool. In addition to presenting strategic alternatives, a well prepared BCG matrix is valuable because it forces objective consideration of the elements of the portfolio in relation to each other.

However, a number of criticisms can be made of the Boston matrix as a marketing management tool. In particular, that:

- The matrix is over-simplified relying as it does on two variables only – market share and market growth.
- Often it is difficult to identify the 'actual' market in which the rate of growth is measured.
- There is an assumption about profitability and market share which may not be the case for all industries.
- The exact information about the largest competitor may not be accessible.

Debriefing Activity 4.7

Since the GE matrix uses several dimensions to assess SBUs instead of only two and is based on return on investment rather than simply cash flow, it is believed that it offers a substantial improvement over the BCG approach. There are, however, limitations associated with the GE matrix approach:

- It only offers broad strategy guidelines, with no indications as to precisely what needs to be done to achieve the strategy.
- There is no precise indication as to how to weight the various elements of market attractiveness or how to score business strengths against these.
- Evaluation and scoring are subjective, as are the points of division in the matrix into high, medium and low segments.
- The technique is much more complex than the BCG approach, and requires more extensive data gathering and processing.
- The approach does not explicitly take account of possible relationships between various SBUs or product market areas.
- There is nothing to prove that there is any relation between market attractiveness and business position, and how these are related to return on investment.

Debriefing Activity 4.8

The approach is similar to the conventional concept of the product life cycle, as it identifies the stage, specifies the characteristics of each stage, and suggests appropriate strategies for each stage. Porter has developed the notion of the industry life cycle further by linking it to the strategic position of the individual organization. This strategic position is categorized in terms of whether the individual organization is a leader or a follower.

Debriefing Activity 4.9

Lack of empirical evidence to support the underpinning ideas is the main criticism, coupled with its very simple approach to strategy selection. There is little doubt that industries do pass through different stages and that individual companies in these industries do have different competitive positions. However, this model suggests that analysing just these two factors enables a correct strategy to be identified and selected, which is of course incorrect, as strategic decisions are much more complex than this model would imply.

Debriefing Activity 4.10

Like the BCG approach, it assumes that the same set of factors is universally applicable for assessing the prospects of any product or business. Relevant factors and their relative importance will vary according to both the firm's products and the individual characteristics of each company. In addition, like the GE portfolio, the matrix does not provide any guidelines on how to implement the strategies suggested in each cell of the matrix.

Debriefing Activity 4.11

The expanded model provides an improved system for classifying and analysing the full range of market situations, no matter what the level of analysis (be it corporate, business division or product/market categories). Classification of products according to this expanded model is meant to reveal the relative competitive position of products, to indicate the rate of market growth and to enable the advancement of strategic alternatives in a general sense.

The problem is that it only gives general and not specific direction, and it does not eliminate the difficulties of defining, say, rates of growth or products and markets. As with other strategic planning tools, the benefits a company can achieve are only as good as the inputs upon which they are based.

The matrix does, however, provide an improved framework, which identifies the cash-flow potential and the investment opportunity for every product offered by a company. It also helps to conceptualize the strategic alternatives of all product/market categories of an organization.

Debriefing Question 4.1

Innovation is important to the survival of an organization. There are many examples of organizations that have suffered by not keeping up with the times. With new technological advances changing the way we live and the sophistication of consumer requirements, products can quickly become obsolete and services can become unnecessary. Recent examples of these include Betamax videos and 45 rpm records.

As a company's products progress along the product life cycle, it is important that new products are developed to keep the company profitable.

Debriefing Question 4.2

Questions regarding the new product development stages have been answered poorly on past examination papers because many students have confused the term with the product life cycle concept. It is important therefore, that you are able to understand each of the following stages of the new product development:

- Initial assessment or idea generation
- Idea screening

- Concept development and testing
- Business analysis
- Product development
- Test marketing and launch
- Commercialization

Debriefing Question 4.3

The Boston Matrix or the BCG matrix classifies products or strategic business units on the basis of their market share relative to that of their competitors and according to the rate of growth in the market as a whole. The matrix is divided into four sections with 'cash cows' having high market share but in low growth markets, 'stars' which are products enjoying high market share in a high growth market, 'question marks' being products with low market share but in a growing market and 'dog' products which have low market share in low growth markets. The split on the horizontal axis is based on a market share relative to that of the industry's largest competitor.

Products are positioned in the matrix as circles with a diameter proportional to their sales revenue. Forecast sales figures are also plotted for each product, which will indicate the potential movement of the product in the matrix. It is then possible to clearly see, in a diagrammatic form, the portfolio of products or businesses and make strategic decisions about them. Each company looks for a balanced portfolio of products, which can easily be recognizable on a Boston matrix, rather than a sheet of pure figures.

Debriefing Question 4.4

The main criticisms of this concept are as follows:

1. This matrix oversimplifies product analysis and relies on two variables only - market share and market growth.
2. Often it is difficult to identify the actual 'market' in which the rate of growth is measured.
3. There is an assumption about profitability and market share which may not be the case for all industries.
4. The exact information about the largest competitor may not be accessible.

Debriefing Question E4

Although this question does not indicate a split in the marks, in fact the question essentially has two distinct parts. The way the question is phrased means that there are probably, however, substantially more marks available for the second part of the question. We would suggest then, something like a 20–25% allocation of the time to the importance of new product development with the remainder of the time being devoted to a discussion of the stages involved in new product development.

The first part of the answer should indicate an awareness of why new product development is important including the operation of the product lifecycle, and the effect of market and technological changes which underpin this. New products are essential to maintain sales and profitability.

On the second part of the question this is a reasonably straight forward discussion of the stages of each part of the new product development process.

NB This answer would have been best structured in the form of a report.

Unit 5

Debriefing Activity 5.3

Clearly your examples may be specific to your own organization, but here are some typical examples of the different types of cost:

1. Fixed costs, e.g. rent and rates, leases, cost of capital.
2. Variable costs, e.g. raw materials, labour, power, transportation.

3. Neither of the above. If you were puzzled by this category of costs, it is because some costs are neither truly fixed nor truly variable, i.e. they are semi-fixed/variable. These are costs that vary to some extent with output/sales. For example, in the lease of some equipment there may be both a fixed and variable element to the cost, e.g. a photocopier.

Debriefing Activity 5.4

1. Using the information provided, Contribution = selling price − variable costs = £20 − £10 = £10
2. Breakeven point = Fixed costs/Contribution = 100,000/10 = 10,000 units

Debriefing Activity 5.5

The effect on breakeven point is as follows:

1. = 6,667 units
2. = 20,000 units

Shown on the breakeven chart we have the following:

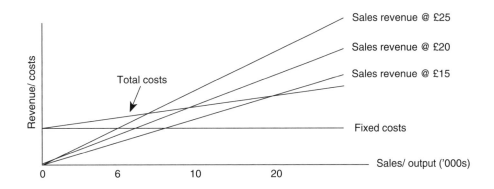

Debriefing Question 5.1

You should have the following answers for the diagrams.

1. Introduction (likely to be highly price-inelastic).
2. Growth (more price-elastic, due to competition).
3. Maturity (less price-elastic, due to brand loyalty).
4. Decline (a return to high price elasticity).

Debriefing Activity 5.6

Examples of markets that fit the range of descriptions in the unit are as follows:

1. Extremely competitive markets, e.g. food retailing, commodity markets, air travel, holidays.
2. Moderate competition, e.g. alcoholic beverages, coffee, toothpaste, detergents.
3. Little or no competition, e.g. privatised utilities.

Debriefing Activity 5.7

Admittedly these are very broad generalizations, but on the information given the indication for prices would be:

The ABC Company wishes to achieve rapid market growth.	Lower
The XYZ Company wants quick returns on capital employed.	Higher
The LPT Company wishes to promote a quality image	Higher
The NYZ Company is targeting socio-economic groups D/E.	Lower

Debriefing Activity 5.8

Do not worry if your list in the activity differs slightly from the one shown below, but in addition to costs, competition, competitors and company considerations, here are examples of other factors:

- Legal/regulatory considerations.
- Dealer and distributor considerations.
- Taxation, e.g. VAT.
- Government subsidies.
- Tariffs/duties.

Debriefing Activity 5.10

The circumstances that suggest price skimming include:

- Few or no competitors.
- High barriers to entry.
- A unique/innovatory product.
- Price inelastic demand.
- No substantial potential scale economies.

Debriefing Activity 5.11

The circumstances that suggest penetration pricing include:

- Extensive competition.
- Few barriers to entry.
- 'Me too' type products.
- High price elasticity.
- Potential for substantial scale economies.

Debriefing Activity 5.12

Where you got very good value for money the marketer probably had set the price too low. You would probably have been prepared to pay more. Where you got very poor value for money, the marketer had probably set the price too high, or at least you paid too much.

Debriefing Question 5.2

Cost-plus pricing or mark-up pricing is where businesses determine the cost of producing their product then add onto it a set percentage or margin – for example 10%.

The strengths of cost-plus pricing are:

- A means of trying to ensure that all overheads (e.g. fixed and product costs) are met. In addition it tries to allow for a profit return on top.
- It should be easy to calculate, as the organization is more certain about costs than demand.
- No need to have to make frequent adjustments to the price as demand changes.
- This method is used in this industry sector and therefore prices tend to be similar and price competition is minimized.
- It can be seen to be fairer to both buyers and sellers.

The weaknesses are:

- This pricing policy takes no account of other elements in the marketing mix, e.g. product, place.
- It does not reflect consumers' perceptions. If a consumer perceives a product as cheap, it is often associated with poor quality.
- It is a cost-based pricing strategy and ignores other factors such as the going rate for similar products. It does not consider different segments, etc.

- It does not consider the 'needs' and 'wants' of customers. This method does not consider competitors prices.
- It may be difficult to identify direct costs and overheads for each item.
- Cost-plus pricing does not consider the elasticity of demand for a product.
- This method only works if the price actually brings in the expected level of sales.

Debriefing Question 5.3

There is a range of information required before the decision about a pricing strategy can be decided. They are as follows:

- The ability to achieve the company's financial objectives.
- The levels of anticipated demand.
- The level of competition and their pricing policies.
- The impact of price on the perceived positioning of the product or service.
- The stage in PLC which the product is currently facing.
- Actual costs such as production, distribution, etc.
- The segments and markets which are being targeted and their income.
- Any legal constraints.
- Positioning strategies.
- The communication aspects of pricing.
- Tariffs, duties, taxation.
- Government subsidies.
- Dealer and distributor information.
- Economic factors, e.g. current trade cycle, levels of interest rates.

Debriefing Question 5.4

A market penetration pricing policy is where the organization sets a relatively low price for the product or service in order to stimulate growth of the market and obtain a large share of it.

The advantages are as follows:

- It should produce larger sales volumes.
- This should lead to an organization gaining a large slice of the market.
- It can prevent competitors from entering the market.

The limitations are as follows:

- It is often difficult to raise price after this policy has been used.
- It is less flexible than using a skimming policy.
- It may not be appropriate due to the costs of R&D and competitors' positions.

Debriefing Question 5.5

There are a number of policies which can be used at each stage of the product life cycle. They are detailed as follows:

Introduction stage	Growth stage	Maturity stage	Decline stage
Skimming policy with high prices, but low profit margin due to high fixed costs	Reduce price to penetrate market further	Price to match or beat competitors	Cut price if not repositioning
Penetration policy to enter the market and gain a high share quickly or to prevent competitors from entering		Retain higher prices in some market segments	Some increases in prices may occur in the late decline stage

Debriefing Question 5.6

Companies usually adjust their basic prices to account for various customer differences and changing situations. Three examples are as follows:

- *Discount and allowance pricing* — this is where the basic price is adjusted to reward customers for responses such as early payment, large or off-season purchases. These can be in the form of cash discounts, quantity discounts for bulk purchases and seasonal discounts for products bought out of season. Trade-in allowances and promotional allowances are price reductions given to encourage purchase.
- *Segmented pricing* — companies will often adjust their basic prices to allow for differences in customers, products and locations; the company sells a product at two or more prices, even though the difference in price is not based on differences in costs. Examples may be where different customers pay different prices for the same product, such as rail travel first class and standard fares. Another example is time pricing where prices vary by the day or the hour, such as telephone companies and 'off-peak' calls.
- *Promotional pricing* — is where companies will temporarily price their products below list price and sometimes below cost prices. Promotional pricing such as loss leaders attract customers, special-event pricing in certain seasons appeals to certain customers. Cash rebates, longer warranties, free maintenance, low-interest pricing policies are all forms of promotional pricing.

Debriefing Question E5

a On this first part of the question note that 'financial' and 'economic' issues only are specified. Financial issues would encompass, for example, cost of production, break even, contribution and profitability. Economic issues relate to in particular, demand and demand elasticity but also competition, disposable income and even government intervention.

b On the second part of the question the examiner was seeking evidence of an appreciation of the need to integrate pricing with the other marketing mix elements. Note here how sometimes the exam questions cut across several areas of the syllabus. Examples of other mix variables and decisions would have included, for example, channel decisions, product quality and branding with its implications for pricing, and the promotional mix in relation to the positioning and pricing.

Unit 6

Debriefing Activity 6.2

The elements of our channel of distribution are as follows:

- Supplier(s): in this case the manufacturer/marketer.
- Customer(s).
- Intermediaries: in this case the retailer.
- Outward flows: in this case goods and services.
- Inward flows: in this case payments and information.

Debriefing Activity 6.3

As you probably guessed, a 'zero-level channel' is a channel with no intermediaries, i.e. the producer/marketer uses 'direct marketing'. This idea of channel length/levels is shown in Figure 6.2.

Debriefing Activity 6.4

There are many reasons why the marketer might use intermediaries. For example:

- Custom in the industry.
- Intermediaries control customer contact.

- Intermediary has superior expertise, skills, resources.
- Too many customers for marketer to reach.

Debriefing Activity 6.5

Examples of types of direct marketing from which you were asked to specify four include:

- Door to door selling.
- In-home marketing, e.g. party selling.
- Mail-order catalogues.
- Direct mail.
- Telemarketing.
- Marketer's own outlets.

Debriefing Activity 6.6

There are a number of reasons for the growth of direct marketing, four of the major ones being:

- Potential for reduced costs/improved profits.
- Speed of delivery.
- Increased control on the part of the marketer.
- Potential for better customer feedback.

Debriefing Question 6.1

The following represent what we feel are the most appropriate types of market coverage for the products listed:

- Rolex watches = Exclusive.
- Cigarettes = Intensive.
- Mid-priced hi-fi = Selective.
- Toilet rolls = Intensive.
- Haute couture fashion = Exclusive.

Debriefing Activity 6.8

Many factors affect channel design and choice, but some of the major ones are:

- Organizational objectives and resources.
- Type of market/buyer, e.g. industrial versus consumer.
- Marketing objectives and strategies.
- Customer requirements/expectations.
- Type of product, e.g. perishable versus non-perishable.
- Channel availability, e.g. the most 'appropriate' channels may simply not be available.
- Competitor considerations.

Debriefing Activity 6.10

Here are just some of the activities you might have on your list:

- Inventory (stock) management.
- Order-processing.
- Warehousing.
- Transport management.
- Materials handling.

You will readily appreciate the potential for savings in these activities.

Debriefing Activity 6.11

You probably managed to think of lots of examples where customer service is affected by a company's physical distribution system. Here are some of the major ones:

- Order cycle time.
- Minimum order size.
- Ability to handle special orders/rush orders (flexibility).
- Consistency of delivery times.
- Degree of damage to delivered products.

Debriefing Question 6.2

The main objective of physical distribution is to decrease costs while increasing service to the customer. The manager will need to consider the order processing, materials handling, warehousing, inventory management and transportation issues. Managers strive for a good balance of service, costs and resources. Therefore, effective planning is paramount to ensure that this happens by determining what level of customer service is acceptable yet realistic in terms of costs. As physical distribution affects every element of the marketing mix, it is important that the customers' needs are at the top of the list.

- *Customer satisfaction*   The key benefits of an effective physical distribution programme should be the offer of a high quality service, which should lead to a significant impact on customer satisfaction. Indeed, companies can differentiate their offerings by considering their physical distribution in relation to their competitors and ensuring a good service level. For example some companies offer guaranteed 'next day' delivery. If managed effectively, it could be possible to position the company's offerings on the basis of the levels of service, which could lead to achieving a sustainable competitive advantage.
- *Company efficiencies*   If the programme is managed effectively, there should be opportunities to ensure reductions in the inventory costs, whilst maintaining a supply of goods adequate for the customers' needs. This should lead to increased profitability.

Debriefing Question 6.3

Different levels of market coverage must be considered when considering the company's objectives and the characteristics/behaviour patterns of the buyers. The marketing manager will need to consider the following issues:

1. *Exclusive distribution*   this is where only one outlet is used in a relatively large geographic area. Using exclusive distribution generally gives a company tighter control of the types of distributors and retailers used. This method is often used when only a limited market is available for products such as Rolls-Royce motor cars. However, when the luxury ice cream Haagen Das was launched this was the distribution policy which was first adopted to communicate the quality positioning of the product.
2. *Intensive distribution*   is where all available outlets are used for distributing a product. This is often appropriate for convenience consumer products such as newspapers, etc. where sales may have a direct relationship to availability.
3. *Selective distribution*   only some outlets in an area are chosen to distribute a product. This is appropriate for durable products such as electrical appliances, as these products are more expensive than convenience goods and consumers are willing to spend more searching time visiting a number of retail outlets to find the best deal.

Debriefing Question 6.4

The key issues which a marketing manager will need to take into account when considering alternative or new distribution channels are as follows:

- Organization's objectives and resources.
- Customers' characteristics, requirements and levels of service.

- Product characteristics such as the size, weight and durability.
- After-sale service.
- Competitors' channels.
- Channel characteristics, such as availability, etc.
- Risk, control, costs involved related to the organization.
- Logistics management issues such as inventory levels, handling issues, warehousing and transportation.
- Impact on other marketing mix elements.

Debriefing Question 6.5

Channel members can be combined and this can lead to stabilized supply, reduced costs and increased coordination of the channel members.

1. *Vertical channel integration* — this is where two or more stages of the channel are under one management. One member of a marketing channel may purchase the operations of another member or perform the functions of the other members thus eliminating the need for such an intermediary. Total vertical integration covers all functions from production to ultimate buyer, for example, oil companies, such as BP, that have their own service station. A vertical marketing system (VMS) is a marketing channel in which a single channel member coordinates or manages channel activities to achieve efficient, low-cost distribution aimed at satisfying target market customers. An example may be drawn from franchise organizations such as McDonald's which are examples of contractual VMSs.

2. *Horizontal channel integration* — is where institutions at the same level of operation are combined under one management. For example, an organization may integrate horizontally by merging with another organization at the same level in a marketing channel level such as the merger of a college with a university. Horizontal integration may enable a firm to generate sufficient sales revenue to integrate vertically as well. This integration allows efficiencies and economies of scale in purchasing, marketing research, etc. although it can lead to a decrease in flexibility and difficulties in coordination.

Debriefing Question 6.6

Direct marketing has been growing recently with the advances in information technology. Organizations have been able to use sophisticated databases to identify their customers' behaviour and characteristics and thus are able to adapt their offerings to increase satisfaction. The use of relationship marketing concepts and new media such as the Internet, DRTV, telemarketing and digital TV, has allowed organizations to build stronger direct relationships with their customers. The ability to communicate effectively and efficiently directly with the customer has allowed a number of organizations to monitor and control their direct marketing efforts thus reducing the use of intermediaries in channels.

An example of this is the Charles Tyrwhitt organization who manufacture and sell quality shirts via the Internet and their direct mail catalogue. This company has grown extensively through the use of new technology. Direct distribution is a growing and important area for all marketers.

Debriefing Question E6

a A good way to start the answer to this question would be to consider how to evaluate and analyse an existing distribution channel which in turn would help highlight the key considerations in evaluating alternatives. The following issues would be particularly important in relation to existing channels: current costs, profitability, degree of competitive edge, appropriateness to new developments and market conditions. In considering alternative channels the following aspects would be important: the length of any proposed alternative distribution channel, the number of intermediaries, the tasks and system for the distribution chain, risks, control and ability to reach target market and impact on other marketing mix elements.

b The second part of the question, the growth of direct marketing, again include a wide number of factors, but in particular developments in powerful databases which have allowed companies to identify their customers and to market to them more directly without the need for intermediaries. In addition advances in communication and information technology have allowed the growth of direct mail, telemarketing and of course the ubiquitous internet, has been a major factor.

Unit 7

Debriefing Activity 7.3

There are a number of ways in which the marketer can obtain feedback from customers regarding the effectiveness of marketing communications. Examples of methods/techniques include:

- Recognition tests.
- Aided recall tests.
- Unaided recall tests.
- Surveys of customer attitudes.

Methods for collecting this information include:

- Customer questionnaires.
- Sales-force feedback.
- Focus groups.

Debriefing Activity 7.4

The major advantages of advertising as a promotional tool include:

- Potentially low cost per target audience contact (reach).
- Allows repetition of message.
- Enables dramatization of company and its products (impact).
- Can be used to build up long-term image.

Debriefing Activity 7.5

The major advantages of personal selling as a promotional tool include:

- Two-way communication with target audience.
- Facilitation of immediate feedback.
- Flexibility – can respond to individual customer needs.
- Allows cultivation of customer relationships.

Debriefing Question 7.1

1. Self-liquidating offer: a promotional campaign where the cost of the sales promotion is covered by income/payments from the customer, e.g. where, say, a kitchen knife is offered at a 'special' price of £1.00 plus five labels when the cost to the marketer of the knives is £1.00.
2. Giveaways: a free gift, e.g. a toy, is included with the product.
3. Coupons: the customer uses coupons obtained from, say, magazines to obtain products at reduced prices.
4. Premiums: items offered free or at a minimum cost for purchasing a product, e.g. free soaps with purchase of perfumes.
5. Dealer loaders: a trade promotion in which retailers that purchase a certain quantity of merchandise receive gifts.
6. Buy-back allowances: again a trade promotion. A certain amount of money is allowed to, say, a retailer according to quantities bought during a promotional deal. For example, if the retailer has purchased say 100 units on special offer, this will qualify for a further additional premium after the initial deal is over.

Debriefing Activity 7.6

The major advantages of publicity/public relations as a promotional tool include the following:

- Can be used to promote a company as a whole and hence all its products.
- Often perceived by target audience as less 'biased' than, say, advertising.
- Potentially low cost.

Debriefing Question 7.2

The initial letters of AIDA stand for:

A – **A**ttention.

I – **I**nterest.

D – **D**esire.

A – **A**ction.

Debriefing Question 7.3

In the innovation-adoption model the customer is said to pass through the following stages:

Awareness – Interest – Evaluation – Trial – Adoption – Post-Adoption Confirmation.

Debriefing Activity 7.10

Here are some examples of promotional messages based on unique selling propositions.

1. 'The chocolate that melts in your mouth and not in your hand.'
2. 'The mint with the hole.'
3. 'The snack you can eat between meals without ruining your appetite.'
4. 'Put a tiger in your tank.'

Debriefing Question 7.4

The four most common methods used for setting promotional budgets are:

- Affordability.
- Percentage of sales.
- Competitive parity.
- Objective and task.

Debriefing Activity 7.12

Among some of the most important factors affecting the choice of promotional mix are the following:

1. Target market/customer type, e.g. industrial versus consumer.
2. Characteristics and cost-effectiveness of each promotional tool.
3. Marketing/sales strategies, e.g. 'push versus pull' strategies.
4. The product life cycle.
5. Availability of promotional tools.
6. Company resources/budgets.

Debriefing Activity 7.13

Examples of innovations in packaging that at the time of their introduction were very successful and gave the marketers using this packaging a competitive advantage include:

- Ring pull cans.
- Pump action toothpaste tubes.
- Flip top cartons for cigarettes.
- Cardboard containers for milk and juice.
- CFC-free aerosols.

Debriefing Question 7.5

When planning a promotional campaign, marketers need to consider the communications strategy, which would probably include push, pull or a combination of both elements.

1. Push strategy – this is where the communication messages are targeted at the channel intermediaries (trade channels) such as dealers, wholesalers, agents, distributors and retailers. This should allow the trade channel members to facilitate the distribution of the products to consumers or end users – thus 'pushing' the products to the consumers. Communications examples may be adverts in the trade press, discount for bulk orders, e.g. 500 cases, dealer competitions for the best sales figures, etc. See Figure 7.6

2. Pull strategy – this is where the communication is directed at the end consumer or buyer. The objective is usually to generate increased awareness, build attitudes and provoke motivation within this group of buyers. This is known as a pull strategy as the buyers should then demand the products from the intermediaries or trade channels. Communication examples may be television adverts, direct mail, sales promotions such as 50% extra free, etc. See Figure 7.7

In reality many organizations use a mixture of both of these strategies, however, they will apportion different weightings of their communications budget to the push and pull strategy.

Debriefing Question 7.6

The elements or tools of the promotion mix are as follows:

- *Advertising* – this will include a range of different types of advertising: to include the trade, consumer and corporate issues. Advertising is an effective tool for raising awareness about a consumer product or service, however, it is not as effective for actually achieving sales. Other elements need to be used with advertising to ensure sales increase.
- *Sales promotions* – includes incentives designed to encourage purchase such as 'buy one get one free', 20% extra free, free offers, etc. These can be aimed at the trade channels, the sales force and the consumers. This element is most effective in actually motivating trials and re-buys.
- *Personal selling* – this type of communication can be very effective. This is where one-to-one contact between the marketer and customer is made, such as the sales rep in an industrial market, telephone sales to consumers, retail sales assistants, missionary selling. This is one of the most effective methods for industrial products as the message can be tailored to each individual buyer as often it is a highly complex and technical product or service. Again, this method is very effective at ensuring actual purchase.
- *Public relations* – these are activities designed to create understanding and goodwill between an organization and its public. A wide range of activities can be classed as public relations such as press conferences, press releases, open days, etc. This method is difficult to evaluate and control. However, press releases are often seen as being more credible than an advert by the consumer and therefore can be used effectively with advertising to raise awareness, especially when launching a new product or repositioning a product/service.
- *Direct mail* – Kotler adds this fifth element to the traditional promotions mix, which can be considered as one of the most effective methods of communication when linked to a company database and loyalty scheme. This method can help in building consumer relationships and is very easy to control and evaluate.

Debriefing Question 7.7

There is a range of issues which the marketer must consider when planning a campaign for an industrial product in relation to a consumer product. The main difference is that usually the industrial product is a technical one, therefore, the communications strategy and promotions mix will need to be different. Some of the key issues about an industrial campaign to consider are as follows:

- There may be different objectives such as informing buyers about new uses, gathering customer and competitor information, etc.
- There are a range of different target audiences such as the members of the decision making unit (DMU).
- The buyer behaviour characteristics for industrial buyers need to be considered, i.e. annual contracts, minimum order levels, etc.
- Often an industrial manufacturer has a smaller promotional budget.
- Appropriateness of media used and reach in targeting the industrial buyer must be considered to ensure that the messages are received.

In most cases, it can be stated that personal selling techniques are more effective for industrial or technical products as the message can be tailored to the needs of the buyer. Therefore, the reliance on advertising is reduced with possibly only a very small amount being conducted in the trade press. Sales promotions will also be important, techniques such as bulk purchase discounts, free trials, etc. will be most effective to ensure purchase.

Debriefing Question 7.8

One of the most basic response hierarchy models is the AIDA model. This model suggests that the buyer passes through four key stages in the buying process – attention, interest, desire and action. This model can be used to help plan the communications objectives and ultimately the promotional mix.

However, this is a very old model, and does not consider a range of issues which are very important to the marketer. Some of these issues which are not considered are related to the influences on the consumer such as perceived risk, level of involvement, environmental issues such as the economy related to disposable income, the buyer's experience of the product previously, competitors strategies, etc. Indeed, this model does not consider a range of very important issues that the marketer will need to understand and so AIDA is very limited in helping us to understand the issues involved.

Debriefing Question 7.9

There has been a growth in the advance of information technology within the past ten years. Indeed, this has had a major impact for marketers planning the promotional mix for their products and services. Some of the key issues are as follows:

- Growth of electronic communications such as the Internet, e-mail, fax, etc. has allowed information to become more rapid and global.
- Increasing power of the computer has allowed the marketer to gather and analyse information about their customers more effectively. Thus the increase in direct mail and loyalty schemes has enabled companies to build individual relationships with customers.
- Digital technology is growing rapidly, with interactive digital television allowing two-way communications. The growth of satellite television has allowed marketers to target very specific segments with their television adverts such as pension plans for the over-50s advertised on the UK Gold channel (Sky). This will also offer marketers the opportunity to evaluate adverts more effectively.
- The increased use of the Internet as a promotional tool for individuals and companies has offered many marketers a further effective promotional tool, resulting in more control and evaluation of the communications. This has also had an impact on direct marketing and increases in direct sales.

It can be seen that there are a wide range of IT advances which have allowed the marketer to plan more interactive, two-way messages which ultimately convert into an increased knowledge about the consumer. This increase in information allows the marketer to tailor the messages to consumer behaviour, which should ultimately lead to more effective promotional strategies.

Debriefing Question E7

a This part of the question is testing the candidate's ability to identify and comment upon each of the stages involved in planning a promotional campaign. The answer should demonstrate an awareness of the need for a systematic approach. The examiner would expect the candidate to comment upon the following stages: identifying the target audience, specifying campaign objectives and defining the USP, selecting the media, scheduling the media, budgeting and evaluation and control.

b Note that the question asks why the promotional tools differ for an industrial product. We can only assume that means differ from a consumer product. Some of the key reasons why the promotional tools would differ include fewer/larger customers, more technical information required, shorter channels of distribution. Communication tools would place more emphasis on the personal tools such as personal selling and less on the impersonal tools such as, for example, advertising.

Unit 8

Debriefing Activity 8.1

The reasons you give in the activity will certainly be very varied: you might feel that there are common faults with a particular product (such as component failure) or with the level of help or support available (buying computers or hi-fi products, for instance). Reasons why these might be difficult to address could relate to other aspects of corporate strategy, e.g., improving the quality of components, or paying and training more skilful and well informed staff may involve unacceptable cost penalties in markets where competition is predominantly based on price. The purpose of the exercise is to make you think about the ways in which these issues are interrelated; keeping customers satisfied is not simply a matter of dealing with individual issues, but formulating policies that take the whole range of 'marketing-mix variables' into account.

Debriefing Activity 8.2

Briefly the main characteristics of the 'customer-care' concept are:

- Interactions between a firm and its customers.
- The 'image' of the firm, or the 'perceptions' customers have of it.
- Gathering information about customer needs and expectations.
- Taking action to meet those needs and fulfil expectations.
- Giving this aspect of the product/service concept a competitive edge.

Debriefing Activity 8.4

The qualities you select will depend on the product of course. What you should get from this exercise is the message that when we actually compare good products with inferior competitors, on most occasions the differences between them do not lie in gross disparities in the generic features of the products, but in the care and attention to the minutiae involved in the choice, purchase and usage process, e.g. in the helpfulness of service personnel, the range of products available to cater for individual tastes, and the details of actual usage. Can the product, say, survive small accidents, or can it be easily cleaned? How are guarantees organized (a simple 'return' system or 'pay and reclaim', which many people dislike)? The list is, and should be, very long, and is likely to be product-specific, at least in part. Another by-product will be the realization that quality is an emergent property of attending to these details, rather than simply a 'checklist' of ways of behaving. Quality is a by-product of a particular philosophy of behaviour.

Debriefing Activity 8.6

The purpose of this activity is to force you to think about what avenues that provide the company with such information actually exist, and how they are used by the companies in question.

Handling complaints, for instance, is traditionally seen as 'firefighting' or deflecting customers who might cause trouble – squashing them, deflating them, placating them, or keeping them quiet. This orientation demands that these avenues should be opened up, extended and treated as a very serious means of gathering important business information, which requires action. Rather than 'applying plasters', complaints should be the occasion for 'fault detection', so that recurrence can be avoided by getting it right first time. There should also, equally importantly, be means for customer credit to be transmitted to the staff. Staff should not only be aware of customers as potential sources of trouble for them, but also as the barometer for their achievements.

Debriefing Activity 8.7

This answer to the activity should bring out:

- The importance of a unified focus in the formulation of strategy and in the design of policies and processes.
- The importance of fostering the idea of achievement, of positive reinforcement for effective action, rather than founding good practice simply on the avoidance of complaints, failure and negative feedback.
- The idea of building up relationships, rather than relying on formal, contractual obligations. Information is the lifeblood of these processes, and flows freely only under conditions of trust.

Debriefing Activity 8.8

Key aspects of the answer to the question in the activity would be:

- Loss of status and power.
- Deskilling or disempowerment.
- Fear of the unfamiliar.

Debriefing Activity 8.10

What is a mission statement for? What is it supposed to accomplish? What are the difficulties in bringing together various and often conflicting aims, and making decisions about priorities and ultimate objectives? This activity should force you to think about the issues that are in play when objectives are formulated.

Debriefing Activity 8.11

This activity tries to make you think about the implications of:

- A common focus.
- Role differentiation.
- Power differences.
- The role of information.

Debriefing Activity 8.12

Examples of service encounters that could be measured in our travel agency example include the following:

- Numbers of customers.
- Numbers of staff.
- Types of enquiry.
- Duration of encounters.
- Waiting time.
- Timing and distribution of customers over the working week.
- Numbers of complaints.
- Types of complaint.
- Outcomes of complaints.
- Customer attitudes.

This list could be greatly extended but each of the elements on our list is relatively easy to measure. Virtually all the tools of marketing research that we discussed in the Unit 'Tools of marketing: research' could be useful here, including:

- Observation.
- Experiment.
- Surveys.

However, some important aspects of service encounters are difficult or even impossible to measure. These include, for example, variations in personnel responses to customers of different kinds (socio-economic, ethnic, gender, age differences); aspects of 'body language' or extra-linguistic communication are also critical but difficult to measure.

Debriefing Activity 8.13

The main points of this activity are to recognize the importance, on the one hand, of the specific features of the business in question, so that a good answer would start by making an audit or inventory of the situational/environmental features, and specifying informational needs as well as objectives; and, on the other hand, of making a fundamental change to cover every aspect of the organization, i.e. to apply a set of core principles from which practice can be derived.

Debriefing Activity 8.15

Examples of issues and problems that might arise in trying to collect information for our wine-bar example include:

- Where should the research be carried out? If information is only collected in the wine bar itself, you may not be gathering information about potential customers who are being discouraged by the problems you want to address.
- This, on the other hand, raises the issue of how to identify such potential customers in the first place.
- What research methods should we use and in particular, what should the balance be between qualitative and quantitative information?
- What will be the costs of the research and what resource constraints will affect the information-gathering process?
- How beneficial will any information collected actually be in planning customer-relations programmes?

Debriefing Question 8.1

There are often many reasons for poor customer care that can lead to problems within an organization, such as the level of service offered. The main reasons for poor customer care can be as follows:

- Poor planning and lack of commitment by management.
- Lack of communication to staff.
- Poor staff motivation.
- Lack of information about customers and the market.
- Poor timing and consideration of the other elements of the marketing mix.
- Poor control of the programme.
- Short-term emphasis.
- Power conflicts.

Debriefing Question 8.2

It is important that a customer care programme is managed effectively and there is an under-standing of total quality management. This should impact on the quality of service, availability, service, support and reliability of service. In essence the following issues should be considered:

- Identify customer needs and perceptions.
- Establish a mission statement.

- Service-level standards and specifications must be specified.
- Establish management processes and communicate this to all staff.
- Define tasks to time factors.
- Establish a basic minimum level.
- Ensure effective response to complaints.
- Management commitment.
- Effective and continuous measurement and control of the programme.

Debriefing Question 8.3

There is a range of clear benefits of an effective, long-term customer-care programme which marketers and top management should appreciate. The benefits are as follows:

- Helps to establish standards.
- Minimize confusion.
- Offer competitive edge.
- Establish TQM quality control.
- Offers value added to customers.
- Promotes better understanding of customers.
- It can motivate staff.
- Helps build customer relationships and improves customer retention.

Debriefing Question 8.4

Total quality management is the combination of the satisfaction of customer needs with the achievement of company objectives. Therefore, TQM gives central place to the customer and satisfying them is the first principle. The concept involves reaching forward to distributors down the chain and back to suppliers in the case of manufactured goods. This is to ensure the quality of all materials, raw and otherwise, and the condition of the product that reaches the ultimate consumer.

Customer-driven quality is often cited as a core value and it is important that marketers understand the implications that all products and service attributes contribute value to the customer and lead to customer satisfaction. Indeed, customer orientation under TQM considers the customer-supplier relationship as well as the external customer.

Therefore, it can be seen that a TQM approach is important for all organizations wishing to truly embrace a customer orientation and it is a key part of customer-care programmes.

Debriefing Question 8.5

It is important that marketers understand the three extra elements of the marketing mix, which are important for services marketing and the implications for customer care. The three extra elements are people, processes and physical evidence.

- *People (internal staff)*   It is important that there is commitment from all staff and that they are motivated. It is important that there is investment in staff in terms of training and development in customer relations, etc., e.g. courtesy from staff. To ensure TQM, internal quality groups should be devised and managed.
- *Process*   Processes should consider the customers' needs and perceptions. There should be customer support systems, TQM systems and good communications. Specifications should be written to ensure specific responses to customer complaints, to ensure minimal waiting times, minimize bottlenecks, etc.
- *Physical evidence*   Physical evidence such as good signage, staff uniforms, informative communications, must be planned and implemented to ensure that the customer-care ethos is achieved.

The integration of these three extended market mix elements is important to maximize the benefits of a customer-care programme and ultimately customer satisfaction.

Debriefing Question E8

a   On the first part of the question your answer should have included practical approaches to customer service and care for this business traveller and could have included issues such as the dissemination of timely communications about the delays, personal assistance for passengers who faced consequential problems and the use of immediate or later compensation measures etc.

b   On this second part of the question you needed to identify and explain the practical steps in establishing an effective customer care programme. The answer would need to include the following:

Identification of customer needs and perceptions, establishing a mission statement, setting service levels, establishing management processes and communicating these to all staff, defining tasks according to time factors, establishing a basic minimum level of service, ensuring that systems for effective responses to complaints were in place, the securing of management and staff commitment, and finally the implementation of effective and continuous measurement.

Unit 9

Debriefing Question 9.1

Some of the marketing advantages smaller companies have over their larger counterparts in the area of new-product development and innovation include:

- Speed.
- Flexibility.
- Better communication between management.
- A tendency to be more creative and entrepreneurial.

Debriefing Question 9.2

Examples of ways (bases) the smaller company can use to specialize in niche markets include:

- Specialization by end use.
- Specialization by customer type
- Specialization by type of product.
- Specialization by geographic area.

Debriefing Activity 9.4

Examples of possible appropriate marketing objectives for our voluntary and not-for-profit organization are as follows:

1. A national police force, e.g. 'To improve public co-operation and support'.
2. A local charity, e.g. 'To increase financial contributions from the local community and secure an increased time commitment from local volunteers'.
3. A church, e.g. 'To increase the average size of congregations and increase financial contributions'.

Debriefing Activity 9.5

Examples of service products include:

- Banking.
- Insurance.
- Hotels.
- Restaurants.
- Air travel.
- Hairdressing.
- Medical care, dental care.

- Home services, e.g. plumbing.
- Management consultancy.
- Industrial cleaning.

Debriefing Activity 9.6

Below is a summary of some of the major marketing implications associated with each of the special characteristics of services:

Characteristic	Marketing implications
PERISHABILITY	The matching of demand and supply becomes very important. Examples of ways in which this matching process can be managed in service marketing include the following: price discounts/special offers to even out demand fluctuations, e.g. off-peak pricing; bargain break holidays; etc. Well managed booking and reservation systems. Development of complementary service products and/or diversification into new markets in order to equate demand and supply. Shared use of facilities/equipment, e.g. hospitals sharing medical scanners, etc.
INTANGIBILITY	Increased importance of promotion and branding. Company/brand image crucial. Increased need to emphasize the benefits rather than features in selling and promotion. Need to look for ways in which to increase the tangibility of the service, e.g. through demonstrations, promotional literature, etc. Difficult to conduct market research for new products. Concept-testing becomes very important.
VARIABILITY	Personnel selection and training very important. Wherever possible all systems, procedures, ingredients, etc., should be standardized. Where necessary/useful, make a marketing feature out of variability, e.g. stress 'customized' aspect.
INSEPARABILITY	Often means that direct sale is the only possible channel of distribution. Scale of operation may be limited unless the service provider can reduce the need for him/her to be physically present, e.g. use of franchises, agents, etc.
NON OWNERSHIP	Lack of ownership needs to be turned to advantage by stressing benefits this gives rise to, e.g. an office-cleaning service company might stress the advantages to the customer of not having to have its own equipment or staff for this purpose.

Debriefing Activity 9.7

In fact virtually every product/market these days has some level of e-commerce activity.

Initially the major applications of e-commerce, and particularly the Internet in consumer markets, were in markets such as books, travel and event tickets, etc. where arguably customers do not need to touch or try on, etc., the product. In addition to the product markets shown on the list, other products/markets where e-commerce techniques and activities are being used include:

- Clothing and footwear.
- Gifts and fancy goods.
- Flowers.

- Garden and outdoor products.
- Furniture.

In short, there is virtually nothing these days that is not being or potentially cannot be marketed using e-commerce and the technologies which underpin it.

Debriefing Activity 9.8

Examples of the sorts of data on customers and an indication of the functions, other than the marketing function which might generate this data include:

- Prices paid – accounts function.
- Product requirements – design function.
- Delivery and out of stock problems – despatch department.
- Customer complaints – switchboard/reception.
- Quality requirements/issues – production department.
- Licensing/brand protection issues – legal department.

Debriefing Activity 9.9

Satellite television enables more sophisticated targeting with respect to advertising because of the following:

- More specialized programmes, albeit with smaller audiences can be linked to special interest groups.
- Satellite television programmes are often broadcast at times when other, terrestrial-based programmes, are not being shown, again allowing access to audiences which would otherwise be difficult to reach.

Debriefing Activity 9.10

Amongst some of the most important reasons why many consumers increasingly feel that automated customer handling operations are annoying and frustrating are:

- Difficulties in getting through in the first instance.
- Having to respond to questions which are not of interest to the caller.
- The time taken to eventually get connected to the person/department being sought.
- The impersonal nature of many of these systems.
- An intense dislike of 'cheesy' piped music.
- A feeling that the organization does not want to talk to its customers.

Debriefing Question 9.1

Although the basic principles of marketing apply irrespective of situation or context, the application of these principles and particularly the selection of, and emphasis given to, the marketing mix tools will differ in different contexts. There are many variations on contexts, but the main different contexts within which marketing activity takes place are the following:

- Fast moving consumer goods (FMCGs)
- Business-to-business
- Large or capital project-based
- Services
- Voluntary and not-for-profit
- Small and medium-sized enterprises (SMEs)
- International

Using these contexts it is possible to demonstrate how the marketing mix tools would vary in terms of selection and emphasis. So, for example, in business-to-business markets there will tend to be more emphasis on personal selling, the provision of technical information and advice, and effective after-sales service. For services the traditional 4Ps of the mix would need to be extended to include People, Process, and Physical evidence. In the international market the emphasis given to the marketing mix tools would need to reflect different environmental and particularly cultural considerations. In large or capital project-based contexts the People and Service elements would be important in the marketing mix. Voluntary and not-for-profit organizations would have less emphasis on price on the marketing mix and indeed may not set prices at all. In SMEs financial and staff limitations mean that expensive advertising campaigns are out of the question and more use will be made of intermediaries rather than employing own sales force to distribute products.

Debriefing Question 9.2

When considering the marketing mix for services, the marketer must include a further range of mix elements to ensure the effectiveness of the marketing plan. In addition to the conventional 4Ps (price, product, place, promotion), there are three further Ps: people, physical evidence and processes. These are discussed below:

- *Price* this refers to the pricing strategy, which should be planned in conjunction with the overall strategy, e.g. market penetration will lead to a lower pricing policy.
- *Product* in the case of services, the product will be intangible, e.g. a pension policy or education.
- *Place* when considering distribution in services marketing, this can often relate to the opening times and availability.
- *Promotion* this is very important for services, as the promotional aspects are often considered as a tangible indication of the service and the use of effective communications is one of the main ways to position the offering.
- *People* the service provider or people/staff of the organization are key factors in the delivery of the service and have major ramifications for customer satisfaction and service quality. It is important that companies are able to implement effective customer-care programmes to build positive relationships.
- *Physical evidence* relates to physical cues about the service, e.g. the staff uniforms and reception areas. It is again important to ensure that the physical evidence, such as signs, is a part of the overall marketing planning.
- *Process* this relates to the systems of delivery for the service, e.g. the parking facilities and booking systems.

Debriefing Question 9.3

An additional layer of complexities and considerations is introduced when a marketer operates in an international environment. A major impact of these complexities and considerations is on the use of the marketing mix elements. Here are just some ways in which the marketing mix elements are affected when the marketer operates in an international environment.

- Products: Different countries have different regulations with regard to, for example, product design and specifications, etc. In addition the usage and therefore customer requirements for a given product may differ between countries. Finally, packaging may need to be changed when marketing in a different country, again to meet legislative or customer use requirements. Because of the cost savings many marketers have attempted to standardise their products and packaging across countries but these cost savings have to be balanced against the need to adapt to different country requirements.
- Price: Marketers face different levels of competition in different countries. Pricing strategies must reflect this. In addition, different countries may be at different levels of economic development and activity. Again these need to be reflected in pricing.
- Place: Different countries may have different channel arrangements, types of intermediaries, infrastructure, etc. Unless the marketer uses direct channels these will affect the distribution element of the mix.
- Promotion: Cultural differences in particular must be reflected in the promotional mix for different countries. Some marketers have tried to standardise the promotion element

of the mix but care needs to be taken with regard to, for example, the use of symbols, signs and language.

- People: Physical evidence, Process: For service products in particular these extended marketing mix elements will need to reflect different country requirements. So, for example, marketing in the USA requires the marketer to pay considerable attention to levels of service support and the process elements for delivery.

Debriefing Question 9.4

The advances in technology have had a major impact on the promotional mix which an organization will be using.

- *Advertising* DRTV advertising has allowed advertising to achieve more than just awareness, data can be captured and responses can lead to converts. The introduction of satellite television and digital technology has allowed for more sophisticated targeting via traditional advertising. The use of the Internet site as an advertising window or banner advertising on other linked sites has been evident in the last five years. The use of CD-ROMs as a vehicle for advertising has been apparent.
- *Sales promotions* the sophistication of databases and the direct mailing of sales promotions has been very powerful for some organizations. The use of the website and the 'free downloadable programme or screen saver' has allowed the marketer to become more creative.
- *Personal selling* the role of personal selling has now declined due to the use of automated customer-handling technology. This has been seen to cut costs whilst not eroding the service to the customer, however, in reality this has not always been effective and many customers are becoming disillusioned.
- *Public relations* the use of the website as a relationship-building tool has been effective for some organizations. For both internal (staff) and external audiences (customers, journalists, community, etc.) it has been easier to communicate using the Internet and mobile technology. For example, internal newsletters can be communicated on the intranet, press releases to journalists can be e-mailed instantly with digital pictures using satellite technology (which has saved days when considering international communications or reporting). The web can be used as an important communication tool in times of crisis management such as disasters or accidents when accurate and instantly changing information to the public will be crucial.

Debriefing Question 9.5

1. *Internet* this can be used in a vast number of ways for marketing purposes. It can be used as an external research tool to access market and competitor information. It can be used as a direct marketing channel and a home-shopping site. It can be used to raise awareness and support other communications tools for specific campaigns. For example, a leading manufacturer of white goods is currently about to use its Internet site as the main promotional tool when launching its new washing machine because it is felt that the Internet can provide more crucial information which the customer will require before making a decision. Therefore, the inside of the machine is 'virtually' available for the customer to interrogate on-line.

   The Internet can also be used by organizations to communicate with other organizations in business-to-business marketing via e-mail. As the ownership of personal computers increases, mobility improves and the cost of Internet use declines, more consumers will also be contactable directly via e-mail instead of mail-shots.

2. *Intranet* this is the use of the internal system of communication throughout an organization. This allows employees access to information, some of which is likely to be restricted. This allows greater management of communication and can be used to advantage for internal newsletters, etc.

3. *Extranet* the extranet is the electronic system where an organization allows a customer on-line access to some of its internal information sources. This allows a sophisticated relationship to be developed and the access and use of such information should allow for mutual economies and enhanced communication. This strategy also encourages trust and commitment between two organizations, such as a supplier and customer. The extranet is used in a growing number of organizations where such access to information has helped in planning sales and logistics down the line. Obviously, there are some potential problems which relate to the level of investment required to allow for this system to work effectively and to the access of information when one organization wishes to terminate the relationship.

Debriefing Question E9

a On this first part of the answer it is important to identify and explain the characteristics of services which distinguish them from physical products including: intangibility, inseparability, perishability, heterogeneity, and ownership. The answer should then go on to identify the key resulting problems for marketers that these differences present encompassing: image problems, service quality, customers' perceptions and expectations, positioning issues, value and customer care.

b The second part of the answer should have considered the extended marketing mix encompassing People, Process and Physical evidence. It is vital to apply these in the context of a small service company though it would not necessarily have to be a management consultancy.

Syllabus

The Marketing Fundamentals module develops a basic knowledge and understanding of marketing, marketing process and the marketing mix. It aims to provide participants with a framework on which to build marketing knowledge and skills through the modules of this Stage, through modules at later Stages and in the workplace.

Participants will not be expected to have any prior knowledge or experience in a marketing role.

Related statements of practice

- Bb.2 Contribute to the production of marketing plans and budgets.
- Db.1 Contribute to the development of products and services.
- Eb.1 Contribute to the development of pricing policies.
- Eb.2 Implement pricing policies.
- Fb.1 Develop effective channels to market.
- Fb.2 Provide support to channel members.
- Hb.1 Contribute to planning and budget preparation.

Learning outcomes

Participants will be able to:

- Explain the development of marketing and the ways it can benefit business and organizations.
- Identify the main steps in, and barriers to, achieving a marketing orientation within the organization.
- Explain the context of, and process for, marketing planning and budgeting including related models.
- Explain the concept of segmentation and the different bases for effective market segmentation.
- Identify and describe the individual elements and tools of the marketing mix.
- Identify the basic differences in application of the marketing mix involved in marketing products and services within different marketing contexts.

Knowledge and skill requirements

Element 1: The development of marketing and market orientation (10%)

1.1 Explain the development of marketing as an exchange process, a philosophy of business, and a managerial function.

1.2 Recognize the contribution of marketing as a means of creating customer value and as a form of competition.

1.3 Appreciate the importance of a market orientation to organizational performance and identify the factors that promote and impede the adoption of a market orientation.

1.4 Explain the role of marketing in co-ordinating organizational resources both within and outside the marketing function.

1.5 Describe the impacts of marketing actions on society and the need for marketers to act in an ethical and socially responsible manner.

1.6 Examine the significance of buyer-seller relationships in marketing and comprehend the role of relationship marketing in facilitating the retention of customers.

Element 2: Marketing planning and budgeting (20%)

2.1 Explain the importance of the marketing planning process and where it fits into the corporate or organizational planning framework.

2.2 Explain the models that describe the various stages of the marketing planning process.

2.3 Explain the concept of the marketing audit as an appraisal of the external marketing environment and an organization's internal marketing operations.

2.4 Describe the role of various analytical tools in the marketing auditing process.

2.5 Explain the value of marketing research and information in developing marketing plans.

2.6 Explain the importance of objectives and the influences on, and processes for setting, objectives.

2.7 Explain the concept of market segmentation and distinguish effective bases for segmenting consumer and business-to-business markets.

2.8 Describe the structure of an outline marketing plan and identify its various components.

2.9 Depict the various management structures available for implementing marketing plans, and understand their advantages and disadvantages.

2.10 Examine the factors that affect the setting of marketing budgets.

2.11 Demonstrate an appreciation of the need to monitor and control marketing activities.

Element 3: The marketing mix and related tools (50%)

3.1 Describe the essential elements of targeting and positioning, and the creation of an integrated and coherent marketing mix.

3.2 Describe the wide range of tools and techniques available to marketers to satisfy customer requirements and compete effectively.

3.3 Explain the development of the extended marketing mix concept to include additional components in appropriate contextual settings: product, price, place (distribution), promotion (communications), people, processes, physical evidence and customer service.

3.4 Demonstrate awareness of products as bundles of benefits that deliver customer value and have different characteristics, features and levels.

3.5 Explain and illustrate the product life cycle concept and recognize its effects on marketing mix decisions.

3.6 Explain and illustrate the principles of product policy: branding, product lines, packaging and service support.

3.7 Explain the importance of introducing new products, and describe the processes involved in their development and launch.

3.8 Explore the range of internal and external factors that influence pricing decisions.

3.9 Identify and illustrate a range of different pricing policies and tactics that are adopted by organizations as effective means of competition.

3.10 Define channels of distribution, intermediaries and logistics, and understand the contribution they make to the marketing effort.

3.11 State and explain the factors that influence channel decisions and the selection of alternative distribution channel options, including the effects of new information and communications technology.

3.12 Describe the extensive range of tools that comprise the marketing communications mix, and examine the factors that contribute to its development and implementation.

3.13 Explain the importance of people in marketing and in particular the contribution of staff to effective service delivery.

3.14 Explain the importance of service in satisfying customer requirements and identify the factors that contribute to the delivery of service quality.

3.15 Examine the effects of information and communication technology on the development and implementation of the marketing mix.

3.16 Explain the importance of measuring the effectiveness of the selected marketing effort and instituting appropriate changes where necessary.

Element 4: Marketing in context (20%)

4.1 Explain the importance of contextual setting in influencing the selection of and emphasis given to marketing mix tools.

4.2 Explain differences in the characteristics of various types of marketing context: FMCG, business-to-business (supply chain), large or capital project-based, services, voluntary and not-for-profit, sales support (e.g. SMEs), and their impact on marketing mix decisions.

4.3 Compare and contrast the marketing activities of organizations that operate and compete in different contextual settings.

4.4 Explain the global dimension in affecting the nature of marketing undertaken by organizations in an international environmental context.

4.5 Explain the existing and potential impacts of the virtual marketplace on the pattern of marketing activities in given contexts.

Related key skills for marketers

- Using ICT and the Internet
- Using financial information and metrics
- Presenting information
- Improving own learning and performance
- Working with others
- Problem-solving
- Applying business law

Assessment

CIM will normally offer two forms of assessment for this module from which centres or participants may choose: written examination and continuous assessment. CIM may also recognize, or make joint awards for, modules at an equivalent level undertaken with other professional marketing bodies and educational institutions.

Overview and rationale

Approach

This module has been designed to provide an introduction to the key concepts of marketing to participants in the Stage 1 qualification, many of whom will have little or no previous experience of the discipline. The knowledge and skills that it sets out to impart essential aspects of marketing theory and practice from which both horizontal and vertical integration in the Stages can take place. Specifically it provides a foundation for Marketing in Practice within Stage 1 and an essential platform for the full gamut of Stage 2 modules.

The themes it adopts as its cornerstones are the twin facets of marketing as a means of conveying **customer value** and as a form of **competition**. These are seen to define the marketing philosophy and function and thus characterize the types of activities involved in marketing. Moreover these themes are recognized as the core of the marketing planning process, which is introduced in this module and is developed in detail in subsequent modules in Stages 2 and 3 (Marketing Planning and Marketing Strategy respectively). A comprehensive examination of the range of marketing techniques available to practitioners is included in the knowledge and skills requirements, along with an assessment of their contribution in achieving specific marketing outcomes. In addition the module introduces the importance of contextual setting in determining the degree of emphasis given to particular marketing activities, and recognizes that organizational characteristics are a key influence on the composition of the marketing mix adopted.

Horizontally, the content of the module has been slimmed down to reduce the degree of overlap found between modules in the current Certificate syllabus. It now includes societal marketing, social responsibility and relationship marketing (from Marketing Environment) as part of the development of marketing. Customer behaviour and care are now dealt with in Customer Communications. Market research planning has been moved to Marketing Environment. The practical application of basic marketing skills is included in Marketing in Practice, which reinforces marketing in context. ICT is not explicit within this syllabus but should be implicit in marketing mix.

In line with the necessity for the future evolution of the syllabus, the elements of the indicative content together with the associated knowledge and skill requirements offer an essential framework in which any such changes may be integrated.

Syllabus content

The balance of weighting allocated to each of the four elements of the syllabus reflect the importance of the area to the achievement of learning and performance outcomes, and the depth and breadth of material to be covered. Although each area may be regarded as a discrete element there are clear progressions and overlaps in the knowledge and skills base considered which has important implications for the delivery of the module.

Element 1: The development of marketing and market orientation

Knowledge and skill requirements here relate to the first two learning outcomes, which focus on the development of marketing and the implementation of a market orientation. This element also includes the new knowledge area of societal marketing the ethical and social responsibility issue. The further new area of relationship marketing is also introduced at this point.

Element 2: Marketing planning and budgeting

The syllabus content in this element relates to the third and fourth learning outcomes that consider the marketing planning and budgeting process, and the market segmentation concept. The material included is intended to provide participants with an overview of marketing planning: the process, benefits, models, components, and implementation. It will be mainly descriptive and illustrative. However it is deemed to be fundamental to developing plans that include programmes of mix activities and thus will enhance meaning and understanding in the study of Element 3. Similarly a grasp of the essentials of segmentation will provide insight into the selection of mix components and overall positioning in accordance with differences in customer requirements and competitive conditions.

Element 3: The marketing mix and related tools

The knowledge and skills areas considered in this element relate directly to the fifth learning outcome which concentrates upon marketing mix activities. The full range of mix components is identified along with some precepts relating to mix formulation and selection. Additionally some reference is made to the effects of new communications techniques and technologies on the operation of various components of the mix.

Element 4: Marketing in context

The sixth learning outcome is covered in this element which examines how the characteristics of organizational and market contexts influences the configuration and implementation of marketing programmes. Specifically it considers a range of contrasting, but related, settings and undertakes to provide a comparative assessment of how differences in context affect marketing activities. The virtual marketplace concept and its implications for organizations and their customers is also considered here.

Delivery approach

For many participants this module will provide their first contact with the essentials of marketing theory and the core components of knowledge. Its intention is to provide value to those that participate from both an immediate practical perspective and a longer-term personal/career development standpoint. To this end studying this module should enable participants to reflect upon the knowledge that they acquire, and enhance their understanding of the role that they play within organizations as well as the activities that they may be involved in. Furthermore it should enable greater understanding of the importance of marketing to a full spectrum of organizations serving markets of differing dimensions.

As a core knowledge and understanding module the preferred form of assessment is proposed to be an examination. This should be borne in mind when developing the learning and teaching strategy for the module.

As the 'spine' of Stage 1 and a foundation module for Stage 2, the indicative content of the syllabus is regarded as being key to future and current understanding in other syllabus areas. It is therefore recommended that the module be taught in the early stages of a programme of study or ideally as a module that runs throughout the full period of this stage of study.

The acquisition of the knowledge and skills components covered is regarded as the main outcome of this module. Specifically, the development of a participant's understanding of the essential principles of marketing theory and the ability to illustrate and apply them in context will guide assessment tasks. Particular emphasis should be given to providing participants with the opportunity to illustrate key concepts through contemporary examples derived from their own or shared work experiences, and case materials from other sources.

Furthermore, although it is expected that learning outcomes should be achieved as discrete goals of attainment, it is also expected that tutors recognize and impart an understanding of the integrated nature of syllabus content. It is therefore important that tutors make a clear link between the customer value and competition precepts, the integrated mix and its components. The ability to develop, resource and implement marketing activities in a planning framework should also be given due consideration. Tutors should endeavour to ensure that a full range of organizational contexts are studied during the course of the module.

The critical importance of the core material for continuous and future study may require a mix of learning strategies including some formative assessment. Deeper learning outcomes such as application and understanding may be developed from the acquired knowledge through research exercises, problem solving activities and case study work.

Reading list

Core texts

Dibb, S., Simkin, L., Pride, W. and Ferrell, O. (2000) *Marketing: Concepts and strategies*. 4th European edition, Abingdon, Houghton Mifflin.

Syllabus guides

CIM (2002) *CIM Companion: Marketing fundamentals*. Cookham, Chartered Institute of Marketing.

BPP (2002) *CIM Study Text: Marketing fundamentals*. London, BPP Publishing.

Ashford, R., Withey, F. and Lancaster, G. (2002) *Marketing Fundamentals Coursebook*. Oxford, Butterworth-Heinemann.

Supplementary readings

Adcock, D., Halborg, C. and Ross, C. (2001) *Marketing: Principles and practice*. 4th edition, Harlow, FT Prentice-Hall.

Blythe, J. (2001) *Essentials of Marketing*. 2nd edition, Harlow, FT Prentice-Hall.

Brassington, F. and Pettitt, S. (2000) *Principles of Marketing*. 2nd edition, Harlow, FT Prentice-Hall.

Chaston, I. (2000) *Entrepreneurial Marketing: Competing by challenging conventions*. London, Palgrave.

Evans, M. and Mouthino, L. (1999) *Contemporary Issues in Marketing*. London, Palgrave.

Hill, E. and O'Sullivan, T. (1999) *Marketing*. 2nd edition. Harlow, Addison Wesley Longman.

Kotler, P., Armstrong, G., Saunders, J. and Wong, V. (2001) *Principles of Marketing*. 3rd European Edition. Harlow, FT/Prentice-Hall.

Lancaster, G., Massingham, L. and Asford, R. (2001) *Essentials of Marketing*. 4th edition, Maidenhead, McGraw-Hill.

Palmer, A. (2000) *Principles of Marketing*. Oxford, Oxford University Press.

Smith, P. (1999) *Great Answers to Tough Marketing Questions*. London, Kogan Page.

BPP (2002) *Marketing Fundamentals: Practice and revision kit*. London, BPP Publishing.

Marketing Fundamentals: Success tape. Learning cassettes by BPP Publishing.